HIDDEN
Maui

HIDDEN
Maui

Ray Riegert

FIRST EDITION

Ulysses Press
BERKELEY, CALIFORNIA

Published by:
ULYSSES PRESS
3286 Adeline Street, Suite 1
Berkeley, CA 94703

Library of Congress Catalog
    Card Number 95-60714
ISBN 1-56975-035-1

Printed in the United States of America
by R.R. Donnelley & Sons

10 9 8 7 6 5 4 3 2 1

PROJECT DIRECTOR: Lee Micheaux
COPY EDITORS: David Sweet, Sayre Van Young
    Frances Bowles, Joanna Pearlman
TYPESETTER: Jennifer Wilkoff
EDITORIAL ASSOCIATES: Mark Rosen, Toby Bielawski
    Kate Baldus
CARTOGRPAHERS: Phil Gardner, Wendy Ann
    Logsdon
COVER DESIGN: Sarah Levin Graphic Design
INDEX: Sayre Van Young
COVER PHOTOGRAPHS: Larry Ulrich and
    Leslie Henriques
BACK COVER photographs: Leslie Henriques

Distributed in the United States by Publishers
Group West, in Canada by Raincoast Books,
and in Great Britain and Europe by World
Leisure Marketing

HIDDEN is a federally registered trademark
of BookPack, Inc.

The author and publisher have made every effort
to ensure the accuracy of information contained
in *Hidden Maui*, but can accept no liability for any
loss, injury, or inconvenience sustained by any
traveler as a result of information or advice
contained in this guide.

For Alice, Keith and Leslie

Acknowledgments

The drawback to being acknowledged in a book about Maui is it means you worked in the office rather than Hawaii. That's not true of my wife, Leslie Henriques, who has been helping me research Maui for years; or Claire Chun who hails from Hawaii.

But project director Lee Micheaux, consultant extraordinaire Bryce Willett, typesetter Jennifer Wilkoff, editorial associates Mark Rosen, Toby Bielawski and Kate Baldus, editor David Sweet, right hand advisor Joy Clark and indexer Sayre Van Young would all I am sure happily trade this meager thanks for a plane ticket to paradise. I am nevertheless extremely grateful to all of them—and to our fabulous new designer, Sarah Levin—and extend a huge *mahalo* to everyone who helped bring this book to press.

Notes to the Reader

At different places throughout the text you will find special listings ◄ *HIDDEN* marked with this hidden symbol. It means that it is a hidden locale, remote region or little-known attraction. It represents a spot that I particularly think you should visit.

Hidden locales may be out along the beach, deep on the rain-forest, or high in the mountains. Sometimes, however, they are right in front of your nose, located near the center of town or in the corner of a shopping area. These kinds of hidden listings are places that are simply overlooked or known only to local residents.

Whether they are secluded places or ones you stumble upon, both types of hidden locales represent the idea behind *Hidden Maui* and all the Hidden guidebooks—to help you escape the beaten tourist track and come in closer contact with the local people and natural environment.

▼▼▼

It is our desire as publishers to create guidebooks that are responsible as well as informative. The danger of exploring hidden locales is that they will no longer be secluded.

We hope that our guidebooks treat people, country and land we visit with respect. We ask that our readers do the same. The hiker's motto, "Walk softly on the Earth," applies to travelers everywhere . . . in the desert, on the beach and in town.

▼▼▼

An alert, adventurous reader is as important as a travel writer in keeping a guidebook up-to-date and accurate. So if you happen upon a great restaurant, discover a hidden locale or (heaven forbid) find an error in the text, we'd appreciate hearing from you. Just write to:

ULYSSES PRESS
3286 Adeline Street, Suite 1
Berkeley, CA 94703

Contents

Maps

Special Features

BEACHES & PARKS ICONS

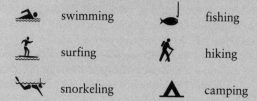

swimming   fishing

surfing   hiking

snorkeling   camping

ONE

The Valley Isle

Residents of Maui, Hawaii's second-largest island, proudly describe their Valley Isle by explaining that "Maui *no ka oi.*" Maui is the greatest. During the last decade, few of the island's visitors have disputed the claim. They return each year, lured by the enchantment of a place possessing 33 miles of public beaches, one of the world's largest dormant volcanoes, beautiful people, a breeding ground for rare humpback whales and a climate that varies from subtropic to subarctic.

Named after one of the most important demigods in the Polynesian pantheon, Maui has retained its mythic aura. The island is famous as a chic retreat and jet-set landing ground. To many people, Maui *is* Hawaii.

But to others, who have watched the rapid changes during the past two decades, Maui is no longer the greatest. They point to the 2.4 million tourists (second only to Oahu) who visited during a recent year, to the condominiums and resort hotels mushrooming along the prettiest beaches and to the increasing traffic over once-rural roads. And they have a new slogan. "Maui is *pau.*" Maui is finished. Overtouristed. Overpopulated. Overdeveloped.

Today, among the island's 102,000 population, it seems like every other person is in the real estate business. On a land mass measuring 729 square miles, just half the size of Long Island, their goods are in short supply. During the 1970s and 1980s, land prices shot up faster than practically anywhere else in the country.

Yet over 75 percent of the island remains unpopulated. Despite pressures from land speculation and a mondo-condo mentality, Maui still offers exotic, untouched expanses for the explorer. Most development is concentrated along the south and west coasts in Kihei, Wailea and Kaanapali. The rest of the island, though more populated than neighboring islands, is an adventurer's oasis.

The second-youngest island in the chain, Maui was created between one and two million years ago by two volcanoes. Haleakala, the larger, rises over 10,000 feet, and offers excellent hiking and camping within its valley. The earlier of the two firepits created the West Maui Mountains, 5788 feet at their highest elevation. Because of their relative age, and the fact they receive 400 inches of rainfall a year, they are more heavily eroded than the smooth surfaces of Haleakala. Between the two heights lies Central Maui, an isthmus formed when the volcanoes flowed together.

The twin cities of Kahului and Wailuku, Maui's commercial and civic centers, respectively, sit in this saddle. Most of the isthmus is planted in sugar, which became king in Maui after the decline of whaling in the 1860s. A road through the cane fields leads south to the sunsplashed resorts and beaches of Kihei and Wailea.

Another road loops around the West Maui Mountains. It passes prime whale-watching areas along the south coast and bisects Lahaina, an old whaling town that is now the island's sightseeing capital. Next to this timeworn harbor stretches the town of Kaanapali with its limitless beaches and endless condominiums. Past these glass-and-steel palisades, near the island's northwest tip, lie hidden beaches, overhanging cliffs and spectacular vistas.

The road girdling Haleakala's lower slopes passes equally beautiful areas. Along the rainswept northeast coast are sheer rock faces ribboned with waterfalls and gorges choked with tropic vegetation. The lush, somnolent town of Hana gives way along the southeast shore to a dry, unpopulated expanse that is always ripe for exploration.

On the middle slopes of Haleakala, in Maui's Upcountry region, small farms dot the landscape. Here, in addition to guavas, avocados and lichee nuts, grow the sweet Kula onions for which the Valley Isle is famous.

Back in the days of California's gold rush, Maui found its own underground nuggets in potatoes: Countless bushels were grown in this area and shipped to a hungry San Francisco market. Today the crop is used to prepare Maui potato chips.

Because of its strategic location between Oahu and Hawaii, Maui has played a vital role in Hawaiian history. Kahekili, Maui's last king, gained control of all the islands except Hawaii before being overwhelmed by Kamehameha in 1790. Lahaina, long a vacation spot for island rulers, became a political center under Hawaii's first three kings and an important commercial center soon after Captain Cook sighted the island in 1778. It served as a supply depot for ships, then as a port for sandalwood exports. By the 1840s, Lahaina was the world capital of whaling. Now, together with the other equally beautiful sections of the Valley Isle, it is a mecca for vacationers.

Maui's magic has cast a spell upon travelers all over the world, making the island a vacation paradise. Like most modern paradises, it is being steadily gilded in plastic and concrete. Yet much of the old charm remains. Some people even claim that the sun shines longer on the Valley Isle than any other place on earth. They point to the legend of the demigod Maui who created his own daylight savings by weaving a rope from his sister's pubic hair and lassoing the sun by its genitals. And many hope he has one last trick to perform, one that will slow the course of development just as he slowed the track of the sun.

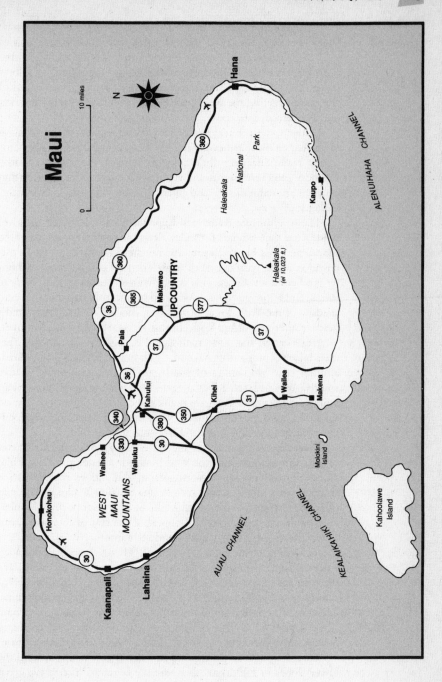

Maui

N

10 miles

0

Hana

360

Haleakala
National
Park

Kaupo

ALENUIHAHA CHANNEL

Haleakala
(el 10,023 ft.)

360

Makawao

UPCOUNTRY

365

36

377

37

Pala

37

Wailea

Makena

36

Kahului

Kihei

31

350

340

380

Walhee

330

Wailuku

30

Molokini
Island

KEALAIKAHIKI CHANNEL

Honokohau

WEST
MAUI
MOUNTAINS

Kahoolawe
Island

30

AUAU CHANNEL

Kaanapali

Lahaina

▼▼▼▼▼▼▼▼▼▼▼

Where to Go

Quite manageable in size, Maui is a destination that can be covered entirely in the course of a short vacation. Each of the island's regions has its strengths, and the areas with the most popular hotels and restaurants are not necessarily the best places for sightseeing. You may find yourself staying on one part of the island, visiting the beaches elsewhere and then setting off in yet another direction to tour.

Lahaina, the cultural heart of the island, is a falsefront whaling town that enjoyed its heyday in the 19th century and today remains rich in tradition. More than anywhere else on the island, Lahaina balances good restaurants and attractive lodgings with nightlife and shopping possibilities. It also offers a lengthy list of historic sightseeing spots.

The neighboring **Kaanapali-Kapalua Area** is a stretch of dove-white sand that extends for miles along the southwest corner of the island. Some of Hawaii's prettiest beaches can be found along this corridor, along with one of the state's densest concentrations of hotels and condominiums. This is where most people stay, and where they spend luxurious days soaking up sunshine. Situated in the wind shadow of the West Maui Mountains, this area enjoys the island's best weather and offers Kodachrome views of Lanai and Molokai.

Hoteliers in the Kaanapali-Kapalua region will tell you that their biggest competitors have set up shop in the **Kihei-Wailea Area**, another strip with miles of pearly beach, this time lining Maui's southeastern quarter. Kihei, a perfect example of development run amuck, is a congeries of strip malls and condominiums. Wailea, on the other hand, is well planned, a trimly manicured landscape dotted with scalloped beaches and five-star hotels.

The commercial center of the Valley Isle sits at the northern end of the isthmus separating the West Maui Mountains and Haleakala. The **Kahului-Wailuku Area** rises from Kahului Harbor, a major shipping area, uphill to the woodframe town of Wailuku. The seat of Maui County government, Wailuku, and neighboring Kahului, lack the beaches and physical appeal of the rest of the island, but offer visitors inexpensive hotels and restaurants.

Sightseeing is spelled with a capital "H" on the **Hana Highway**. Curving along the rain-doused northeastern coast, this magnificent drive curves past rainforests, seacliffs and checkerboard taro plantations to the idyllic village of Hana. Here you'll find friendly inns, a few restaurants and some of the most absorbing scenery in Hawaii. Local residents, looking out on the luxurious flora and tumbling terrain, lovingly call it "Heavenly Hana." It's not an exaggeration.

Maui's **Upcountry**, a band of ranchland that wraps around the lower slopes of Haleakala, is where the beach culture of the coast gives way to an Old-West society of cattlemen and Hawaiian-style cowboys, or *paniolos*. Angus and Hereford cattle roam these cool, moist slopes and eye-catching wildflowers grow with abandon.

SEASONS   5

You have to climb 10,000 feet, but upon arriving at the summit in **Haleakala National Park**, you may discover there is a place on Maui even more alluring than "Heavenly Hana." This is, after all, the "House of the Sun," a dormant volcano that is home to eerie occurrences and legendary sunrises. Often standing above the clouds and vaulting high beyond the surrounding countryside, Haleakala is definitely the place on Maui closest to heaven.

As much as Maui has to offer, Maui County has something more. Two additional islands in fact. Lanai and Molokai—both long linked historically to the Valley Isle, and lying nearer to Maui than any other islands in the chain—are part of the county administered from Wailuku. Since they are so closely tied to the larger island, and offer such fascinating day-trip destinations, they have been given their own chapters in *Hidden Maui*.

Directly to the west, lying in Maui's wind shadow, sits the smallest and most secluded island. **Lanai** is an explorer's paradise, with a network of jeep trails leading to hidden beaches and scenic mountain ridges. There are only 2000 people and about 20 miles of paved road here. If you're seeking an idyllic retreat, this is the place.

Molokai, slightly larger but nearly as remote, provides another extraordinary hideaway. With white-sand beaches, a mountainous interior and a large population of Hawaiians, the "Friendly Isle" retains a unique sense of old Hawaii. Here you can visit a leper colony on the windswept Kalaupapa Peninsula, a pilgrimage that could prove to be the most inspiring of all your experiences in Hawaii.

When to Go
SEASONS

There are two types of seasons on Maui, one keyed to tourists and the other to the climate. The peak tourist seasons run from mid-December until Easter, then again from mid-June through Labor Day. Particularly around the Christmas holidays and in August, the visitors centers are crowded. Prices increase, hotel rooms and rental cars become harder to reserve and everything moves a bit more rapidly.

If you plan to explore the island during these seasons, make reservations several months in advance; actually, it's a good idea to make advance reservations whenever you visit. Without doubt, the off-season is the best time to hit the island. Not only are hotels more readily available, but campsites and hiking trails are also less crowded.

Climatologically, the ancient Hawaiians distinguished between two seasons—*kau*, or summer, and *hooilo*, or winter. Summer extends from May to October, when the sun is overhead and the temperatures are slightly higher. Winter brings more variable winds and cooler weather.

The important rule to remember about Maui's beautiful weather is that it changes very little from season to season but varies dramatically from place to place. The average yearly temperature is about 75°, and during the coldest weather in January and the warmest in August, the thermometer rarely moves more than 5° or 6° in either direction. Similarly, sea water temperatures range comfortably between 74° and 80° year-round.

A key aspect to this luxurious semitropical environment is the trade wind that blows with welcome regularity from the northeast, providing a natural form of air conditioning. When the trades stop blowing, they are sometimes replaced by *kona* winds carrying rain and humid weather from the southwest. These are most frequent in winter, when the island receives its heaviest rainfall.

While summer showers are less frequent and shorter in duration, winter storms are sometimes quite nasty. I've seen it pour for five consecutive days, until hiking trails disappeared and local streets were awash. If you visit in winter, particularly from December to March, you're risking the chance of rain.

A wonderful factor to remember through this wet weather is that if it's raining where you are, you can often simply go someplace else. And I don't mean another part of the world, or even a different island. Since the rains generally batter the northeastern section of the island, you can usually head over to the south or west coast for warm, sunny weather. Or if you seek cooler climes, head up to the mountains; for every thousand feet in elevation, the temperature drops about 3°. If you climb high enough on Maui, you might even encounter snow!

CALENDAR OF EVENTS

Something else to consider in planning a visit to Maui is the amazing lineup of annual cultural events. For a thumbnail idea of what's happening when, check the calendar below. You might just find that special occasion to climax an already dynamic vacation.

JANUARY   **Kihei-Wailea Area**   The Four Seasons Resort Wailea sponsors the **Celebration of Whales**, an international gathering with discussions, whale watching, entertainment and an art exhibit.

Molokai   Molokai Makahiki kicks off the New Year with traditional Hawaiian games for kids and adults.

FEBRUARY   **Throughout Maui**   **Chinese New Year** is celebrated at various locations throughout the island with dancing, music, martial arts demonstration, food booths and fireworks. Front Street in Lahaina is a choice spot to enjoy the festivities.

Kahului-Wailuku Area   **Art Maui** is a month-long juried art show featuring new work by local artists. It's held at the Maui Arts and Cultural Center on Kahului Beach Road.

MARCH   **Throughout Maui**   You can volunteer to help the Pacific Whale Foundation count humpbacks during the **Great Whale Count**.

Kahului-Wailuku Area The **Maui Marathon** is run from the Maui Shopping Mall in Kahului to Whalers Village in Kaanapali in early March.

Hana Highway The **East Maui Taro Festival** is a celebration of the staple of the Hawaiian diet.

Throughout Maui Buddhist temples mark **Buddha Day**, the luminary's birthday, with special services. Included among the events are pageants, dances and flower festivals.

APRIL

Kahului-Wailuku Area In early April, the Valley Isle Road Runners Association sponsors the **Iao Valley 10K Run**.

Hana Highway The **O'Neill Pro Board Windsurfing Competition** is a popular ten-day tournament that's held at Hookipa Beach Park.

Throughout Maui **Lei Day** is celebrated by people wearing flower leis and colorful Hawaiian garb. This island-wide festival featuring lei-making contests and Hawaiian entertainment is held on May 1.

MAY

Upcountry and Haleakala **Seabury Hall Craft Fair** in Makawao offers local arts and crafts, food booths and live entertainment.

Lanai The **Pineapple Festival,** held in Lanai City, features contemporary Hawaiian music, pineapple cooking contests and arts and crafts.

Molokai Celebrate the birth of hula on the Friendly Isle with performances, music and Hawaiian food at **Molokai Hula Piko**.

Throughout Maui **Kamehameha Day,** honoring Hawaii's first king, is celebrated June 11 with parades, chants, hula dances and exhibits.

JUNE

Kaanapali-Kapalua Area The **Kapalua Music Festival** features chamber music by internationally acclaimed artists.

Upcountry and Haleakala Staged at the Eddie Tam Center in Makawao, the **Annual Upcountry Fair** is where the 4-H crowd swings into action. Enjoy the live entertainment and local delicacies and, if you're an aspiring performer, don't miss the Star Search.

Kaanapali-Kapalua Area More than 100 different wines from California, Oregon and Washington, as well as Australia, are sampled at the **Kapalua Wine and Food Symposium**.

JULY

Kahului-Wailuku Area The **Maui Jaycees Carnival,** akin to a county fair, comes to the Maui War Memorial Sports Complex in Wailuku. Local entertainment, games, rides and commercial booths are part of the fun. The Maui War Memorial Sports Complex also hosts the **Fourth of July Fireworks Extravaganza,** which features eats, explosives and live entertainment.

Upcountry and Haleakala In addition to fireworks, Maui celebrates the Fourth of July with the **Makawao Parade and Rodeo**.

AUGUST   **Throughout Maui** Buddhists perform colorful **Bon Dances** every weekend to honor the dead. On August 21, locals celebrate **Admission Day**, the date in 1959 when Hawaii became the 50th state.

Kaanapali-Kapalua Area In addition to a raw-onion–eating contest, you'll find food booths containing onion dishes from local restaurants, live music, a farmer's market and a cookoff where people can enter their favorite Maui onion recipe at the **Maui Onion Festival**, held at the Kaanapali Beach Resort.

Molokai Visitors to Molokai won't want to miss the **Molokai Ranch Rodeo**, a full two-day rodeo with barbecues and live bands.

SEPTEMBER   **Kaanapali-Kapalua Area** Hawaii's largest tennis purse is the prize on which everyone keeps their eyes at the **Kapalua Tennis Open Tournament**. A six-person relay across the nine-mile channel from Lanai to Kaanapali draws 50 international swimming teams to the **Maui Channel Relay Swim**.

Kahului-Wailuku Area The six-person **Hana Relay**, a 54-mile swim from Kahului to Hana, is one of autumn's more challenging events.

Hana Highway A popular event on the east side of the island is the **Haku Mele Celebration**. Staged in Hana's Plantation House, it provides yet another opportunity to enjoy traditional island entertainment and food.

Upcountry and Haleakala Maui Cycle to the Sun is the ultimate uphill challenge: a 38-mile bike ride from the ocean to the 10,023-foot peak of Haleakala. Covering the same route is the **Haleakala Run to the Sun**.

Molokai A lantern parade and block party are two events that highlight **Aloha Week**.

OCTOBER   **Throughout Maui** The highlight of Hawaii's cultural season is the **Aloha Week** festival, a series of week-long celebrations featuring parades, street parties and pageants.

Lahaina The **Lahaina Halloween Hoolaulea** is a memorable street party with a parade, food fair, music and dancing on Front Street.

Kaanapali-Kapalua Area The **Hyatt Regency Maui Kaanapali Classic** Tournament draws top stars from the PGA Tour.

Kahului-Wailuku Area The **Maui County Fair** features agricultural exhibits, ethnic foods and arts-and-crafts displays at the Kahului fairgrounds.

Lanai Aloha Week is celebrated with a parade, a block party, a beach party and activities honoring the various ethnic groups on the Pineapple Isle.

NOVEMBER   **Kaanapali-Kapalua Area** An $800,000 purse draws the best golfers on the professional tour to the **Lincoln Mercury Kapalua International PGA Golf Tournament**.

Kahului-Wailuku Area Hawaiian and other crafts are showcased at the **Lokahi Pacific Christmas Craft Fair**, held at the War Memorial Sports Complex in Wailuku.

Hana Highway The **Aloha Classic Windsurfing** competition at Hookipa Beach on the Hana Highway is the last of three events on the Pro Boardsailing Association World Tour.

Upcountry and Haleakala In Makawao, the **Maui County Rodeo Finals** bring together the top cowboys from Molokai and Maui.

Throughout Maui Buddha's enlightenment is commemorated with **Bodhi Day** ceremonies and religious services.

DECEMBER

Kaanapali-Kapalua Area Hawaiian arts and crafts, music and dance are highlighted at the **Na Mele O Maui Festival**.

Kihei-Wailea Area Santa is the center of attention at the **Wailea Christmas Festival**, staged in the Wailea Shopping Village.

Upcountry and Haleakala Christmas arts and crafts are the star attractions at the **Hui Noeau Christmas House** in Makawao.

The **Hawaii Visitors Bureau**, a state-run agency, is a valuable resource from which to obtain free information on Maui and the rest of Hawaii. With offices nationwide, the Bureau can help plan your trip and then offer advice once you reach Maui. The Valley Isle office is called the **Maui Visitors Bureau ~** 1727 Wili Pa Loop, Wailuku; 244-3530. On the mainland, you can contact the **Hawaii Visitors Bureau** at 350 Fifth Avenue, Suite 1827, New York, NY 10118 ~ 212-947-0717, 800-353-5846.

Before You Go

VISITORS CENTERS

Another excellent resource is the **Hawaii State Library Service**. With a network of libraries on Maui, this government agency provides facilities for residents and nonresidents alike. The libraries are good places to find light beach-reading material as well as books on Hawaii. Visitors can check out books by simply applying for a library card with a valid identification card.

Or boot up the computer and link up with "**Maui On-Line.**" A service of Channel 7, The Visitor Channel, this web page is more like a web book, with a wealth of information on lodging, dining, transportation, beaches and outdoor activities. Their Internet address is http:\\maui.net\~mol; 661-1111, fax 661-9700.

In planning a Maui sojourn, one potential moneysaver is the package tour, which combines air transportation with a hotel room and other amenities. Generally, it is a style of travel that I avoid. However, if you can find a package that provides air transportation, a hotel or condominium accommodation and a rental car, all at one low price—it is worth considering. Just try to avoid the packages that preplan your entire visit, dragging you around on air-conditioned tour buses. Look for the package that provides only the

PLANNING AHEAD

bare necessities, namely transportation and lodging, while allowing you the greatest freedom.

However you decide to go, be sure to consult a travel agent. They are professionals in the field, possessing the latest information on rates and facilities and their service to you is free.

PACKING   When I get ready to pack for a trip, I sit down and make a list of everything I'll need. It's a very slow, exact procedure: I look in closets, drawers and shelves, and run through in my mind the activities in which I'll participate, determining which items are required for each. After all the planning is complete and when I have the entire inventory collected in one long list, I sit for a minute or two, basking in my wisdom and forethought.

Then I tear the hell out of the list, cut out the ridiculous items I'll never use, halve the number of spares among the necessary items and reduce the entire contents of my suitcase to the bare essentials.

Before I developed this packing technique, I once traveled overland from London to New Delhi carrying two suitcases and a knapsack. I lugged those damned bundles onto trains, buses, jitneys, taxis and rickshaws. When I reached Turkey, I started shipping things home, but by then I was buying so many market goods that it was all I could do to keep even.

I ended up carrying so much crap that one day, when I was sardined in a crowd pushing its way onto an Indian train, someone managed to pick my pocket. When I felt the wallet slipping out, not only was I unable to chase the culprit—I was so weighted down with baggage that I couldn't even turn around to see who was robbing me!

Over 75 percent of Maui is undeveloped!

I'll never travel that way again, and neither should you. Particularly when visiting Hawaii, where the weather is mild, you should pack very light. The airlines permit two suitcases and a carry-on bag; try to take one suitcase and maybe an accessory bag that can double as a beach bag. Dress styles are very informal in the islands, and laundromats are frequent, so you don't need a broad range of clothing items, and you'll require very few extras among the essential items.

Remember, you're packing for a semitropical climate. Take along a sweater or light jacket for the mountains and something to protect against rain. But otherwise, all that travelers on Maui require are shorts, bathing suits, lightweight slacks, short-sleeved shirts and blouses and summer dresses or *muumuus*. Rarely do visitors require sport jackets or formal dresses. Wash-and-wear fabrics are the most convenient.

For footwear, I suggest soft, comfortable shoes. Low-cut hiking boots or tennis shoes are preferable for hiking; for beachgoing, there's nothing as good as sandals.

There are several other items to squeeze in the corners of your suitcase—sunscreen, sunglasses, a towel and, of course, your copy of *Hidden Maui*. You might also consider packing a mask, fins and snorkel and a camera.

If you plan on camping, you'll need most of the equipment required for mainland overnighting. On Maui, you can get along quite comfortably with a lightweight tent and sleeping bag. You'll also need a knapsack, canteen, camp stove and fuel, mess kit, first-aid kit (with insect repellent, water purification tablets and Chapstick), toilet kit, a pocket knife, hat, waterproof matches, flashlight and ground cloth.

LODGING

Accommodations on Maui range from funky cottages to highrise condominiums. You'll find inexpensive family-run hotels, middle-class tourist facilities and world-class resorts.

Whichever you choose, there are a few guidelines to help save money. Try to visit during the off-season, avoiding the high-rate periods during the summer and from Christmas to Easter. Rooms with mountain views are less expensive than ocean view accommodations. Generally, the farther a hotel is from the beach, the less it costs. Another way to economize is by reserving a room with a kitchen. In any case, try to reserve far in advance.

Throughout this book, hotels are described according to price category. *Budget* hotels have rooms starting from $50 or less per night for two people. *Moderate* facilities begin somewhere between $50 and $90. *Deluxe* hotels offer rates starting from $90 to $130. *Ultra-deluxe* establishments rent accommodations at prices above $130.

Bed-and-Breakfast Inns   The bed-and-breakfast business on Maui becomes more diverse and sophisticated every year. Today there are several referral services that can find you lodging on Maui or any of the other islands. Claiming to be the biggest clearinghouse in the state, **Bed & Breakfast Honolulu (Statewide)** represents over 300 properties, including about 75 on Maui. ~ 3242 Kaohinani Drive, Honolulu, HI 96817; 595-7533, 800-288-4666, fax 595-2030.

The original association, **Bed & Breakfast Hawaii**, claims over 150 locations, many on Maui. This Kauai-based service was founded in 1976 and is well known throughout Hawaii. ~ P.O. Box 449, Kapaa, HI 96746; 822-7771, 800-733-1632, fax 822-2723.

You can also try **Affordable Accommodations**, which is actually based in Maui. ~ 2825 Kauhale Street, Kihei 96753; 879-7865. Or call **All Islands Bed & Breakfast**, an Oahu-based reservation service that claims to represent more than 150 bed and breakfasts on Maui alone. ~ 823 Kainui Drive, Kailua, HI 96734; 263-2342, 800-542-0344, fax 263-0308.

While the properties represented by these agencies range widely in price, **Hawaii's Best Bed & Breakfasts** specializes in small, upscale accommodations on all the islands. With about 100 places to choose from, it places guests in a variety of privately owned facilities; most are deluxe in price. About two dozen of the places are on Maui. ~ P.O. Box 563, Kamuela, HI 96743; 885-4550, 800-262-9912, fax 885-0559.

CONDOS

Many people visiting Maui, especially those traveling with families, find that condominiums are often cheaper than hotels. While some hotel rooms come with kitchenettes, few provide all the amenities of condominiums. A condo, in essence, is an apartment away from home. Designed as studio, one-, two- or three-bedroom apartments, they come equipped with full kitchen facilities and complete kitchenware collections. Many also feature washer-dryers, dishwashers, air conditioning, color televisions, telephones, lanais and community swimming pools. Utilizing the kitchen will save considerably on your food bill; by sharing the accommodations among several people, you'll also cut your lodging bill.

DINING

A few guidelines will help you chart a course through Maui's countless dining places. Each restaurant entry is described as budget, moderate, deluxe or ultra-deluxe in price. Dinner entrées at *budget* restaurants usually cost $8 or less. The ambience is informal café style and the crowd is often a local one. *Moderately* priced restaurants range between $8 and $16 at dinner and offer pleasant surroundings, a more varied menu and a slower pace. *Deluxe* establishments tab their entrées above $16, featuring sophisticated cuisines, plush decor and more personalized service. *Ultra-deluxe* restaurants generally price above $24 and the service is comparable to the food.

TRAVELING WITH CHILDREN

Maui is an ideal vacation spot for family holidays. The pace is slow, the atmosphere casual. A few guidelines will help ensure that your trip to the islands brings out the joys rather than the strains of parenting, allowing everyone to get into the *aloha* spirit.

Use a travel agent to help with arrangements; they can reserve spacious bulkhead seats on airlines and determine which flights are least crowded. They can also seek out the best deals on inexpensive condominiums, saving you money on both room and board.

Planning the trip with your kids stimulates their imagination. Books about travel, airplane rides, beaches, whales, volcanoes and Hawaiiana help prepare even a two-year-old for an adventure. This preparation makes the "getting there" part of the trip more exciting for children of all ages.

And "getting there" means a long-distance flight. Plan to bring everything you need on board the plane—diapers, food, toys, books and extra clothing for kids and parents alike. I've found it helpful to carry a few new toys and books as treats to distract my son and daughter when they get bored. I also pack a few snacks.

Allow extra time to get places. Book reservations in advance and make sure that the hotel or condominium has the extra crib, cot or bed you require. It's smart to ask for a room at the end of the hall to cut down on noise. And when reserving a rental car, inquire to see if they provide car seats and if there is an added charge. Hawaii has a strictly enforced car seat law.

The mermaid goddess Wewehi lives in the waters off Maui. You can't miss her—she'll be the only swimmer wearing *limu-loloa*, a reddish-colored seaweed.

Besides the car seat you may have to bring along, also pack shorts and T-shirts, a sweater, sun hat, bathing suits, sundresses and waterproof sandals. A stroller with sunshade for little ones helps on sightseeing sojourns; a shovel and pail are essential for sandcastle building. Most important, remember to bring a good sunblock. The quickest way to ruin a family vacation is with a bad sunburn. Also plan to bring indoor activities such as books and games for evenings and rainy days.

Most towns have stores that carry diapers, food and other essentials. However, prices are much higher in Hawaii. To economize, some people take along an extra suitcase filled with diapers and wipes, baby food, peanut butter and jelly, etc.

A first-aid kit is always a good idea. Also check with your pediatrician for special medicines and dosages for colds and diarrhea. If your child does become sick or injured on Maui, contact a local doctor or the **Maui Memorial Hospital** at 242-2343. There is also a **Poison Control Center in Honolulu,** which can be reached at 800-362-3585.

Hotels often provide access to babysitters. In the Kaanapali area you can try **Babysitting Services of Maui** for bonded sitters. On occasion, they also have sitters in Kihei. ~ 661-0558.

Some resorts and hotels have daily programs for kids during the summer and holiday seasons. Hula lessons, lei making, storytelling, sandcastle building and various sports activities keep *keikis* (kids) over six happy while also giving Mom and Dad a break. As an added bonus, these resorts offer family plans, providing discounts for extra rooms or permitting children to share a room with their parents at no extra charge. Check with your travel agent.

WOMEN TRAVELING ALONE

It is sad commentary on life in the United States, but women traveling alone must take precautions. It's entirely unwise to hitchhike and probably best to avoid inexpensive accommodations on the outskirts of town; the money saved does not outweigh the risk. Bed and breakfasts and good hotels are generally your safest bet for lodging.

If you are hassled or threatened in some way, never be afraid to scream for assistance. It's a good idea to carry change for a phone call. In case of an emergency, you can call the **Sexual Assault Hotline** at 808-242-4357.

GAY & LESBIAN TRAVELERS

The island of Maui is at the cutting edge of gay culture in at least one regard: While the rest of the state debates a law that would legalize same-sex marriages, Maui has been home for years to **Royal Hawaiian Weddings**. This Valley Isle institution arranges beautiful gay wedding ceremonies set in lush tropical surroundings. ~ P.O. Box 424, Puunene, HI; 875-0625.

Local wags also point out that ever since the days of Hawaiian royalty, Maui has been a favorite playground for island queens. Seriously now, after Oahu, Maui has more exclusively gay and gay-friendly facilities than any other island. This includes an impressive concentration of gay and lesbian bed and breakfasts. Maui also offers some of Hawaii's best beaches, including **Little Makena**, a gay nude beach in the Kihei-Wailea district.

For information on the gay and lesbian scene on Maui, contact **Both Sides Now**. They can provide details on lodging, upcoming events and social gatherings. ~ P.O. Box 5042, Kahului, HI 96732; 244-4566. Lesbians can also call **Contact Dykes**. ~ 879-2971.

Women can contact the **Women's Events Hotline** for goings-on around the island. ~ 573-3077. Another organization is **Women Helping Women,** a domestic violence shelter. ~ 579-9581.

The Valley Isle is even home to "the only gay and lesbian surfing school in the world," the **Maui Surfing School**. Lessons are held at the south end of Lahaina. ~ 875-0625. (See the surfing section in Chapter Two for more information.)

If you're looking for someone to guide you above the water, contact **Personal Maui**. It's run by a fellow named Dan Keen, who gives tours (in your rental car) and can help introduce you to Maui's hidden realms. ~ 572-1589.

Nightlife centers around **Hamburger Mary's**, a restaurant and bar in Wailuku. **Blue Tropix** in Lahaina goes gay every Sunday afternoon and evening. There's a drag show every Thursday night at **Casanova Italian Restaurant** in Makawao. Proceeds go to the Maui AIDS Foundation. The gay and lesbian bed and breakfasts are concentrated in Kihei, along the Hana Highway and in the Upcountry region.

For more information on nightlife and lodging see area chapters or "gay-friendly travel" in the index.

SENIOR TRAVELERS

Maui is a hospitable place for senior citizens to visit. Countless museums, historic sights and even restaurants and hotels offer senior discounts that can cut a substantial chunk off vacation costs. For a small fee, the national park system's Golden Age Passport, which must be applied for in person, allows free admission for anyone 62 and older to the national park facilities on the island. Once purchased, the passport is good for life.

The **American Association of Retired Persons** (AARP) offers membership to anyone over 50. AARP's benefits include travel discounts with a number of firms. ~ 3200 East Carson Street, Lakewood, CA 90712; 310-496-2277, 800-424-3410.

Be extra careful about health matters. Consider carrying a medical record with you—including your medical history and current medical status as well as your doctor's name, phone number and address. Make sure your insurance covers you while you are away from home.

DISABLED TRAVELERS

The **Commission on Persons with Disabilities** publishes a survey of the city, county, state and federal parks in Hawaii that are accessible to disabled people. They also provide "Aloha Guides to Accessibility," which covers Maui as well as the other islands, and gives information on various hotels, shopping centers and restaurants that are accessible. ~ 919 Ala Moana Boulevard, Room 101, Honolulu, HI 96814; 586-8121.

The **Society for the Advancement of Travel for the Handicapped** provides information for travelers with disabilities. ~ 347 5th Avenue, #610, New York, NY, 10016; 212-447-7284. The **Maui Center for Independent Living** also offers helpful information. ~ 1464-D Lower Main Street, Room 105, Wailuku, HI 96793; 808-242-4966. **Travelin' Talk**, a network of people and organizations, also provides assistance. ~ P.O. Box 3534, Clarksville, TN 37043; 615-552-6670.

Be sure to check in advance when making room reservations. Some hotels feature facilities for those in wheelchairs.

FOREIGN TRAVELERS

Passports and Visas   Most foreign visitors are required to have a passport and a tourist visa to enter the United States. Contact your nearest United States Embassy or Consulate well in advance to obtain a visa and to check on any other entry requirements.

Customs Requirements   Foreign travelers are allowed to carry in the following: 200 cigarettes (1 carton), 50 cigars, or 2 kilograms (4.4 pounds) of smoking tobacco; one liter of alcohol for personal use only (you must be 21 years of age to bring in alcohol); and US$100 worth of duty-free gifts that include an additional quantity of 100 cigars. You may bring in any amount of currency, but must fill out a form if you bring in over US$10,000. Carry any prescription drugs in clearly marked containers. (You may have to produce a written prescription or doctor's statement for the customs officer.) Meat or meat products, seeds, plants, fruits and narcotics are not allowed to be brought into the United States. Contact the **United States Customs Service** for further information. ~ 1301 Constitution Avenue NW, Washington, DC 20229; 202-927-6724.

Driving   If you plan to rent a car, an international driver's license should be obtained prior to arrival. Some rental car companies require both a foreign license and an international driver's license. Many car rental agencies require that the lessee be at least 25 years of age; all require a major credit card.

Currency   United States money is based on the dollar. Bills come in six denominations: $1, $5, $10, $20, $50 and $100. Every dollar is divided into 100 cents. Coins are the penny (1 cent), nickel (5 cents), dime (10 cents) and quarter (25 cents).

You may not use foreign currency to purchase goods and services in the United States. Consider buying traveler's checks in dollar amounts. You may also use credit cards affiliated with an American company such as Interbank, Barclay Card, VISA and American Express.

Electricity and Electronics   Electric outlets use currents of 110 volts, 60 cycles. For appliances made for other electrical systems, you need a transformer or adapter. Travelers who use laptop computers for telecommunication should be aware that modem configurations for U.S. telephone systems may be different from their European counterparts. Similarly, the U.S. format for videotapes is different from that in Europe; U.S. Park Service visitors centers and other stores that sell souvenir videos often have them available in European format.

Weights and Measurements   The United States uses the English system of weights and measures. American units and their metric equivalents are as follows: 1 inch = 2.5 centimeters; 1 foot (12 inches) = 0.3 meter; 1 yard (3 feet) = 0.9 meter; 1 mile (5280 feet) = 1.6 kilometers; 1 ounce = 28 grams; 1 pound (16 ounces) = 0.45 kilogram; 1 quart (liquid) = 0.9 liter.

▼▼▼▼▼▼▼▼▼▼▼▼ Chances are you'll be flying through Honolulu on your way
Transportation into Maui. The **Honolulu International Airport** is served by
American Airlines, Canada 3000, Canadian Pacific Airlines,
BY AIR China Airlines, Continental Airlines, Delta Air Lines, Hawaiian Airlines, Korea Airlines, New Zealand Air, Northwest Airlines, Quantas, Philippine Airlines, TWA and United Airlines.

Three airports serve Maui—Kahului Airport, Kapalua-West Maui Airport and Hana Airport.

The **Kahului Airport** is the main landing facility and should be your destination if you're staying in the Central Maui region or on the southeast coast in the Kihei-Wailea area. United Airlines, Delta Air Lines and a couple of charter companies offer nonstop service from the mainland. American Airlines stops in Honolulu en route.

If you land in Kahului, you'll arrive at a bustling airport that has been expanded. I never realized how popular Maui was until I first pushed through the mobs of new arrivals here. In addition to the masses, you'll find a coffee shop and lounge, newsstand, gift shop, lei stand, baggage service and information booth (872-3893).

Kapalua-West Maui Airport serves the Lahaina-Kaanapali area. Aloha Island Air, Mahalo Air and Trans Air fly into the facility.

Hana Airport, really only a short landing strip and a one-room terminal, sits near the ocean in Maui's lush northeastern corner. Aloha Island Air and Air Molokai land in this isolated community. And don't expect very much ground transportation waiting for you. There is no bus service, though there is a car rental agency.

During the 19th century, sleek clipper ships sailed from the West Coast to Hawaii in about 11 days. Today, you'll be traveling by a less romantic but far swifter conveyance—the jet plane. Rather than days at sea, it will be about five hours in the air from California, nine hours from Chicago or around 11 hours if you're coming from New York.

Whichever carrier you choose, ask for the economy or excursion fare and try to fly during the week; weekend flights are generally higher in price. To qualify for lower-price fares, it is sometimes necessary to book your flight two weeks in advance and to stay over a Saturday night. Generally, however, the restrictions are minimal. Children under two years of age can fly for free, but they will not have a seat of their own. Each passenger is permitted two large pieces of luggage plus a carry-on bag. Shipping a bike or surfboard will cost extra.

Since cruise ships are the only commercial boats serving Maui and all five of the other Hawaiian Islands, most of the transportation between islands is by plane. **Aloha Airlines**, the state's major carrier, provides frequent inter-island jet service. If you're looking for smooth, rapid, comfortable service, this is certainly it. You'll be buckled into your seat, offered a free soft drink or low-cost cocktail and whisked to your destination within about 20 minutes.

Without doubt, the best service aboard any inter-island carrier is on Aloha Airlines. They have an excellent reputation for flying on time. I give them my top recommendation.

Now that you know how to fly quickly and comfortably, let me tell you about the most exciting way to get from Honolulu to Maui or to fly from Maui to other neighbor islands. Several small air-

GETTING BETWEEN ISLANDS

PARADISE FOR TWO

Want to get married but can't decide where or when? Simply pick up the phone and call **A Wedding Made In Paradise**. These ready-to-please consultants will help you choose the location on Maui and the minister. They'll even plan the ceremony.
~ Kihei; 879-3444.

lines—such as **Aloha Island Air, Air Molokai** and **Mahalo Air**—fly twin-engine propeller planes. These small airplanes travel at low altitudes and moderate speeds over the islands. Next to chartering a helicopter, they are the finest way to see Hawaii from the air.

Hawaii's grand oceanliner tradition is carried on today by **American Hawaii Cruises**. Sailing the SS *Independence* and the SS *Constitution*, they cruise the inter-island waters, docking at Maui, the Big Island, Kauai and Pier 2 in Honolulu. The cruises are week-long affairs that evoke memories of the old steamship era. ~ 2 North Riverside Plaza, Chicago, IL 60606; 800-765-7000.

One of the few ferry services in Hawaii is provided by **Sea Link of Hawaii**. Their 118-foot *Maui Princess* provides trips daily between Maui and Molokai. ~ 533-6899.

Another ferry, **Expeditions** operates out of Maui and links Lahaina with Manele Bay on Lanai. There are five boats per day in each direction. The 45-minute trip provides a unique way to travel between the islands. ~ P.O. Box 10, Lahaina, HI 96767; 661-3756.

CAR RENTALS

Renting a car is as easy on Maui as anywhere. The island supports at least several rental agencies, which compete fiercely with one another in price and quality of service. So before renting, shop around: check the listings in this book, and also look for the special temporary offers that many rental companies sometimes feature.

There are several facts to remember when renting a car. First of all, a major credit card is very helpful; if you lack one, you'll often have to leave a cash deposit on the car. Also, some agencies don't rent at all to people under 25. Regardless of your age, many companies charge several dollars a day extra for insurance. The insurance is optional and expensive, but if you don't take it you're liable for the first several thousand dollars in accident damage. So before leaving home, check to see how much coverage your personal insurance policy provides for rental cars and, if necessary, have a clause added that will include rental car protection.

Rates fluctuate with the season; slack tourist seasons are great times for good deals. Also, three-day, weekly and monthly rates are almost always cheaper than daily rentals; cars with standard shifts are generally less than automatics; and compacts are more economical than the larger four-door models.

Naturally, the most convenient means of renting a car is through one of the outfits at the airport. The problem with these companies, however, is that you pay for the convenience. In Kahului, the airport car-rental agencies are as follows: **Andres Rent A Car** (877-5378), **Avis Rent A Car** (871-7575, 800-331-1212), **Budget Rent A Car** (871-8811, 800-527-0700), **Dollar Rent A Car** (877-2731, 800-800-4000), **Hertz Rent A Car** (877-5167, 800-654-3131) and **National Interrent** (871-8851, 800-227-7368).

Then there are the agencies located away from the airport. Some of them will provide airport pick-up service when your plane arrives. I recommend that you check in advance and reserve a car from an outfit that extends this service. The others might be a little cheaper, but I've never considered the inconvenience worth the savings. Without a ride you'll be confronted with the Catch-22 situation of getting to your car. Do you rent a car in which to pick up your rental car? Take a bus? Or are you supposed to hitchhike?

Enough said. The rental agencies outside the airport include several companies that rent older model cars at very competitive rates. Two of these are **Word of Mouth Rent A Used Car** (877-2436, 800-533-5929) and **VIP Car Rentals** (877-2054, 800-367-6080).

If you find yourself in the Lahaina-Kaanapali area wanting to rent a car, try **Avis Rent A Car** (661-4588, 800-331-1212), **Budget Rent A Car** (661-8721, 800-527-0700), **Dollar Rent A Car** (667-2651, 800-800-4000), **Hertz Rent A Car** (661-3195, 800-654-3131) or **National Interrent** (667-9737, 800-227-7368). Among these agencies, Dollar is located at the Kapalua West Maui Airport, and Budget and Hertz are near the airport.

Dollar Rent A Car is the sole company in Hana. ~ 248-8237, 800-800-4000

Kihei is served by **Avis Rent A Car** (879-1980, 800-654-3131) and **Kihei Rent A Car** (879-7257).

Note: Many rental agencies will forbid you from driving the road from Hana around the southeast side of the island because it is sometimes in poor condition.

JEEP RENTALS

Generally, I don't recommend renting a jeep. They're more expensive and less comfortable than automobiles, and won't get you to very many more interesting spots. In addition, the rental car collision insurance provided by most credit cards does not cover jeeps. If you hit the rainy season though, and want to explore the back roads, it can't hurt. Except in extremely wet weather when roads are muddy, all the places mentioned in this book can be reached by car.

If, like most visitors to Maui, you arrive at the airport in Kahului, you certainly won't want for car rental agencies. There are quite a few with booths right at the airport. A number of others are located around town.

There are several companies on the island of Maui that rent four-wheel-drive vehicles. Some outfits offering jeeps are **Adventures Rent A Jeep** (190 Papa Place, Kahului; 877-6626, 800-701-5337) and **Budget Rent A Car** (871-8811, 661-8721, 800-527-0700).

MOTOR SCOOTER RENTALS

A & B Moped Rental rents mopeds by the hour, day or week. These vehicles provide an exhilarating and economical way to explore the area. Though they are not intended for long trips or busy roadways, they're ideal for short jaunts to the beach. ~ 3481 Lower Honoa-piilani Road, Honokowai; 669-0027.

PUBLIC TRANSIT

There is almost no general transportation on Maui and the little that is provided lies concentrated in one small sector of the island. The **Lahaina Express** (661-8748) travels between Lahaina and Kaanapali. Picking up the baton in Kaanapali, the **Kaanapali Trolley** (667-7411) runs through this popular resort area. **Akina Bus Service** (879-2828) operates buses in the town of Lahaina.

Speedy Shuttle (875-8070) offers transportation from Kahului Airport to resorts on the island. (It's recommended that you call at least a day in advance, though last-minute pickups are available.) **Alii's Coach** (879-4853) provides transportation throughout the whole island, including to airports.

AERIAL TOURS

Much of Maui's best scenery is reached via serpentine roads or steep mountain drives. While the views are stunning, the best way to get a bird's-eye view is from the air. Helicopters, fixed-wing aircraft and gliders all make it easy to see the volcanic uplands, waterfall splashed cliffs and dreamy back-country beaches.

There's also a west Maui/Molokai flight highlighting the tallest waterfall in the state, Molokai's Kahiwa. **Hawaii Helicopters** offers tours ranging from 30 minutes to five hours. The longer tours stop in Hana for 45 minutes to three hours, offering a chance to explore this verdant area's beaches and waterfalls via van. ~ Kahului Heliport; 877-3900.

At **American Pacific Air** you can choose between a 45-minute tour of West Maui or a one-hour-and-40-minute circle tour of the entire island aboard four- and six-seater Cessnas. ~ Kahului Airport; 871-8115.

For aerobatic flights and scenic tours in an open cockpit aircraft, try **Biplane Barnstormers**. Trips range from 20 minutes to an hour and 40 minutes and reach a wide variety of destinations around the island. A special 30-minute aerobatic flight, guaranteed to knock your socks off, includes barrel rolls, loops and four-leaf clovers. ~ 878-2860.

For those who'd prefer to experience their helicopter tour without leaving the ground, **Incredible Journeys!** offers a simulated flight. This virtual reality view of Maui explores the entire island via what claims to be the "world's first" helicopter tour simulator. The film quality is imperfect, but it's an interesting experience nonetheless. ~ Hyatt Regency Maui, 200 Nohea Kai Drive, Kaanapali; 661-0092.

TWO

The Land
and Outdoor Adventures

Maui is part of the Hawaiian archipelago that stretches more than 1500 miles across the North Pacific Ocean. Composed of 132 islands, Hawaii has eight major islands, including Maui, clustered at the southeastern end of the chain. Together these larger islands are about the size of Connecticut and Rhode Island combined. Only seven are inhabited: the eighth, Kahoolawe, served until recently as a bombing range for the U.S. Navy. Another island, Niihau, is privately owned and off-limits to the public.

Located 2500 miles southwest of Los Angeles, Maui is on the same 20th latitude as Hong Kong and Mexico City. It's two hours earlier in Maui than in Los Angeles, four hours before Chicago and five hours earlier than New York. Since Hawaii does not practice daylight-saving, this time difference becomes one hour greater during the summer months.

Maui, in a sense, is a small continent. Volcanic mountains rise in the interior, while the coastline is fringed with coral reefs and white-sand beaches. The northeastern face, buffeted by trade winds, is the wet side. The contrast between this side and the island's southwestern sector is sometimes startling. Maui's Hana region, for instance, is one of the wettest spots in the United States, but the southern side of the island resembles Arizona. Dense rainforests in the northeast are teeming with exotic tropical plants, while across the island you're liable to see cactus growing in a barren landscape!

For years, sugar was king in Maui, the most lucrative part of the island's economy. Today, tourism is number one. More than 2.4 million travelers worldwide visit Maui every year. It's now a $10.9 billion business that expanded exponentially during the 1970s and 1980s.

Marijuana is now Hawaii's foremost cash crop, flourishing on Maui, Hawaii and Kauai and representing a $3.4 billion business. Of course, no Chamber of Commerce report will list the demon weed as Hawaii's prime crop. Officially, sugar is still tops. While the $252 million sugar industry is small potatoes compared with tourism, Hawaii remains one of America's largest sugar-producing states. But sugar, like everything on Maui and elsewhere in the islands, is threatened by urban development. A ton of water is required to produce a pound of sugar.

Pineapple is another crop that's ailing. Stiff competition from the Philippines, where labor is cheap and easily exploitable, has reduced pineapple plantations on Maui and other islands to a few relatively small operations.

The islands do a booming business in macadamia nuts, orchids, anthuriums, guava nectar and passion-fruit juice. Together, with the cattle business, these industries have created a viable economy in the 50th state. The per capita income on Maui and throughout Hawaii is greater than the national average, and the standard of living is generally higher.

GEOLOGY

More than 25 million years ago a fissure opened along the Pacific floor. Beneath tons of seawater molten lava poured from the rift. This liquid basalt, oozing from a hot spot in the earth's center, created a crater along the ocean bottom. As the tectonic plate that comprises the ocean floor drifted over the earth's hot spot, numerous other craters appeared. Slowly, in the seemingly endless procession of geologic time, a chain of volcanic islands, stretching almost 2000 miles and including the idyllic island of Maui, emerged from the sea.

On the continents it was also a period of terrible upheaval. The Himalayas, Alps and Andes were rising, but these great chains would reach their peaks long before the Pacific mountains even touched sea level. Not until a few million years ago did these underwater volcanoes break the surface and become islands. By then, present-day plants and animals inhabited the earth, and apes were rapidly evolving into a new species.

Maui's first volcano, now the West Maui Mountains, rose above the waves about two million years ago. It was another million years before Haleakala first appeared. Gradually, lava flows from these two firepits joined together, creating the archipelago's second-largest island.

For many millennia, the mountains continued to grow. The forces of erosion cut into them, creating knife-edged cliffs and deep valleys. Then plants began germinating: mosses and ferns, springing from windblown spores, were probably first, followed by seed plants carried by migrating birds and on ocean currents. The steep-walled valleys provided natural greenhouses in which unique species evolved, while transoceanic winds swept insects and other life from the continents.

Some islands never survived this birth process: the ocean simply washed them away. The first islands that did endure, at the northwestern end of the Hawaiian chain, proved to be the smallest. Today these islands, with the exception of Midway, are barren uninhabited atolls. The volcanoes of Maui and its sister islands, far to the southeast, became the mountainous archipelago generally known as the Hawaiian Islands.

FLORA   Many of the plants you'll see on Maui are not indigenous. In fact, much of the lush vegetation of this tropical island found its way here from locations all over the world. Sea winds, birds and seafaring settlers brought many of the seeds, plants, flowers and trees from the islands of the South Pacific, as well as from other, more distant regions. Over time, some plants adapted to Maui's unique ecosystem and climate, creating strange new lineages and evolving into a completely new ecosystem. This process has long interested scientists, who consider the Hawaiian Islands one of the best natural labs for studies of plant evolution.

With several distinct biological regions, there's much more to Maui than lush tropics. Rainforests give way to dry forests, and to coastal habitats where the vegetation is specially suited to withstand wind and salt. Higher in altitude are the bogs, pools of standing water containing rare life forms that have been forced to adapt to a difficult environment. Highest in altitude is the alpine zone, consisting of bare volcanic surfaces scattered with clumps of low-growing herbs and shrubs. Subzero temperatures, frost and even snow help keep this region desolate.

Sugar cane arrived in Hawaii with the first Polynesian settlers, who appreciated its sweet juices. By the late 1800s, sugar cane was well established as a lucrative crop. The pineapple was first planted on Maui in 1903 and the island now harvests over 50 percent of the state's pineapples. A member of the bromeliad family, this spiky plant is actually a collection of beautiful pink, blue and purple flowers, each of which develops into fruitlets. The pineapple is a collection of these fruitlets, grown together into a single fruit that takes 14 to 17 months to mature. Sugar cane and pineapple are still the main crops on Maui, although competition from other countries and environmental problems caused by pesticides have taken their toll.

Visitors to Maui will find the island a perpetual flower show. Two flowers the island is particularly known for are the protea and the carnation. Originally from Australia and South Africa, the protea comes in varying shapes, sizes and colors, each unique. They are found mostly on the leeward slopes of Haleakala, where the altitude, cool nights and dry volcanic soil provide the perfect growing conditions for this exotic plant. Carnations grow in abundance in the Kula area, where the fields are filled with color and the air is often heady with the flowers' distinctive perfume. But it is the sweetly scented plumeria, delicate orchids, exotic ginger, showy birds of paradise, highly fragrant gardenias and the brightly hued hibiscus that run riot on Maui and add color and fragrance to the island. Scarlet and purple bougainvillea vines, and the aromatic lantana, with its dense clusters of flowers, are also found in abundance.

One of Maui's unique plants is the silversword. Delicate looking, this silvery green plant is actually very hardy. It thrives on the moonscape of Haleakala, 6000 to 10,000 feet above sea level. Very adaptable, it can survive in extreme hot and cold temperatures with little moisture. Its silvery hairs reflect the sun and its leaves curl inward, protecting the stalk and creating a sort of bowl where rain is collected and stored. The plant lives from five to more than thirty years, waiting until the right moment before sprouting a three- to six-foot stalk composed of hundreds of small, reddish flowers—and then it dies. In the same family as the sunflower, this particular type of silversword lives only on Haleakala and has been close to extinction for many years. Now protected, it is currently making a comeback.

Although many people equate the tropics with the swaying palm tree, Maui is home to a variety of exotic trees. The famed banyan tree, known for pillarlike aerial roots that grow vertically downward from the branches, spreads to form a natural canopy. When the roots touch the ground, they thicken, providing support for the tree's branches to continue expanding. The candlenut tree, originally brought to Hawaii from the South Pacific islands, is big, bushy and prized for its nuts, which can be used for oil or polished and strung together to make leis. With its cascades of bright yellow or pink flowers, the cassia tree earns its moniker—the shower tree.

SEAWEED GATHERING

Few Westerners think of seaweed as food, but it's very popular today among the Japanese, and it once served as an integral part of the Hawaiian diet. It's extremely nutritious, easy to gather and very plentiful. Rocky shores are the best places to find the edible species of seaweed. Some of them float in to shore and can be picked up; other species cling stubbornly to rocks and must be freed with a knife; still others grow in sand or mud. Low tide is the best time to collect seaweed: more plants are exposed, and some can be taken without even getting your feet wet.

Covered with tiny pink blossoms, the canopied monkeypod tree has fernlike leaves that close up at night.

Found in a variety of shapes and sizes, the ubiquitous palm does indeed sway to the breezes on white-sand beaches, but it also comes in a short, stubby form featuring more frond than trunk. The fruit, or nuts, of these trees are prized for their oil, which can be utilized for making everything from margarine to soap. The wood (rattan, for example) is often used for making furniture.

MAUI WOWIE For decades, Maui has been known for its sparkling beaches and lofty volcanoes. Agriculturally, the island has grown famous by producing sugar cane and pineapples. But during the past several decades, Maui and the other islands in the chain have become renowned for another crop, one that some deem a sacrament and others a sin.

In the islands it's commonly referred to as *pakalolo*. Mainlanders know it more familiarly by the locales in which it grows—Maui Wowie, Kona Gold, Puna Butter and Kauai Buds. Because of Hawaii's lush tropical environment, marijuana grows year-round and has become the state's number-one cash crop (and one of its largest law enforcement problems).

Now that marijuana is big business, ripoffs have become a harrowing problem in Hawaii. Growers often guard their crops with guns and booby traps. Because of this armed protection, it can be very dangerous to wander through someone's dope patch. It might be on public land far from the nearest road, but in terms of the explorer's personal safety, a marijuana plantation should be treated as the most private property imaginable. In the words of the islanders, it is strictly *kapu*.

FRUITS AND VEGETABLES There's a lot more to Maui's tropical wonderland than gorgeous flowers and overgrown rainforests. The island is also teeming with edible plants. Roots, fruits, vegetables, herbs and spices grow like weeds from the shoreline to the mountains. Following is a list of some of the more commonly found.

Avocado: Covered with either a tough green or purple skin, this pear-shaped fruit sometimes weighs as much as three pounds. It grows on ten- to forty-foot-high trees, and ripens from June through November.

Bamboo: The bamboo plant is actually a grass with a sweet root that is edible and a long stem frequently used for making furniture. Often exceeding eight feet in height, bamboo is green until picked, when it turns a golden brown.

Banana: Polynesians use banana trees not only for food but also for clothing, roofing, medicines, dyes and even alcohol. The fruit, which grows upside down on broad-leaved trees, can be harvested as soon as the first banana in the bunch turns yellow.

Breadfruit: This large round fruit grows on trees that reach up to 60 feet in height. Breadfruit must be boiled, baked or fried.

Coconut: The coconut tree is probably the most important plant in the entire Pacific. Every part of the towering palm is used. Most people are concerned only with the hard brown nut, which yields delicious milk as well as a tasty meat. If the coconut is still green, the meat is a succulent jellylike substance. Otherwise, it's a hard but delicious white rind.

Guava: A roundish yellow fruit that grows on a small shrub or tree, guavas are extremely abundant in the wild. They ripen between June and October.

Mango: Known as the king of fruits, the mango grows on tall shade trees. The oblong fruit ripens in the spring and summer.

Each Hawaiian island has its own official flower; the Valley Isle's blossom is the pink Maui rose.

Maui onion: Resembling an ordinary yellow onion in size and color, these bulbs are uncommonly sweet and mild. They are grown on the south side of Haleakala in rich volcanic soil, and enjoy enough sun and altitude to make them very sweet. A member of the lily family, the Maui onion is best eaten raw.

Mountain apple: This sweet fruit grows in damp, shaded valleys at an elevation of about 1800 feet. The flowers resemble fluffy crimson balls; the fruit, which ripens from July to December, is also a rich red color.

Papaya: This delicious fruit, which is picked as it begins to turn yellow, grows on unbranched trees. The sweet flesh can be bright orange or coral pink in color. Summer is the peak harvesting season.

Passion fruit: Oval in shape, this tasty yellow fruit grows to a length of about two or three inches. It's produced on a vine and ripens in summer or fall.

Taro: The tuberous root of this Hawaiian staple is pounded, then made into a grayish purple paste known as *poi*. One of the most nutritious foods, it has a rather bland taste. The plant has wide, shiny, thick leaves with reddish stems; the root is white with purple veins.

On Maui, it seems there is more wildlife in the water and air than on land. A scuba diver's paradise, the ocean is a promised land for many creatures. Coral, colorful fish and migrating whales are only part of this underwater community. Sadly, many of Hawaii's coral reefs have been dying mysteriously in the last few years. No one is sure why, but many believe this is partially due to runoff from pesticides used in agriculture.

For adventure lovers, Maui offers excellent opportunities for whale watching. Every year, humpback whales converge in the warm waters off the island to give birth to their calves. They begin their migration in Alaska and can be spotted in Hawaiian waters from

FAUNA

November through May. The humpback, named for its practice of showing its dorsal fin when diving, is quite easy to spy. Measuring 45 feet and weighing over 40 tons, humpbacks feed in shallow waters, usually diving for periods of no longer than 15 minutes. They often sleep on the surface and breathe fairly frequently.

Humpbacks are quite playful, and are seen leaping, splashing and flapping their 15-foot tails over their backs. The best time for whale watching is from January to April. Unlike other whales, humpbacks have the ability to sing. Loud and powerful, their songs carry above and below the water for miles. The songs change every year, yet, incredibly, all the whales always seem to know the current one.

Maui is also home to many rare and endangered birds. Like the flora, the birds on this island are highly specialized. Hawaii's state bird, the nene, or Hawaiian goose, is a cousin to the Canadian goose and mates for life. Extinct on Maui for many years, several birds were reintroduced here in the late 1950s. There's still some doubt as to whether they'll survive on their own in the wild. The only place they currently live, besides the Big Island, is on Haleakala. The slopes of Haleakala are also home to two other endangered birds: the crested honeycreeper and the parrotbill.

There *are* a few birds native to Hawaii that have thus far avoided the endangered species list. Two of the most common birds are the yellow-green *amakihi* and the red *iiwi*.

Known in Hawaiian mythology for its protective powers, the *pueo*, or Hawaiian owl, a brown-and-white-feathered bird, resides in Haleakala crater. The *koae kea*, or "tropic bird," also lives on Haleakala and in the crater. Resembling a seagull in size, it has a long, thin white tail and a striking striping pattern on the back of the wings.

Another common bird is the *iwa*, or frigate, a very large creature measuring three to four feet in length, with a wing span averaging

PRESERVING MAUI

With the current interest in ecology, even Maui's resorts are becoming environmentally aware. Most have instituted recycling and conservation programs. The Maui Land and Pineapple Company, owner of Kapalua, has awarded The Nature Conservancy a conservancy easement on 8000 acres on the slopes of Puu Kukui, a western Maui summit. The Ritz-Carlton hotel offers a variety of "eco-packages," where a dollar of each guest's bill is donated to The Nature Conservancy, and the Aston Wailea Resort saves seven million gallons of water annually by recycling water and is a pesticide-free resort.

seven feet. The males are solid black, while the females have a large white patch on their chest and tail. A predatory bird, they're easy to spot raiding the nesting colonies of other birds along the offshore rocks. If you see one, be careful not to point at it; legend has it that it's bad luck. Other birds that make Maui their home are the Hawaiian stilt and the Hawaiian coot—both water birds—along with the black noddy, American plover and wedge-tailed shearwater.

Not many wild four-footed creatures roam the island. Deer, feral goats and pigs were brought to the islands early on and have found a home in the forests. Some good news for people fearful of snakes: There is nary a serpent (or a sea serpent) on the island, although lizards such as skinks and geckos abound.

One can only hope that with the renewed interest in Hawaiian culture, and growing environmental awareness, Hawaii's plants and animals will continue to exist as they have for centuries.

Outdoor Adventures

SCUBA & SKINDIVING

The opportunities for adventuring on the Valley Isle are numerous and the conditions for several activities are outstanding. Whale watching, for example, is top-notch on Maui as humpbacks return each year to the waters off Lahaina to give birth. For cyclists, there are thrilling rides down the slopes of Haleakala and challenging courses on Hana's curving coast. Maui is also home to several of the world's premier windsurfing spots including Hookipa Beach on the island's north shore. (For information on outdoor adventures on Lanai and Molokai see chapters Ten and Eleven respectively.)

Maui offers a wide variety of snorkeling and diving opportunities ranging from Black Rock off Kaanapali to Honolua Bay not to mention Olowalu, Ahihi–Kinau Reserve, and Ulua Beach. While most of the dive operators are located near the island's south coast resorts, there are also good diving and snorkeling opportunities on the north shore at Paia's Baldwin Beach Park, as well as Hana's Waianapanapa State Park. From Maui it's also easy to reach neighboring destinations such as the Molokini Crater Marine Preserve and reefs off Lanai. One area off Lanai—Cathedrals—is considered the best dive site in Hawaii.

MOLOKINI   Molokini, a crescent-shaped crater off Maui's southern coast, offers one of the island's great snorkeling adventures. Every day dozens of boatloads of people pull up to dive the remarkably clear waters. Visibility typically ranges between 80 and 150 feet, conditions so clear you can spot fish before even entering the water. During winter months, you're also likely to see the humpback whales cavorting nearby.

Makena Boat Partners operates the 46-foot *Kai Kanani,* which departs from Makena Beach, and goes closer to the largely submerged volcano than other touring vessels. ~ 879-7218. Other companies operating excursions include **Lahaina Divers** at 143 Dickenson Street, Lahaina ~ 667-7496 and **Maui Classic Charters** at 1215 South Kihei Road, Kihei ~ 879-8188. You can also sail to the islet on the **Silent Lady**, a 64-foot whaling schooner. Most tours include snorkeling equipment, food and drinks in the price of admission. ~ Maalaea Harbor; 242-6499.

LAHAINA   **Extended Horizons** offers trips to Lanai for divers of varying abilities, and snorkelers can come along. ~ Mala Wharf, Lahaina; 667-0611.

Ocean Riders Adventure Rafting specializes in all-day snorkeling trips to Lanai. ~ Mala Wharf, Lahaina; 661-3586.

Lahaina Divers Inc. is another well-liked dive operator. ~ 143 Dickenson Street, Lahaina; 667-7496.

KIHEI-WAILEA AREA   **Bill's Scuba Shop Underwater Habitat** runs scuba and snorkeling trips off Wailea Point, Holoa Point and Molokini Crater. Certification classes and night dives are available. ~ 36 Keala Place, Kihei; 879-3483.

For weather forecasts on Maui, call 877-5111; marine conditions, 877-3477.

Molokini Divers features scuba and snorkeling trips to this popular islet. Visibility of 150 feet makes this marine preserve a favorite place to splash down. ~ Kihei Boat Harbor, Kihei; 879-0055.

Another recommended tour operator that also rents equipment is **Maui Dive Shop** ~ Azeka Place Shopping Center, South Kihei Road, Kihei, 879-3388; and Kihei Town Center, South Kihei Road, Kihei, 879-1919.

Well-known by underwater photographers, **Mike Severns Diving** runs trips for certified divers to Molokini and Makena. His dives focus on the southwest rift of Haleakala, a fascinating place to study marine life. Led by informative biologists, these trips are an excellent way to see Maui's hidden marine life. ~ Kihei Boat Ramp, Kihei; 879-6596.

Maui Sun Divers provides all gear and offers everything from beginner trips to certification classes to night dives. ~ Kihei; 879-3337.

Interested in learning underwater photography? Sign on with **Ed Robinson's Diving Adventures**. A prominent oceanic photographer, Robinson leads excursions aboard the *Seadiver II* and *Manakai* to the Lanai Cathedrals, Molokini and other favored dive sites. ~ Kihei; 879-3584.

SURFING & WINDSURFING   If you must go down to the sea again, why not do it on a board. Popular spots include Honolua Bay on the northwest coast, Hookipa Beach near Paia and Kanaha Beach Park in the Kahului area, as well as Napili Bay and Maalaea on the south coast. You can also take beginner lessons in the Lahaina area.

LAHAINA   A good place to start is **Maui Surfing School**. Andrea Thomas and her staff offer small classes and free board rental, and guarantee you'll be able to surf after one lesson. ~ Adjacent to Lahaina Harbor; 875-0625.

KAANAPALI-KAPALUA AREA The **Kaanapali Windsurfing School** offers surfing and windsurfing lessons on the adjacent beach. Ninety-minute windsurfing lessons come with a guarantee of success. Four-person surfing classes are also offered, weather permitting. Rentals are available. ~ Whalers Village, Kaanapali; 667-1964.

KAHULUI-WAILUKU AREA **Mistral High Wind Center** is a full-service windsurfing school that can even plan complete windsurfing holidays. ~ 261 Dairy Road, Kahului; 871-7753.

Similar opportunities await at **Windsurfing West**. Here the lessons include video replay (instant feedback) at the water's edge and are guaranteed to have you up and sailing in no time. ~ 415 Dairy Road, Kahului; 871-8733.

Thanks to a convenient radio communication system, instructors at the **Court Larnard Windsurfing School** at the Maui Windsurfing Company remain in constant contact with their students. Lessons are at Kanaha Beach Park, which has a protected area ideal for beginners. Safe, onshore winds blow you back toward the beach. Rentals are also available. ~ 520 Keolani Place, Kahului; 877-4816.

You can buy windsurfing gear at **Lightning Bolt**, the oldest surf shop on Maui. ~ 55 Kaahumanu Avenue, Kahului; 877-3484.

FISHING

Fishing in Hawaii is superb year-round, and the offshore waters are crowded with many varieties of edible fish. For deep-sea fishing you'll have to charter a boat, and freshwater angling requires a license, which can be obtained at sportfishing stores. For information on seasons, licenses and official regulations, check with the Aquatic Resources Division of the State Department of Land and Natural Resources.

Beaches and rocky points are usually good places to surf-cast; the best times are during the incoming and outgoing tides. Successful baits include octopus, eel, lobster, crab, frozen shrimp and sea worms. You can also fish with lures. The ancient Hawaiians used pearl shells to attract the fish and hooks, some made from human bones, to snare them. Your friends will probably be quite content to see you angling with store-bought artificial lures.

The deep blue sea around Maui can be nirvana for sportfishing enthusiasts. Choose between party boats, diesel cruisers and yachts custom-designed for trolling. All outfits provide equipment and bait. Just bring your own food and drinks and you're in business. If it's not too rough, your skipper may head for the productive game fishing waters between Maui and the Big Island. If conditions are choppy, you're more likely to fish the leeward side of the island or off neighboring Lanai.

There is also good fishing from the shore in many places. *Ulua*, *papio* and threadfin are the most common catches, but you'll also find goatfish, triggerfish, leatherback, milkfish, *moano*, big-eyed scad, bonefish, mullet and mountain bass. For information on the best places for offshore fishing, ask at local fishing stores, or try the following beaches: Hoaloha Park, Launiupoko State Wayside Park, Honokowai Beach Park, D. T. Fleming Park, Honokohau Beach, Keawakapu Beach, Poolenalena Beach Park, Black Sands Beach, Little Beach and Waianapanapa State Park.

LAHAINA   Ideal for groups up to four, **Robalo-One** is a stable 23-foot vessel that hits speeds up to 40 miles per hour in pursuit of game fish. You'll catch snapper, wrasse, barracuda or jack crevalle on half-day trips. ~ Lahaina Harbor; 661-0480.

Lucky Strike Charters fishes for marlin, mahimahi, wahoo and tuna with light and medium tackle. Light-tackle bottom fishing is also available. ~ Lahaina Harbor; 661-4606.

Islander II and **Hinatea** are matching sportfishing boats offering identical trips into coastal waters. On half- and full-day trips you'll fish for marlin, tuna, mahimahi, wahoo and shark. ~ Lahaina Harbor; 667-7548.

KIHEI-WAILEA AREA   In the Kihei area, contact **Carol Ann Charters** for half- and full-day fishing trips great for catching marlin, tuna, mahimahi and *ono*. ~ Maalaea Harbor; 877-2181.

Rascal Charters fishes for ahi, *ono*, mahimahi and marlin. Half- and full-day trips aboard a 31-foot vessel include game and bottom fishing. ~ Maalaea Harbor; 874-8633.

TORCH-FISHING   The old Hawaiians often fished at night by torchlight. They fashioned torches by inserting nuts from the *kukui* tree into the hollow end of a bamboo pole, then lighting the flammable nuts. When fish swam like moths to the flame, the Hawaiians speared, clubbed or netted them. Today, locals use flashlights.

CRABBING   There are two important crab species in Hawaii—Kona crabs and Samoan crabs. The Kona variety are found in relatively deep water, and can usually be caught only from a boat. Samoan crabs inhabit sandy and muddy areas in bays and near river mouths. All that most local people use to catch them is a net fastened to a round wire hoop and secured by a string. The net is lowered to the bottom; then, after a crab has gone for the bait, the entire contraption is raised to the surface.

SQUIDDING   Between June and December, squidding is a popular Hawaiian sport. Actually, the term is a misnomer: squid inhabit deep water and are not usually hunted. What you'll really be after are octopuses. There are two varieties in Hawaii, both of which are com-

The New Travel

Travel today is becoming a personal art form. A destination no longer serves as just a place to relax: it's also a point of encounter. To many, this new wave in travel customs is labeled "adventure travel" and involves trekking glaciers or sweeping along in a hang glider; to others, it connotes nothing more daring than a restful spell in a secluded resort. Actually, it's a state of mind, a willingness not only to accept but seek out the uncommon and unique.

Few places in the world are more conducive to this imaginative new travel than Maui. Several organizations on the island cater specifically to people who want to add local customs and unusual adventures to their vacation itineraries.

The Nature Conservancy of Hawaii, a nonprofit conservation organization, conducts natural history day hikes of Maui and Molokai. Led by expert guides, small groups explore untrammeled beaches, a rainforest and an ancient bog. The tours provide a singular insight into the plant and animal life of the islands. Reservations should be made at least one month in advance. ~ P.O. Box 1716, Makawao, HI 96768; 572-7849 on Maui and 553-5236 on Molokai.

Eye of the Whale features a ten-day tour of Kauai, Maui and the Big Island, including hiking and snorkeling. ~ P.O. Box 1269, Kapaa, HI 96755; 808-889-0227, 800-659-3544.

Hike Maui leads day hikes all around the Valley Isle. Ranging from five to ten hours in duration, these treks can be custom designed to your interests. ~ P.O. Box 330969, Kahului, HI 96733; 879-5270.

Maui Hiking Safaris sets out from Kahului at 8:00 a.m. and 2:00 p.m. on full-day and half-day adventures. With a guide and no more than six hikers, they explore the 1790 lava flow as well as rainforests and natural pools. The guides identify local flora and talk about Hawaiiana and volcanology. ~ P.O. Box 11198, Lahaina, HI 96761; 573-1716.

Open Eye Tours & Photos, led by nature photographer Barry Fried, provides custom-designed tours from a base in Maui's Upcountry. On the menu of outdoor adventures are visits to sacred healing places, gardens, petroglyphs, rainforests and, of course, some very photogenic waterfalls. ~ P.O. Box 324, Makawao, HI 96768; 572-3483.

When you're ready to take up the challenge of this new style of free-wheeling travel, check with these outfits. Or plan your own trip. To traditional tourists, Hawaii means souvenir shops and fast-food restaurants. But for those with spirit and imagination, it's a land of untracked beaches and ancient volcanoes waiting to be explored.

monly found in water three or four feet deep: the *hee*, a grayish-brown animal that changes color like a chameleon, and the *puloa*, a red-colored mollusk with white stripes on its head. Both are nocturnal and live in holes along coral reefs. The Hawaiians used to pick up the octopus, letting it cling to their chest and shoulders. When they were ready to bag their prize, they'd dispatch the creature by biting it between the eyes. Today, most people feel more comfortable spearing the beast.

SHELLFISH   Among Hawaii's many natural food sources are the shellfish that inhabit coastal waters. Oysters and clams, which use their muscular feet to burrow into sand and soft mud, are collected along the bottom of Hawaii's bays. Lobsters, though illegal to spear, are taken with short poles to which cable leaders and baited hooks are attached. Locals also gather limpets. These tiny black shellfish, locally known as *opihi*, cling tenaciously to rocks in areas of very rough surf. The Hawaiians gather them by leaping into the water after one set of waves breaks, then jumping out before the next set arrives. Being a coward myself, I simply order them in Hawaiian restaurants.

SHELL HUNTING   With over 1500 varieties of shells washing up on its beaches, Hawaii has some of the world's finest shelling. The miles of sandy beach along Maui's south shore are a prime area for handpicking free souvenirs. Along the shores are countless shell specimens with names like horned helmet, Hebrew cone, Hawaiian olive and Episcopal miter. Or you might find glass balls from Japan and sun-bleached driftwood.

Beachcombing is the easiest method of shell gathering. Take along a small container and stroll through the backwash of the waves, watching for ripples from shells lying under the sand. You can also dive in shallow water where the ocean's surge will uncover shells.

It's tempting to walk along the top of coral reefs seeking shells and other marine souvenirs, but these living formations maintain a delicate ecological balance. Reefs in Hawaii and all over the planet are dying because of such plunder. In order to protect this underwater world, try to collect only shells and souvenirs that are adrift on the beach and no longer necessary to the marine ecology.

The best shelling spots along Maui's south shore are Makena, Kihei beaches, Maalaea Bay, Olowalu, the sandy stretch from Kaanapali to Napili Bay, D. T. Fleming Park and Honolua Bay. On the north coast, the stretch from Waiehu to Waihee (west of Kahului) and the beaches around Hana are the choicest hunting grounds.

After heavy rainfall, watch near stream mouths for Hawaiian olivines and in stream beds for Maui diamonds. Olivines are small, semiprecious stones of an olive hue. Maui diamonds are quartz stones and make beautiful jewelry. The best places to go diamond hunting are near the Kahului Bay hotel strip and in Olowalu Stream.

From mid-December until the middle of May, it is prime whale-watching season on Maui. Humpback whales, measuring about 40 feet and weighing over 40 tons, migrate as many as 4000 miles from their summer home in Alaska. On the journey south, they consume tons of krill and tiny fish, then fast while in Hawaii. It is in the waters off Maui that they give birth to their young, babies that can weigh as much as three tons and gain up to 100 pounds a day.

Eager to protect the whales who winter in these waters, local officials have forced power craft to keep their distance from these cetaceans. But these restrictions are not so severe as to unduly interfere with the many sailing vessels that offer whale-watching opportunities off the Maui coast. You can also enjoy dive trips or pure performance rides on these beautiful vessels.

A prime area for whale watching lies along Honoapiilani Highway between Maalaea Bay and Lahaina, particularly at McGregor Point. So while you're visiting Maui, always keep an eye peeled seaward for vaporous spume and a rolling hump. The place you're standing might suddenly become an ideal crow's-nest.

About 2000 of the world's 10,000 humpbacks make the annual migration to Maui's southwestern coast each year. Today they are an endangered species, protected by federal law from whalers. Several local organizations study these leviathans and serve as excellent information sources.

The **Pacific Whale Foundation** issues daily reports over local radio stations during whale season. This same organization conducts "eco-adventure cruises," the profits from which help fund their whale protection projects. They have snorkeling tours to Molokini and whale-watching cruises, both led by marine naturalists. Most interesting is their dolphin adventure, where you skindive Lanai's untouched coral reefs and see spinner and bottlenose dolphins in one of the island's many hidden coves. ~ 101 North Kihei Road, Kihei; 879-8860. To contact their whale hotline call 800-942-5311.

LAHAINA **Sentinel Yacht Charters** specializes in sailing adventures. They also offer six-person whale-watching trips aboard a 41-foot sloop, as well as snorkeling excursions, sunset trips and joysailing. Special trips include Molokai and Lanai. ~ Lahaina Harbor; 661-8110.

Scotch Mist Sailing Charters offers half-day snorkeling trips to Lanai, as well as trips to the coral gardens of west Maui. Whale watching and champagne sunset sails are also available. ~ Lahaina Harbor; 661-0386.

First Class runs snorkeling, performance and sunset sailing trips. ~ Lahaina Harbor; 667-7733.

Windjammer Cruises has a 70-foot, three-masted schooner ideal for sunset dinner sails. You can dine on island cuisine, listen to live Polynesian entertainment and take in the views of Kahoolawe, Molokai and Lanai. ~ 505 Front Street, Lahaina; 661-8600.

Or, for a more intimate experience, try the six-passenger **Cinderella**, a 50-foot yacht. ~ Maalaea Harbor; 242-2779.

Trilogy Excursions receives high praise from repeat clients who climb aboard the 50-foot catamaran for excursions to Lanai. Once on the nearby island, they can swim and snorkel Hulopoe Bay Marine Reserve, enjoy a Hawaiian barbecue and tour Lanai City. ~ 180 Lahainaluna Road, Lahaina; 661-4743.

Island Marine Activities offers whale-spotting cruises from mid-December to May. ~ 113 Prison Street, Lahaina; 661-8397.

KAANAPALI-KAPALUA AREA   **Kapalua Kai** is a popular catamaran offering picnic-and-snorkeling and sunset sails. It sails Maui's most scenic waters and features whale-watching excursions in winter months. ~ Kaanapali; 667-5980.

PARA-SAILING & HANG GLIDING

Lahaina and Kaanapali Beach are perfect places to become airborne. Wonderful views of Maui's west side and neighboring Molokai add to the fun. The typical parasailing trip includes 30 to 45 minutes shuttling out and back to the launch point and eight to ten minutes in the air.

Parasail Kaanapali riders rise as high as 900 feet. ~ Mala Wharf; 669-6555. UFO **Parasailing** lets you ascend up to 800 feet and, if you wish, fly with a companion. ~ Whalers Village, Kaanapali; 661-7836. For hang gliding from some of the most beautiful spots on the island, try **Hang Gliding Maui** ~ Makawao; 572-6557.

KAYAKING

A sport that's growing in popularity, kayaking is an exciting way to explore the waters.

KAANAPALI-KAPALUA AREA   Kayaks are available from **Kaanapali Windsurfing School** ~ Whalers Village, Kaanapali; 667-1964.

KAHULUE-WAILUKU AREA   In Central Maui, **Maui Sea Kayaking** offers day trips to Maui and Lanai and full-moon trips to Molokini. Or they'll lead you on an overnight "romance" retreat, for which a guide will arrange a seaside campsite that is off-the-beaten-track and inaccessible by car. In the morning, the guide will return to prepare your breakfast and lead the way back to civilization. They also lead surfers to beaches good for surfing. ~ Puunene; 572-6299.

KIHEI-WAILEA AREA   A place to learn this adventure sport is **Kelii's Kayak Tours**. Guided tours include the Makena-La Perouse area on Maui's south shore, a north shore tour exploring the Honolua Bay/Honokohau area and a sunset excursion along Papawai Point.

Along the way you might spot dolphins, flying fish or whales. ~ 158 Lanakila Place, Kihei; 874-7652.

Kayak rentals and tours can also be arranged through **South Pacific Kayaks**. Their guided trips include snorkeling, and you're likely to see whales, sea turtles and dolphins. ~ 2439 South Kihei Road, Kihei; 875-4848.

RAFTING

Rafting trips are the adventurous way to enjoy the Maui coast. Easily combined with dive and whale-watching trips, these sturdy craft are a great way to reach hidden coves and beaches.

LAHAINA Hawaiian **Rafting Adventures** operates half- and full-day trips to Lanai. ~ 1223 Front Street, Lahaina; 661-7333. Whale-watching trips are great fun in the winter months.

Ocean Riders Adventure Rafting will take you out to Lanai and, weather permitting, Molokai, for a glorious day of snorkeling. All trips are aboard rigid-hull inflatable boats. ~ Mala Wharf, Lahaina; 661-3586.

Another company offering tours is **Captain Steve's Rafting Excursions**, which heads out regularly in search of tropical fish, dolphins and exotic birdlife. One trip not to miss circumnavigates Lanai. ~ Mala Wharf, Lahaina; 667-5565.

KIHEI-WAILEA AREA Blue Water Rafting offers both rafting and snorkeling trips to Molokini. ~ Kihei Boat Ramp, Kihei; 879-7238.

RIDING STABLES

Maui's volcanic landscape, beaches and sculptured valleys are choice sites for equestrian excursions. A variety of rides are available across the island—from the shoreline of Hana to the slopes of Haleakala, you can count on seeing wildlife, lava fields and those famous Maui sunsets.

KIHEI-WAILEA AREA **Makena Stables** leads trail rides across the scenic 20,000-acre Ulupalakua Ranch on the south slope of Haleakala. As you cross this rugged ranchland you may spot axis deer, Hawaiian owls and pheasants. Mountain trails cross a 200-year-old lava flow. Choose among three-hour, four-hour and all day rides, including one to the Tedeschi winery. ~ 7299 South Makena Road, Makena; 879-0244.

HANA HIGHWAY **Oheo Stables** offers three-hour outings up the backside of Haleakala. Trips ascend through a tropical rainforest and include views of waterfalls and the Kipahulu Valley. Highlights include the view from Pipiwai lookout above Oheo Gulch. ~ Hana Highway, one mile south of National Park Headquarters at Pools of Ohea; 667-2222.

UPCOUNTRY AND HALEKALA Hit the trail on Maui's north shore with **Adventures on Horseback** and you'll ride along 300-foot cliffs, see lush rainforests and take a break to swim in waterfall-fed pools. ~ Makawao; 242-7445.

At **Thompson Ranch and Riding Stables** ride through pasture-land on short day and sunset trips that offer views of the other islands. With special arrangements the full-day Haleakala ride enters the volcano at 10,000 feet. ~ Thompson Road, Kula; 878-1910.

For tours of Haleakala National Park, contact **Pony Express Tours**, which leads half- and full-day horseback trips through the wilderness area. ~ 667-2200. On the weekends **Charlie's Trail Rides and Pack Trips** provides overnight horseback trips from Kaupo through Haleakala. ~ 248-8209.

GOLF

With more than a dozen public and private courses, Maui is golf heaven. Choices on the Valley Isle range from country club links to inexpensive community courses. Also, several resorts offer a choice of championship courses ideal for golfers looking for a change of pace. These are open to the public for a hefty fee.

KAANAPALI-KAPALUA AREA   The **Kaanapali Golf Courses** are among the island's finest. The championship par-71 North Course, designed by golf course architect Robert Trent Jones Sr., has a slight incline. The easier South Course is intersected by Maui's popular sugar cane train. ~ Kaanapali Beach Resort, Kaanapali; 661-3691.

With three courses, the **Kapalua Golf Club** is one of the best places to golf on Maui. For a real challenge, try the par-73 Plantation Course, built in the heart of pineapple country. The oceanfront Bay Course was created by Arnold Palmer himself. The Village Course ascends into the foothills. ~ 300 Kapalua Drive, Kapalua; 669-8044.

KIHEI-WAILEA AREA   The **Wailea Golf Club**, located in the heart of the Wailea Resort complex, offers three courses, all with ocean views. The 18-hole "blue course" heads uphill along the slopes of Haleakala. The more challenging "emerald course" has slightly more difficult greens. The "gold course" is the longest and most challenging, with 93 bunkers. There are two clubhouses on the premises. ~ 100 Wailea Golf Club Drive; 879-2966.

Located next to the Maui Prince Resort, **Makena Golf Course** has two 18-hole courses. Designed by Robert Trent Jones Jr., the "North" and "South" courses are intended to blend into the natural Hawaiian landscape while offering high-challenge golf. Rolling terrain and beautiful views of the neighbor islands make these links a treat. ~ 5415 Makena Alanui Road, Wailea; 879-3344.

KAHULUI-WAILUKU AREA   **Waiehu Municipal Golf Course** is the island's only publicly owned course. With a front nine on the shoreline and a challenging back nine along the mountains, this course offers plenty of variety. Other amenities include a driving range and practice green. ~ Kahekili Highway, Waiehu; 243-7400.

Sandalwood is one of Maui's newest courses. Somewhat hilly, this par-72 course was designed by Nelson Wright. Three holes have lakes or ponds. There's a restaurant and pro shop on the premises, as well as a practice range, a chipping green and three putting greens. ~ 2500 Honoapiilani Highway, Wailuku; 242-7090.

In the same area, the private **Grand Waikapu Valley Country Club** is an 18-hole gem offering great ocean views. Water features abound on this course. ~ 244-7090.

HANA HIGHWAY The **Maui Country Club** is a relatively easy nine-hole course open to the public on Mondays. ~ 48 Nonohe Place, Paia; 877-7893.

UPCOUNTRY AND HALEAKALA The upcountry **Pukalani Country Club**, on the slopes of Haleakala, is an 18-hole public course. Bring a jacket or sweater because these links can get cool or windy. Boasting the highest elevation of all Maui's courses, this one is a sleeper (with great views). ~ 360 Pukalani Street; 572-1314.

TENNIS

If you're an avid tennis fan, or just in the mood to whack a few balls, you're in luck. Public tennis courts are easily found throughout the island. Almost all are lighted and convenient to major resort destinations.

LAHAINA In the Lahaina area, you'll enjoy the courts at the **Lahaina Civic Center** ~ 1840 Honoapiilani Highway; or at **Malu-ulu-olele Park** on Front and Shaw streets.

KAANAPALI-KAPALUA AREA Popular resorts in the area that open their courts to the public include the **Hyatt Regency Maui** ~ 200 Nohea Kai Drive, Kaanapali; 661-1234; and the **Maui Marriott** ~ 100 Nohea Kai Drive, Kaanapali; 667-1200.

The **Kapalua Tennis Garden** offers ten hard courts. ~ 100 Kapalua Drive, Kapalua; 669-5677.

KIHEI-WAILEA AREA There are public courts at **Kalama Park** on Kihei Road and **Maui Sunset Condominiums** on Waipulani Road.

Makena Resort Tennis Club is a favorite resort that lets the public use their courts. ~ Makena Resort, 5400 Makena Alanui Drive, Makena; 879-8777.

Wailea Tennis Club has eleven hard courts, three of which have lights. ~ 131 Wailea Iki Place, Wailea; 879-1958;

KAHULUI-WAILUKU AREA In the Kahului area, try the courts at the **Kahului Community Center** on Onehee and Uhu streets and the **Maui Community College** on Kaahumanu and Wakea avenues. In Wailuku, try **Wailuku War Memorial** at 1580 Kaahumanu Avenue, or the public courts at Wells and Market streets.

HANA HIGHWAY In the Hana area try the **Hana Ball Park**.

UPCOUNTRY AND HALEAKALA Popular upcountry courts are found at the **Eddie Tam Memorial Center** in Makawao and the **Pukalani Community Center** in Pukalani.

For general information, call the County Department of Parks and Recreation at 243-7389.

BICYCLING   If you've ever wanted to zip down a mountainside or go off-road in volcanic highlands, you've come to the right place. While Maui is best known for its downhill cycling trips, there are also many other challenging adventures. For example, you can enjoy the remote route from Hana to Ulupalakua or head from Kapalua to Wailuku via Kahakuloa.

Chris' Bike Adventures runs such intriguing trips as the Haleakala Wine Trek, a tour of the mountain's remote backside and a trip along the island's hidden northwest coast, complete with off-road biking. Unlike other bike tours, this company lets riders bicycle at their own pace. Half- and full-day trips include gourmet lunch. ~ Kula; 871-2453.

At **Maui Downhill**, you'll enjoy sunrise day-trips and mid-morning runs on Haleakala. The sunrise run is a beautiful 38-mile trip from the crater to sea level. Other, less strenuous trails also offer great views of the mountain, ranchlands and verdant forests. ~ 199 Dairy Road, Kahului; 871-2155.

Similar trips are offered by **Cruiser Bob's Haleakala Downhill**. Equipment includes full-face helmets, windbreaker pants and custom megabrakes. ~ 99 Hana Highway, Paia; 579-8444.

Another company operating Haleakala downhill bike tours is **Maui Mountain Cruisers**, which serves breakfast or lunch on morning or midday rides. ~ 296 Alamaha, Kahului; 871-6014.

For those of you who prefer to go it alone, the **Bike Shop** has a store in Kahului that both rents and sells bikes and accessories, and also does repair work. ~ 111 Hana Highway; 877-5848.

OCEAN
SAFETY   For swimming, surfing and scuba diving, there's no place quite like Maui. With endless miles of white-sand beach, the island attracts aquatic enthusiasts from all over the world. They come to enjoy Maui's colorful coral reefs and matchless surf conditions.

Many water lovers, however, never realize how dangerous the sea can really be. Particularly in Hawaii, where waves can reach 30-foot heights and currents flow unobstructed for thousands of miles, the ocean is sometimes as treacherous as it is spectacular. Dozens of people drown every year in Hawaii, many others are dragged from the crushing surf with broken backs, and countless numbers sustain minor cuts and bruises.

These accidents can be entirely avoided if you approach the ocean with a respect for its power as well as an appreciation of its beauty. All you have to do is heed a few simple guidelines. First, never turn your back on the sea. Waves come in sets: one group may be small and quite harmless, but the next set could be large enough to sweep you out to sea. Never swim alone.

Don't try to surf, or even bodysurf, until you're familiar with the sports' techniques and precautionary measures. Be extremely careful when the surf is high.

If you get caught in a rip current, don't swim against it: swim across it, parallel to the shore. These currents, running from the shore out to sea, can often be spotted by their ragged-looking surface water and foamy edges.

Around coral reefs, wear something to protect your feet against coral cuts. Recommended are the inexpensive Japanese *tabis*, or reef slippers. If you do sustain a coral cut, clean it with hydrogen peroxide, then apply an antiseptic or antibiotic substance. This is also a good procedure for octopus bites.

Maui has more miles of swimmable beach than any of the other islands in the chain.

When stung by a Portuguese man-of-war or a jellyfish, mix unseasoned meat tenderizer with alcohol, leave it on the sting for ten or twenty minutes, then rinse it off with alcohol. The old Hawaiian remedies, which are reputedly quite effective, involve applying urine or green papaya.

If you step on the sharp, painful spines of a sea urchin, soak the affected area in very hot water for 15 to 90 minutes. Another remedy calls for applying urine or undiluted vinegar. If any of these preliminary treatments do not work, consult a doctor.

Oh, one last thing. The chances of encountering a shark are about as likely as sighting a UFO. But should you meet one of these ominous creatures, stay calm. He'll be no happier to see you than you are to confront him. Simply swim quietly to shore. By the time you make it back to terra firma, you'll have one hell of a story to tell.

HIKING

Many people complain that Maui is overdeveloped. The wall-to-wall condominiums lining the Kaanapali and Kihei beachfront can be pretty depressing to the outdoors lover. But happily there is a way to escape. Hike right out of it.

The Valley Isle has many fine trails that lead through Hana's rainforest, Haleakala's magnificent valley, up to West Maui's peaks and across the south shore's arid lava flows. Any of them will carry you far from the madding crowd. It's quite simple on Maui to trade the tourist enclaves for virgin mountains, untrammeled beaches and eerie volcanic terrain. One note: A number of trails pass preserved cultural or historical sites. Please do not disturb these in any way. For more information, contact the Division of Forestry and Wildlife, Na Ala Hele Trails and Access Program. ~ 54 South High Street, Room 101, Wailuku, HI 96793; 243-5352.

Most trails you'll be hiking are composed of volcanic rock. This is a very crumbly substance, so be extremely cautious when climbing rock faces. In fact, you should avoid steep climbs if possible. Stay on the trails: Maui's dense undergrowth makes it very easy to get lost. If you get lost at night, stay where you are. Because of the low latitude, night descends rapidly here; there's practically no twilight. Once darkness falls, it can be very dangerous to move around.

You should also be careful to purify all drinking water. And be extremely cautious near streambeds as flash-flooding sometimes occurs, particularly on the windward coast. This is particularly true during the winter months, when heavy storms from the northeast lash the island.

It's advisable to wear long pants when hiking in order to protect your legs from rock outcroppings, insects and spiny plants. Also, if you're going to explore Haleakala volcano, be sure to bring cold-weather gear; temperatures are often significantly lower than at sea level and this peak occasionally receives snow.

You might want to obtain hiking maps; they are available from **Hawaii Geographic Maps & Books**. ~ P.O. Box 1698, Honolulu, HI 96806; 538-3952.

If you're uncomfortable about exploring solo, you might consider an organized tour. The **National Park Service** provides information to hikers interested in exploring Haleakala or other sections of the island. What follows is a basic guide to most of Maui's major trails. ~ Haleakala National Park, P.O. Box 369, Makawao, Maui, HI 96768; 572-9306.

KAHULUI-WAILUKU AREA   The main hiking trails in this Central Maui region lie in Iao Valley, Kahului and along Kakekili Highway (Route 340).

Iao Stream Trail (1 mile) leads from the Iao Valley State Monument parking lot for half a mile along the stream. The second half of the trek involves wading through the stream or hopping across the shoreline rocks. But your efforts will be rewarded with some excellent swimming holes en route. You might want to plan your time so you can relax and swim.

Not far from the Kahului Airport on Route 360, birdwatchers will be delighted to find a trail meandering through the **Kanaha Pond Wildlife Sanctuary**. This jaunt follows two loop roads, each one mile long, and passes the natural habitat of the rare Hawaiian stilt and the Hawaiian coot. The trails in the Kanaha Pond area are closed during bird-breeding season (April–August). Permits are necessary from the State Division of Forestry. ~ 243-5352.

Northwest of Kahului, along the Kahekili Highway, are two trails well worth exploring, the **Waihee Ridge Trail** and **Kahakuloa Valley Trail**.

Waihee Ridge Trail (3 miles) begins just below Maluhia Boy Scout Camp outside the town of Waihee. The trail passes through a guava thicket and scrub forest and climbs 1500 feet en route to a peak overlooking West and Central Maui. The trail summit is equipped with a picnic table rest stop.

KIHEI-WAILEA AREA   **King's Highway Coastal Trail** (5.5 miles) follows an ancient Hawaiian route over the 1790 lava flow and is considered a desert region. The trail begins near La Perouse Bay at the end of the rugged road that connects La Perouse Bay with Makena Beach and Wailea. It heads inland through groves of *kiawe* trees, then skirts the coast and finally leads to Kanaloa Point. From this point the trail continues across private land. Because segments of the trail pass through the Ahihi-Kinau Natural Reserve, which has stricter regulations, call or write Na Ala Hele (above) for more information.

HANA HIGHWAY Hana-Waianapanapa Coastal Trail (3 miles), part of the ancient King's Highway, skirts the coastline between Waianapanapa State Park and Hana Bay. Exercise extreme caution near the rocky shoreline and cliffs. The trail passes a *heiau*, sea arch, blowhole and numerous caves while winding through lush stands of *hala* trees.

Waimoku Falls Trail (2 miles) leads from the bridge at Oheo Gulch up to Waimoku Falls. On the way, it goes by four pools and traverses a bamboo forest. (Mosquito repellent advised.) Contact Haleakala National Park Headquarters for information on this trail.

UPCOUNTRY The main trails in Maui's beautiful Upcountry lie on Haleakala's southern slopes. They branch out from Polipoli Spring State Recreation Area through the Kula and Kahikinui Forest Reserves.

Redwood Trail (1.7 miles) descends from Polipoli's 6200-foot elevation through impressive stands of redwoods to the ranger's cabin at 5300 feet. There is a dilapidated public shelter in the old CCC camp at trail's end. A four-wheel drive is required to reach the trailhead.

Plum Trail (2.3 miles) begins at the CCC camp and climbs gently south to Haleakala Ridge Trail. The route passes plum trees as well as stands of ash, redwood and sugi pine. There are shelters at both ends of the trail.

Tie Trail (0.5 mile) descends 500 feet through cedar, ash and sugi pine groves to link Redwood and Plum Trails. There is a shelter at the Redwood junction.

Polipoli Trail (0.6 mile) cuts through cypress, cedars and pines en route from Polipoli Campground to Haleakala Ridge Trail.

Boundary Trail (4.4 miles) begins at the cattle guard marking the Kula Forest Reserve boundary along the road to Polipoli. It crosses numerous gulches planted in cedar, eucalyptus and pine. The trail terminates at the ranger's cabin.

Waiohuli Trail (1.4 miles) descends 800 feet from Polipoli Road to join Boundary Trail. Along the way it passes young pine and grasslands, then drops down through groves of cedar, redwood and ash. There is a shelter at the Boundary Trail junction.

Skyline Road (6.5 miles) begins at 9750 feet, near the top of Haleakala's southwest rift, and descends more than 3000 feet to the top of Haleakala Ridge Trail. The trail passes a rugged, treeless area resembling the moon's surface. Then it drops below timberline at 8600 feet and eventually into dense scrub. The unobstructed views of Maui and the neighboring islands are awesome. Bring your own water.

Haleakala Ridge Trail (1.6 miles) starts from Skyline Trail's terminus at 6550 feet and descends along Haleakala's southwest rift to 5600 feet. There are spectacular views in all directions and a shelter at trail's end.

(For Haleakala volcano trails, see Chapter Nine.)

CAMPING Camping on Maui usually means pitching a tent, reserving a cabin or renting a camper. Throughout the island there are secluded spots and beaches, and numerous county, state and federal parks. All the campsites, together with hiking trails, are described in the following chapters; it's a good idea to consult those detailed listings when planning your trip.

Before you set out to camp, there are a few very important matters that I want to explain more fully. First, bring a campstove: firewood is scarce in most areas and soaking wet in others.

Another problem that you're likely to encounter are those nasty varmints that buzz in your ear just as you're falling asleep—mosquitoes. Maui contains neither snakes nor poison ivy, but it has plenty of these dive-bombing pests. Like me, you probably consider that it's always open season on the little bastards.

With most of the archipelago's other species, however, you'll have to be a careful conservationist. You'll be sharing the wilderness with pigs, goats, tropical birds, deer and mongooses, as well as a spectacular array of exotic and indigenous plants. They exist in one of the world's most delicate ecological balances. There are more endangered species in Hawaii than in all the rest of the United States. So keep in mind the maxim that the Hawaiians try to follow. *Ua mau ke ea o ka aina i ka pono:* The life of the land is preserved in righteousness.

Though extremely popular with adventurers, Maui has very few official campsites. The laws restricting camping here are more strictly enforced than on other islands. The emphasis on this boom island favors condominiums and resort hotels rather than outdoor living, but you can still escape the concrete congestion at several parks and unofficial campsites (including one of the most spectacular tenting areas in all Hawaii—Haleakala Wilderness Area).

Camping at **county parks** requires a permit. These are issued for a maximum of three nights at each campsite, and cost $3 per person per night, children 50¢. Permits can be obtained at War Memorial Gym adjacent to Baldwin High School, Route 32, Wailuku, or by writing the Department of Parks and Recreation Permit Department, 1580 Kaahumanu Avenue, Wailuku, Maui, HI 96793; 243-7389.

State park permits are free and allow camping for five days. They can be obtained at the Division of State Parks in the State Building, High Street, Wailuku, or by writing the Division of State Parks. ~ 54 South High Street, Room 101, Wailuku, Maui, HI 96793; 243-5354. You can also rent cabins at Wainapanapa and Polipoli state parks through this office.

If you plan on camping in the Haleakala Wilderness Area, you must obtain a permit on the day you are camping. You can do so at Haleakala National Park headquarters, located on the way to the valley. These permits are allocated on a first-come, first-served basis.

Remember, rainfall is heavy along the northeast shore around Hana, but infrequent on the south coast. Also, Haleakala gets quite cold; you'll need heavy clothing and sleeping gear.

It is best to bring along your own camping gear, but in a pinch check **Maui Expeditions**, which sells and rents supplies. ~ Kihei Commercial Center, 300 Ohukai, Kihei; 875-7470. **Maui Sporting Goods** has a large selection of gear for sale. ~ 92 North Market Street, Wailuku; 244-0011. **Gaspro Inc.** sells a limited amount of camping equipment. ~ 365 Hanakai Street, Kahului; 877-0056.

THREE

History and Culture

POLYNESIAN ARRIVAL The history of Maui, complex and dynamic as it is, actually began after that of other islands in the chain. Perhaps as early as the third century, Polynesians sailing from the Marquesas Islands, and then later from Tahiti, landed near the southern tip of the Big Island. By about 800 A.D., Polynesians from the Marquesas and Society Islands arrived on Maui. In Europe, mariners were rarely venturing outside the Mediterranean Sea, and it would be centuries before Columbus happened upon the New World. Yet in the Pacific, entire families were crossing 2500 miles of untracked ocean in hand-carved canoes with sails woven from coconut fibers. The boats were formidable structures, catamaran-like vessels with a cabin built on the platform between the wooden hulls. Some were a hundred feet long and could do twenty knots, making the trip to Hawaii in a month.

The Polynesians had originally come from the coast of Asia about 3000 years before. They had migrated through Indonesia, then pressed inexorably eastward, leapfrogging across archipelagoes until they finally reached the last chain, the most remote—Hawaii.

These Pacific migrants were undoubtedly the greatest sailors of their day and stand among the finest in history. When close to land they could smell it, taste it in the seawater, see it in a lagoon's turquoise reflection on the clouds above an island. They knew the courses of 150 stars. From the color of the water they determined ocean depths and current directions. They had no charts, no compasses, no sextants; sailing directions were simply recorded in legends and chants. Yet Polynesians discovered the Pacific, from Indonesia to Easter Island, from New Zealand to Hawaii. They made the Vikings and Phoenicians look like landlubbers.

On Maui, the seaborne colonizers established a line of kings who ruled the island for several centuries. Among them was Hua, a 12th-century monarch who earned a reputation for being a fierce warrior. According to legend, he angered the Hawaiian gods by murdering a priest and felt the holy wrath in the form of an island-wide drought. In desperation, Hua moved to the Big Island in search of fresh water, but the gods made sure the drought traveled with him.

CAPTAIN COOK They were high islands, rising in the northeast as the sun broke across the Pacific. First one, then a second, and finally, as the tall-masted ships drifted west, a third island loomed before them. Landfall! The British crew was ecstatic. It meant fresh water, tropical fruits, solid ground on which to set their boots and a chance to carouse with the native women. For their captain, James Cook, it was another in an amazing career of discoveries. The man whom many call history's greatest explorer was about to land in one of the last spots on earth to be discovered by the West.

He would name the place for his patron, the British earl who became famous by pressing a meal between two crusts of bread. The Sandwich Islands. Later they would be called Owhyhee, and eventually, as the Western tongue glided around the uncharted edges of a foreign language, Hawaii.

It was January 1778. The English army was battling a ragtag band of revolutionaries for control of the American colonies, and the British Empire was still basking in a sun that never set. The Pacific had been opened to Western powers over two centuries before, when a Portuguese sailor named Magellan crossed it. Since then, the British, French, Dutch and Spanish had tracked through in search of future colonies.

They happened upon Samoa, Fiji, Tahiti and the other islands that spread across this third of the globe, but somehow they had never sighted Hawaii. Even when Cook finally spied it, he little realized how important a find he had made. Hawaii, quite literally,

MAUI THE GOD

So many legends have grown up around the demigod Maui, the island's namesake, that many believe the mischievous deity actually existed. According to popular legend, he created the Hawaiian chain by hooking the islands and pulling them up from the bottom of the ocean. It was also Maui who learned the secrets of firemaking from a mud hen and shared them with men and women across the island.

was a jewel in the ocean, rich in fragrant sandalwood, ripe for agricultural exploitation and crowded with sea life. But it was the archipelago's isolation that would prove to be its greatest resource.
Strategically situated between Asia and North America, it was the
only place for thousands of miles where whalers, merchants and
bluejackets could go for provisions and rest.

Cook was 49 years old when he shattered Hawaii's quiescence.
The Englishman hadn't expected to find islands north of Tahiti.
Quite frankly, he wasn't even trying. It was his third Pacific voyage
and Cook was hunting bigger game, the fabled Northwest Passage
that would link this ocean with the Atlantic.

But these mountainous islands were still an interesting find. He
could see by the canoes venturing out to meet his ships that the
lands were inhabited; when he finally put ashore on Kauai, Cook
discovered a Polynesian society. He saw irrigated fields, domestic
animals and high-towered temples. The women were bare-breasted,
the men wore loincloths. As his crew bartered for pigs, fowls and
bananas, he learned that the natives knew about metal and coveted
iron like gold.

If iron was gold to these "Indians," then Cook was a god. He
soon realized that his arrival had somehow been miraculously
timed, coinciding with the Makahiki festival, a wild party celebrat-
ing the roving deity Lono whose return the Hawaiians had awaited
for years. Cook was a strange white man sailing monstrous ships—
obviously he was Lono. The Hawaiians gave him gifts, fell in his
path and rose only at his insistence.

But even among religious crowds, fame is often fickle. After
leaving Hawaii without ever visiting Maui, Cook sailed north to the
Arctic Sea, where he failed to discover the Northwest Passage.

As the winter of 1778 approached, the British sea captain determined to steer a course south once more, spending the season in
the Sandwich Islands. On November 25, at a latitude of 20° 55', as
day broke across the Pacific, he first sighted Maui. To Western eyes
it was an exotic locale, vaulting 10,000 feet above the waves with
a peak that rose through the clouds.

By noon, canoes filled with local natives, including the great
Maui chief, Kahekili, visited the English explorers, presenting them
with elaborate feather cloaks and small pigs. By the next day, Cook
had departed, sailing east to the Big Island.

He arrived at the tail end of another exhausting Makahiki festival. By then the Hawaiians had tired of his constant demands for
provisions and were suffering from a new disease that was obviously carried by Lono's archangelic crew—syphilis. This Lono was
proving to be something of a freeloader.

Tensions ran high. The Hawaiians stole a boat. Cook retaliated
with gunfire. A scuffle broke out on the beach and in a sudden

violent outburst, which surprised the islanders as much as the interlopers, the Hawaiians discovered that their god could bleed. The world's finest mariner lay face down in foot-deep water, stabbed and bludgeoned to death.

Cook's end marked the beginning of an era. He had put the Pacific on the map, his map, probing its expanses and defining its fringes. In Hawaii he ended a thousand years of solitude. The archipelago's geographic isolation, which has always played a crucial role in Hawaii's development, had finally failed to protect it, and a second theme had come into play—the islands' vulnerability. Together with the region's "backwardness," these conditions would now mold Hawaii's history. All in turn would be shaped by another factor, one which James Cook had added to Hawaii's historic equation: the West.

KAMEHAMEHA AND KAAHUMANU The next man whose star would rise above Hawaii was present at Cook's death. Some say he struck the Englishman, others that he took a lock of the great leader's hair and used its residual power, its mana, to become king of all Hawaii.

Kamehameha was a tall, muscular, unattractive man with a furrowed face, a lesser chief on the powerful island of Hawaii. When he began his career of conquest a few years after Cook's death, he was a mere upstart, an ambitious, arrogant young chief. But he fought with a general's skill and a warrior's cunning, often plunging into the midst of a melee. He had an astute sense of technology, an intuition that these new Western metals and firearms could make him a king.

In Kamehameha's early years, Maui and the other islands were composed of many fiefdoms. Several kings or great chiefs, continually warring among themselves, ruled individual islands. At times, a few kings would carve up one island or a lone king might seize several. Never had one monarch controlled all the islands.

Among the most powerful was the Maui chief, Kahekili. He was, according to the historian Gavan Daws, "one of the last of the older generation of chiefs, raised in the tradition of warriors who roasted their enemies and used the skulls of the dead for filth pots." With the Valley Isle as a power base, he seized Oahu, torturing its chiefs and killing his own foster son. By 1786 he also controlled Molokai and Lanai.

During that same year, Captain Jean-François de La Pérouse, sailing under orders from the king of France, became the first Westerner to set foot on Maui.

Other players were entering the field: Westerners with ample firepower and towering ships. During the decade following Cook, only a handful arrived, mostly Englishmen and Americans, and they did not yet possess the influence they soon would wield. However, even a few foreigners were enough to upset the balance of power. They sold weapons and hardware to the great chiefs, making several of them more powerful than any of the others had ever been. War was imminent.

Kamehameha stood in the center of the hurricane. Like any leader suddenly caught up in the terrible momentum of history, he never quite realized where he was going or how fast he was moving. And he cared little that he was being carried in part by Westerners who would eventually want something for the ride. Kamehameha was no fool. If political expedience meant Western intrusion, then so be it. He had enemies among chiefs on the other islands; he needed the guns.

Hawaiian craftsmen produced the world's finest featherwork, weaving thousands of tiny feathers into golden cloaks and ceremonial helmets.

During the 1780s, Kahekili thwarted two attacks on Maui. But when two white men came into Kamehameha's camp in 1790, he had the military advisers to complement a fast expanding arsenal. Within months he cannonaded Maui. Attacking also with war canoes, he drove the forces of Kahekili's son, Kalanikupule, from Kahului up into the sharp-walled confines of Iao Valley.

In 1792, Kamehameha seized the Big Island by inviting his main rival to a peaceful parley, then slaying the hapless chief. By 1795, he had consolidated his control of Maui, grasped Molokai and Lanai and begun reaching greedily toward Oahu. He struck rapidly, landing near Waikiki and sweeping inland, forcing his enemies to their deaths over the precipitous cliffs of the Nuuanu Pali.

The warrior had become a conqueror, establishing his new capital in Lahaina and controlling all the islands except Kauai, which he finally gained in 1810 by peaceful negotiation. Kamehameha proved to be as able a bureaucrat as he had been a general. He became a benevolent despot who, with the aid of an ever-increasing number of Western advisers, expanded Hawaii's commerce, brought peace to the islands and moved his people inexorably toward the modern age.

He came to be called Kamehameha the Great, a wise and resolute leader who gathered a war-torn archipelago into a kingdom. But with the revisionist history of the 1960s and 1970s, as Third World people questioned both the Western version of events and the virtues of progress, Kamehameha began to resemble Benedict Arnold. He was seen as an opportunist, a megalomaniac who permitted the Western powers their initial foothold in Hawaii. He used their technology and then, in the manner of great men who depend on stronger allies, was eventually used by them.

As long a shadow as Kamehameha cast across the islands, the event that most dramatically transformed Hawaiian society occurred after his death in 1819. The kingdom had passed to Kamehameha's son Liholiho, but Kamehameha's favorite wife, Kaahumanu, usurped the power. Liholiho was a prodigal son, dissolute, lacking self-certainty, a drunk. A native of Maui, Kaahumanu was a woman for all seasons, a canny politician who combined brilliance with boldness, the feminist of her day. She had infuriated Kamehameha by eating forbidden foods and sleeping with other chiefs, even when he placed a taboo on her body and executed her lovers. She drank liquor, ran away, proved completely uncontrollable and won Kamehameha's love.

It was only natural that when he died, she would take his mana, or so she reckoned. Kaahumanu gravitated toward power with the drive of someone whom fate has unwisely denied. She carved her own destiny, announcing that Kamehameha's wish had been to give her a governmental voice. There would be a new post and she would fill it, becoming in a sense Hawaii's first prime minister.

And if the power, then the motion. Kaahumanu immediately marched against Hawaii's belief system, trying to topple the old idols. For years she had bristled under a polytheistic religion regulated by taboos, or *kapus*, which severely restricted women's rights. Now Kaahumanu urged the new king, Liholiho, to break a very strict *kapu* by sharing a meal with women.

Since the act might help consolidate Liholiho's position, it had a certain appeal to the king. Anyway, the *kapus* were weakening: these white men, coming now in ever greater numbers, defied them with impunity. Liholiho vacillated, went on a two-day drunk before gaining courage, then finally sat down to eat. It was a last supper, shattering an ancient creed and opening the way for a radically new divinity. As Kaahumanu had willed, the old order collapsed, taking away a vital part of island life and leaving the Hawaiians more exposed than ever to foreign influence.

Already Western practices were gaining hold. Commerce from Lahaina, Honolulu and other ports was booming. There was a fortune to be made dealing sandalwood to China-bound merchants, and the chiefs were forcing the common people to strip Hawaii's forests. The grueling labor might make the chiefs rich, but it gained the commoners little more than a barren landscape. Western diseases struck virulently. The Polynesians in Hawaii, who numbered 300,000 in Cook's time, were extremely susceptible. By 1866, their population had dwindled to less than 60,000. It was a difficult time for the Hawaiian people.

MISSIONARIES AND MERCHANTS Hawaii was not long without organized religion. The same year that Kaahumanu shattered tradition, a group of New England missionaries boarded the brig *Thaddeus* for a voyage around Cape Horn. It was a young company—many were in their twenties or thirties—and included a doctor, a printer and several teachers. They were all strict Calvinists, fearful that the second coming was at hand and possessed of a mission. They were bound for a strange land called Hawaii, 18,000 miles away.

Hawaii, of course, was a lost paradise, a hellhole of sin and savagery where men slept with several wives and women neglected to wear dresses. To the missionaries, it mattered little that the Hawaiians had lived this way for centuries. The churchmen would save these heathens from hell's everlasting fire whether they liked it or not.

The delegation arrived in Kailua on the Big Island in 1820 and then spread out, establishing important missions in Lahaina and Honolulu. Soon they were building schools and churches, conducting services in Hawaiian and converting the natives to Christianity.

The missionaries rapidly became an integral part of Hawaii, despite the fact that they were a walking contradiction to everything Hawaiian. They were a contentious, self-righteous, fanatical people whose arrogance toward the Hawaiians blinded them to the beauty and wisdom of island lifestyles. Where the natives lived in thatch homes open to the soothing trade winds, the missionaries built airless clapboard houses with New England–style fireplaces. While the Polynesians swam and surfed frequently, the new arrivals, living near the world's finest beaches, stank from not bathing. In a region where the thermometer rarely drops much below 70 degrees, they wore long-sleeved woolens, ankle-length dresses and claw-hammer coats. At dinner they preferred salt pork to fresh beef, dried meat to fresh fish. They considered coconuts an abomination and were loath to eat bananas.

And yet the missionaries were a brave people, selfless and God-fearing. Their dangerous voyage from the Atlantic had brought them into a very alien land. Many would die from disease and overwork; most would never see their homeland again. Bigoted though they were, the Calvinists committed their lives to the Hawaiian people. They developed the Hawaiian alphabet, rendered Hawaiian into a written language and, of course, translated the Bible. Theirs was the first printing press west of the Rockies. They introduced Western medicine throughout the islands and created such an effective school system that, by the mid-19th century, 80 percent of the Hawaiian population was literate. Unlike almost all the other white people who came to Hawaii, they not only took from the islanders, they also gave.

But to a missionary, *giving* means ripping away everything repugnant to God and substituting it with Christianity. They would have to destroy Hawaiian culture in order to save it. Though instructed by their church elders not to meddle in island politics, the missionaries soon realized that heavenly wars had to be fought on earthly battlefields. Politics it would be. After all, wasn't government just another expression of God's bounty?

They allied with Kaahumanu and found it increasingly difficult to separate church from state. Kaahumanu converted to Christianity, while the missionaries became government advisers and helped pass laws protecting the sanctity of the Sabbath. Disgusting practices such as hula dancing were prohibited.

Politics can be a dangerous world for a man of the cloth. The missionaries were soon pitted against other foreigners who were quite willing to let the clerics sing hymns, but were adamantly opposed to permitting them a voice in government. Hawaii in the 1820s had become a favorite way station for the whaling fleet. As the sandalwood forests were destroyed, the island merchants began looking for other industries. By the 1840s, when over 500 ships a year anchored in Hawaiian ports, whaling had become the islands' economic lifeblood. On Maui, the population soared to 35,000 and the economy boomed.

In the 1840s, more American ships visited Hawaii than any other port in the world.

Like the missionaries, the whalers were Yankees, shipping out from bustling New England ports. But they were a different cut of Yankee: rough, crude, boisterous men who loved rum and music and thought a lot more of fornicating with island women than saving them. After the churchmen forced the passage of laws prohibiting prostitution, the sailors rioted along the waterfront and fired cannons at the mission homes. When the smoke cleared, the whalers still had their women. When the authorities tried to crack down on debauchery in Lahaina, a band of sailors from the whaling ship *Daniel*, brandishing a black flag, forced the local missionary to barricade himself in his house. Fearing for his life, he was finally rescued by a group of Hawaiians who drove the sailors back to their ship.

It was during the 1840s that Maui, led by a governor who placed money before mores, became a center for wild living. Lahaina, according to the missionaries, was the capital of sin, something of a seaside Sodom.

Religion simply could not compete with commerce, and other Westerners were continuously stimulating more business in the islands. By the mid-19th century, as Hawaii adopted a parliamentary form of government, American and British fortune hunters were replacing missionaries as government advisers. It was a time when anyone, regardless of ability or morality, could travel to the islands and become a political powerhouse literally overnight. A consumptive American, fleeing the mainland for reasons of health, became chief justice of the Hawaiian Supreme Court while still in his twenties. Another lawyer, shadowed from the East Coast by a checkered past, became attorney general two weeks after arriving.

The situation was no different internationally. Hawaii was subject to the whims and terrors of gunboat diplomacy. The archipelago was solitary and exposed, and Western powers were beginning to eye it covetously. In 1843, a maverick British naval officer actually annexed Hawaii to the Crown, but the London government later countermanded his actions. Then, in the early 1850s, the threat of American annexation arose. Restless Californians, fresh from the gold fields and hungry for revolution, plotted unsuccessfully in Honolulu. Even the French periodically sent gunboats in to protect their small Catholic minority.

Finally, the three powers officially stated that they wanted to maintain Hawaii's national integrity. But independence seemed increasingly unlikely. European countries had already begun claiming other Pacific islands, and with the influx of Yankee missionaries and whalers, Hawaii was being steadily drawn into the American orbit.

THE SUGAR PLANTERS   There is an old Hawaiian saying that describes the 19th century: The missionaries came to do good, and they did very well. Actually the early evangelists, few of whom profited from their work, lived out only half the maxim. Their sons would give the saying its full meaning.

This second generation, quite willing to sacrifice glory for gain, fit neatly into the commercial society that had rendered their fathers irrelevant. They were shrewd, farsighted young Christians who had grown up in Hawaii and knew both the islands' pitfalls and potentials. They realized that the missionaries had never found Hawaii's pulse, and they watched uneasily as whaling became the lifeblood of the islands. Certainly it brought wealth, but whaling was too tenuous—there was always a threat that it might dry up entirely. A one-industry economy would never do; the mission boys wanted more. Agriculture was the obvious answer, and eventually they determined to bind their providence to a plant that grew wild in the islands—sugar cane.

In the years following the California gold rush of 1849, Maui's agricultural products were in particularly high demand. Prevailing winds persuaded many captains rounding Cape Horn en route to San Francisco to reprovision in Maui. Fresh fruits and vegetables, not to mention sugar cane plants, were plentiful and business for Upcountry farms expanded until the region earned the nickname *Nu Kaliponi*, or New California.

The first sugar plantation was actually started on Kauai in 1835 and on Maui in 1849, but not until the 1870s did the new industry blossom. By then, the Civil War had wreaked havoc with the whaling fleet, and a devastating winter in the Arctic whaling grounds practically destroyed it. The mission boys, who prophesied the storm, weathered it comfortably. They had already begun fomenting an agricultural revolution.

By the early 1860s, James Campbell had built Maui's first large sugar mill. Soon the center of island activity moved from Lahaina to the plantation town of Paia. A narrow-gauge railroad began operating between Kahului and Paia, and the island's population, which had been largely Polynesian and Caucasian, became increasingly Asian.

Agriculture, of course, means land, and in the 19th century practically all Hawaii's acreage was held by the king and the chiefs. So in 1850, the mission sons, together with other white entrepreneurs, pushed through the Great Mahele, one of the slickest real estate laws in history. Rationalizing that it would grant chiefs the liberty to sell land to Hawaiian commoners and white men, the mission sons established a Western system of private property.

The Hawaiians, who had shared their chiefs' lands communally for centuries, had absolutely no concept of deeds and leases. What resulted was the old $24-worth-of-beads story. The benevolent Westerners wound up with the land, while the lucky Hawaiians got practically nothing. Large tracts were purchased for cases of whiskey; others went for the cost of a hollow promise. The entire island of Niihau, which is still owned by the same family, sold for $10,000. It was a bloodless coup, staged more than 40 years before the revolution that would topple Hawaii's monarchy. In a sense it made the 1893 uprising anticlimactic. By then Hawaii's future would already be determined: white interlopers would own four times as much land as Hawaiian commoners.

On Maui, James Makee established a plantation on the slopes of Haleakala that sprawled across 1000 acres and produced up to 800 tons of sugar a year. His Rose Ranch, at Ulupalakua, became a lavish center of fashionable living. A piano and an organ were imported to entertain those guests uninterested in the bowling alley and tennis court.

Following the Great Mahele, the mission boys, along with other businessmen like Makee, were ready to become sugar planters. The

SPRECKELSVILLE

You have doubtless been losing sleep wondering how the old plantation town of Spreckelsville got its name. The moniker derives from Claus Spreckels, known locally as the Sugar King. This 19th-century robber baron combined business with politics, won the hearts and votes of Hawaii's leaders and came to dominate the islands' sugar industry. Once, when the Hawaiian cabinet refused to grant him water rights, Spreckels lent a sum of money to King Kalakaua, who reciprocated by naming another cabinet. Spreckels also put His Majesty heavily into debt at the card table, forcing the legislature to retire the king's gambling debts with a special loan.

mana once again was passing into new hands. Obviously, there was money to be made in cane, a lot of it, and now that they had land, all they needed was labor. The Hawaiians would never do. Cook might have recognized them as industrious, hardworking people, but the sugar planters considered them shiftless. Disease was killing them off anyway, and the Hawaiians who survived seemed to lose the will to live. Many made appointments with death, stating that in a week they would die; seven days later they were dead.

Foreign labor was the only answer. In 1850, the Masters and Servants Act was passed, establishing an immigration board to import plantation workers. Cheap Asian labor would be brought over. It was a crucial decision, one that would ramify forever through Hawaiian history and change the very substance of island society. Between 1850 and 1930, 180,000 Japanese, 125,000 Filipinos, 50,000 Chinese and 20,000 Portuguese immigrated. They transformed Hawaii from a chain of Polynesian islands into one of the world's most varied and dynamic locales, a meeting place of East and West.

The Chinese were the first to come, arriving in 1852 and soon outnumbering the white population. Initially, with their long pigtails and unusual habits, the Chinese were a joke around the islands. They were poor people from southern China whose lives were directed by clan loyalty. They built schools and worked hard so that one day they could return to their native villages in glory. They were ambitious, industrious and—ultimately—successful.

Too successful, according to the sugar planters, who found it almost impossible to keep the coolies down on the farm. The Chinese came to Hawaii under labor contracts, which forced them to work for five years. After their indentureship, rather than reenlisting as the sugar bosses had planned, the Chinese moved to the city and became merchants. Worse yet, they married Hawaiian women and were assimilated into the society.

These coolies, the planters decided, were too uppity, too ready to fill social roles that were really the province of white men. So in the 1880s, they began importing Portuguese. But the Portuguese thought they already *were* white men, while any self-respecting American or Englishman of the time knew they weren't.

The Portuguese spelled trouble, and in 1886 the sugar planters turned to Japan, with its restricted land mass and burgeoning population. The new immigrants were peasants from Japan's southern islands, raised in an authoritarian, hierarchical culture in which the father was a family dictator and the family was strictly defined by its social status. Like the Chinese, they built schools to protect their heritage and dreamed of returning home someday; but unlike their Asian neighbors, they only married other Japanese. They sent home for "picture brides," worshiped their ancestors and emperor and paid ultimate loyalty to Japan, not Hawaii.

The Japanese, it soon became evident, were too proud to work long hours for low pay. Plantation conditions were atrocious; workers were housed in hovels and frequently beaten. The Japanese simply did not adapt. Worst of all, they not only bitched, they organized, striking in 1909.

So in 1910, the sugar planters turned to the Philippines for labor. For two decades the Filipinos arrived, seeking their fortunes and leaving their wives behind. They worked not only with sugar cane but also with pineapples, which were becoming a big business in the 20th century. They were a boisterous, fun-loving people, hated by the immigrants who preceded them and used by the whites who hired them. The Filipinos were given the most menial jobs, the worst working conditions and the shoddiest housing. In time, another side of their character began to show—a despondency, a hopeless sense of their own plight, their inability to raise passage money back home. They became the untouchables of Hawaii.

The sugar industry on Maui, and throughout the islands, was dominated by a sugar refiner named Claus Spreckels, from San Francisco. Buying in to a Maui sugar plantation in 1877, he set his sights on the isthmus that separates Haleakala from the West Maui Mountains. Two other sugar planters, Samuel T. Alexander and Henry P. Baldwin, sons of missionaries, who founded Alexander & Baldwin, one of Hawaii's largest companies, were already digging a 17-mile-long irrigation ditch to their Haiku plantation.

Spreckels, also known as the "Sugar King," manipulated Hawaii's real monarch with bribes and loans into granting him invaluable water rights. Neither Baldwin nor Alexander was any match for "His Royal Saccharinity." By 1880, Maui began yielding the Sugar King's first crop.

REVOLUTIONARIES AND ROYALISTS Sugar, by the late 19th century, was king. It had become the center of island economy, the principal fact of life for most islanders. Like the earlier whaling industry, it was drawing Hawaii ever closer to the American sphere. The sugar planters were selling the bulk of their crops in California; having already signed several tariff treaties to protect their American market, they were eager to further strengthen mainland ties. Besides, many sugar planters were second-, third- and fourth-generation descendants of the New England missionaries; they had a natural affinity for the United States.

There was, however, one group that shared neither their love for sugar nor their ties to America. To the Hawaiian people, David Kalakaua was king, and America was the nemesis that had long threatened their independence. The whites might own the land, but the Hawaiians, through their monarch, still held substantial political power. During Kalakaua's rule in the 1870s and 1880s, anticolonialism was rampant.

The sugar planters were growing impatient. Kalakaua was proving very antagonistic; his nationalist drumbeating was becoming louder in their ears. How could the sugar merchants convince the United States to annex Hawaii when all these silly Hawaiian royalists were running around pretending to be the Pacific's answer to the British Isles? They had tolerated this long enough. The Hawaiians were obviously unfit to rule, and the planters soon joined with other businessmen to form a secret revolutionary organization. Backed by a force of well-armed followers, they pushed through the "Bayonet Constitution" of 1887, a self-serving document that weakened the king and strengthened the white landowners. If Hawaii was to remain a monarchy, it would have a Magna Carta.

The first president of Hawaii, Sanford Dole, was a missionary boy whose name eventually became synonymous with pineapples.

But Hawaii would not be a monarchy long. Once revolution is in the air, it's often difficult to clear the smoke. By 1893, Kalakaua was dead and his sister, Liliuokalani, had succeeded to the throne. She was an audacious leader, proud of her heritage, quick to defend it and prone to let immediate passions carry her onto dangerous ground. At a time when she should have hung fire, she charged, proclaiming publicly that she would abrogate the new constitution and reestablish a strong monarchy. The revolutionaries had the excuse they needed. They struck in January, seized government buildings and, with four boatloads of American marines and the support of the American minister, secured Honolulu. Liliuokalani surrendered.

It was a highly illegal coup; legitimate government had been stolen from the Hawaiian people. But given an island chain as isolated and vulnerable as Hawaii, the revolutionaries reasoned, how much did it really matter? It would be weeks before word reached Washington of what a few Americans had done without official sanction, then several more months before a new American president, Grover Cleveland, denounced the renegade action. By then the revolutionaries would already be forming a republic.

Not even revolution could rock Hawaii into the modern age. For years, an unstable monarchy had reigned; now an oligarchy composed of the revolution's leaders would rule. Officially, Hawaii was a democracy; in truth, the Chinese and the Japanese were hindered from voting, and the Hawaiians were encouraged not to bother. Hawaii, reckoned its new leaders, was simply not ready for democracy.

More than ever before, the sugar planters, alias revolutionaries, held sway. By the early 20th century, they had linked their plantations into a cartel, the Big Five. It was a tidy monopoly composed of five companies that owned not only the sugar and pineapple industries, but also the docks, shipping companies and many of the stores. Most of these holdings, happily, were the property of a few interlocking, intermarrying mission families—the Doles, Thurstons, Alexanders, Baldwins, Castles, Cookes and others—who had found heaven right here on earth. They golfed together and dined together, sent their daughters to Wellesley and their sons to Yale. All were proud of their roots, and as blindly paternalistic as their forefathers. It was their destiny to control Hawaii, and they made very certain, by refusing to sell land or provide services, that mainland firms did not gain a foothold in their domain.

What was good for the Big Five was good for Hawaii. Competition was obviously not good for Hawaii. Although the Chinese and the Japanese were establishing successful businesses in Honolulu and some Chinese were even growing rich, they posed no immediate threat to the Big Five. And the Hawaiians had never been good at capitalism. By the early 20th century, they had become one of the world's most urbanized groups. But rather than competing with white businessmen in Honolulu, unemployed Hawaiians were forced to live in hovels and packing crates, cooking their poi on stoves fashioned from empty oil cans.

Political competition was also unhealthy. Hawaii was ruled by the Big Five, so naturally it should be run by the Republican Party. After all, the mission families were Republicans. Back on the mainland, the Democrats had always been cool to the sugar planters, and it was a Republican president, William McKinley, who eventually annexed Hawaii. The Republicans, quite simply, were good for business.

The Big Five set out very deliberately to overwhelm any political opposition. When the Hawaiians created a home-rule party around the turn of the century, the Big Five shrewdly co-opted it by running a beloved descendant of Hawaii's royal family as the Republican candidate. On the plantations they pitted one ethnic group against another to prevent the Asian workers from organizing. Then, when labor unions finally formed, the Big Five attacked them savagely. In 1924, police killed 16 strikers on Kauai. Fourteen years later, in an incident known as the "Hilo massacre," the police wounded 50 picketers.

The Big Five crushed the Democratic Party by intimidation. Polling booths were rigged. It was dangerous to vote Democratic—workers could lose their jobs, and if they were plantation workers, that meant losing their houses, as well. Conducting Democratic meetings on the plantations was about as easy as holding a hula dance in an old missionary church. The Democrats went underground.

Those were halcyon days for both the Big Five and the Republican Party. In 1900, only five percent of Hawaii's population was white. The rest comprised races that rarely benefited from Republican policies. But for the next several decades, even during the Depression, the Big Five kept the Republicans in power.

While the New Deal swept the mainland, Hawaii clung to its colonial heritage. The islands were still a generation behind the rest of the United States—the Big Five preferred it that way. There was nothing like the status quo when you were already in power. Other factors that had long shaped Hawaii's history also played into the hands of the Big Five. The islands' vulnerability, which had always favored the rule of a small elite, permitted the Big Five to establish a formidable cartel. Hawaii's isolation, its distance from the mainland, helped protect their monopoly.

THE JAPANESE AND THE MODERN WORLD All that ended on December 7, 1941. The Japanese bombers that attacked Pearl Harbor sent shock waves through Hawaii that are still rumbling today. World War II changed all the rules of the game, upsetting the conditions that had determined island history for centuries.

Ironically, no group in Hawaii would feel the shift more thoroughly than the Japanese. When the emperor declared war on the United States, 160,000 Japanese-Americans were living in Hawaii, fully one-third of the islands' population. On the mainland, Japanese-Americans were rounded up and herded into relocation camps. But in Hawaii that was impossible; there were simply too many, and they made up too large a part of the labor force.

Many were second-generation Japanese, *nisei*, who had been educated in American schools and assimilated into Western society. Unlike their immigrant parents, the *issei*, they felt few ties to Japan. Their loyalties lay with America and, when war broke out, they determined to prove it. They joined the U.S. armed forces and formed a regiment, the 442nd, which became the most frequently decorated outfit of the war. The Japanese were heroes, and when the war ended many heroes came home to the United States and ran for political office. Men like Dwight Eisenhower, Daniel Inouye, John Kennedy and Spark Matsunaga began winning elections.

By the time the 442nd returned to the home front, Hawaii was changing dramatically. The Democrats were coming to power. Leftist labor unions won crucial strikes in 1941 and 1946. Jack Burns, an ex-cop who dressed in tattered clothes and drove around Honolulu in a beat-up car, was creating a new Democratic coalition.

TORA! TORA! TORA!

Although Oahu was devastated by the Japanese attack on Pearl Harbor, Maui suffered but a single casualty. A week after the Pacific war began, the Maui Pineapple Company was hit by a pair of Japanese submarine shells. Total damage: $700.

Burns, who would eventually become governor, recognized the potential power of Hawaii's ethnic groups. Money was flowing into the islands—first military expenditures and then tourist dollars—and non-whites were rapidly becoming a new middle class. The Filipinos still constituted a large part of the plantation workforce, and the Hawaiians remained disenchanted, but the Japanese and the Chinese were moving up fast. Together they constituted a majority of Hawaii's voters.

Burns organized them, creating a multiracial movement and thrusting the Japanese forward as candidates. By 1954, the Democrats controlled the legislature, with the Japanese filling one out of every two seats in the capital. Then, when Hawaii attained statehood five years later, the voters elected the first Japanese ever to serve in Congress. Today one of the state's U.S. senators and a congressman are Japanese. On every level of government, from municipal to federal, the Japanese predominate. They have arrived. The mana, that legendary power coveted by the Hawaiian chiefs and then lost to the sugar barons, has passed once again—to a people who came as immigrant farm-workers and stayed to become the leaders of the 50th state.

The Japanese and the Democrats were on the move, but in the period from World War II until the present day, everything was in motion. Hawaii was in upheaval. Jet travel and a population boom shattered the islands' solitude. While in 1939 about 500 people flew to Hawaii, now more than seven million land every year. The military population escalated as Oahu became a key base not only during World War II but throughout the Cold War and the Vietnam War, as well. Hawaii's overall population exploded from about a half-million just after World War II to over one million today.

No longer did the islands lag behind the mainland; they rapidly acquired the dubious quality of modernity. Hawaii became America's 50th state in 1959, Honolulu grew into a bustling high-rise city, and condominiums mushroomed along Maui's beaches. In 1961, the Kaanapali area of Maui became the first resort complex to be built on a neighbor island.

CREAMED ONIONS

Everyone knows about the shortages and rationing during World War II. But few have heard about the great Maui surplus. It seems that in May 1942, as local farmers were about to harvest a bumper crop of sweet Maui onions, a shipment of 900 tons of onions arrived on the island. The local populace responded with an innovative "Maui Onion Week," touting delights such as "creamed onions." Onion breath had become patriotic!

Outside investors swallowed up two of the Big Five corporations, and several partners in the old monopoly began conducting most of their business outside Hawaii. Everything became too big and moved too fast for Hawaii to be entirely vulnerable to a small interest group. Now, like the rest of the world, it would be prey to multinational corporations.

By the 1980s, Hawaii would also be of significant interest to investors from Japan. In a few short years they succeeded in buying up a majority of the state's luxury resorts, including every major beachfront hotel in Waikiki and a number of resorts on Maui, sending real estate prices into an upward spiral that did not level off until the early 1990s.

One element that has not plateaued during the current decade is the Native Hawaiian movement. Nativist sentiments were spurred in January 1993 by the 100th anniversary of the American overthrow of the Hawaiian monarchy. Over 15,000 people turned out to mark the illegal coup. Later that year, President Clinton signed a statement issued by Congress formally apologizing to the Hawaiian people. Then in 1994, the United States Navy returned the island of Kahoolawe to the state of Hawaii. Long a rallying symbol for the Native Hawaiian movement, the unoccupied island had been used for decades as a naval bombing target.

Today, with its own Native American movement, average house prices over $300,000 and an inflation factor that saw prices rise over 200 percent in 20 years, Hawaii has finally arrived. It is so much a part of the United States that one segment of the population is advocating secession. An island chain that slept for centuries has been awakened by the forces of change and is in turn beginning to disrupt the complacency of the forces that have long kept it dormant.

Hawaii, according to Polynesian legend, was discovered by ▼▼▼▼▼▼▼▼▼▼
Hawaii-loa, an adventurous sailor who often disappeared on **Culture**
long fishing trips. On one voyage, urged along by his navigator, Hawaii-loa sailed toward the planet Jupiter. He crossed the "many-colored ocean," passed over the "deep-colored sea," and eventually came upon "flaming Hawaii," a mountainous island chain that spewed smoke and lava.

History is less romantic. The Polynesians who found Hawaii were probably driven from their home islands by war or some similar calamity. They traveled in groups, not as lone rangers, and shared their canoes with dogs, pigs and chickens, with which they planned to stock new lands. Agricultural plants such as coconuts, yams, taro, sugar cane, bananas and breadfruit were also stowed on board.

Most important, they transported their culture, an intricate system of beliefs and practices developed in the South Seas. After undergoing the stresses and demands of pioneer life, this traditional lifestyle was transformed into a new and uniquely Hawaiian culture.

It was based on a caste system that placed the *alii*, or chiefs, at the top and the slaves, *kauwas*, on the bottom. Between these two groups were the priests, *kahunas*, and the common people, *maka-ainanas*. The chiefs, much like feudal lords, controlled all the land and collected taxes from the commoners who farmed it. Each island was divided like a pie into wedge-shaped plots, *ahupuaas*, which extended from the ocean to the mountain peaks. In that way, every chief's domain contained fishing spots, village sites, arable valleys and everything else necessary for the survival of his subjects.

Life centered around the *kapu*, a complex group of regulations that dictated what was sacred or profane. For example, women were not permitted to eat pork or bananas; commoners had to prostrate themselves in the presence of a chief. These strictures were vital to Hawaiian religion; *kapu* breakers were directly violating the will of the gods and could be executed for their actions. And there were a lot of gods to watch out for, many quite vindictive. The four central gods were *Kane*, the creator; *Lono*, the god of agriculture; *Ku*, the war god; and *Kanaloa*, lord of the underworld. They had been born from the sky father and earth mother, and had in turn created many lesser gods and demigods who controlled various aspects of nature.

> People often refer to Maui's racial mixes as a "chop suey" blend of humanity.

It was, in the uncompromising terminology of the West, a stone-age civilization. Though the Hawaiians lacked metal tools, the wheel and a writing system, they managed to include within their short inventory of cultural goods everything necessary to sustain a large population on a chain of small islands. They fashioned fish nets from coconut fibers, made hooks out of bone, shell and ivory, and raised fish in rock-bound ponds. The men used irrigation in their farming. The women made clothing by pounding mulberry bark into a soft cloth called tapa, dyeing elaborate patterns into the fabric. They built peak-roofed thatch huts from native *pili* grass and *lauhala* leaves. The men fought wars with spears, slings, clubs and daggers. The women used mortars and pestles to pound the roots of the taro plant into poi, the islanders' staple food.

The West labeled these early Hawaiians "noble savages." Actually, they often lacked nobility. The Hawaiians were cannibals who sometimes practiced human sacrifice and often used human bait to fish for sharks. They constantly warred among themselves and would mercilessly pursue a retreating army, murdering as many of the vanquished soldiers as possible.

But they weren't savages either. The Hawaiians developed a rich oral tradition of genealogical chants and created beautiful lilting songs to accompany their hula dancing. The Hawaiians helped develop the sport of surfing. They also swam, boxed, bowled and devised an intriguing game called *konane*, a cross between checkers and the Japanese game of *go*. They built hiking trails from coral and lava, and created an elemental art form in the images—petro-glyphs—that they carved into rocks along the trails.

They also achieved something far more outstanding than their varied arts and crafts, something that the West, with its awesome knowledge and advanced technology, has never duplicated. The Hawaiians on Maui and other islands created a balance with nature. They practiced conservation, establishing closed seasons on certain fish species and carefully guarding their plant and animal resources. They led a simple life, without the complexities the outside world would eventually thrust upon them. It was a good life: food was plentiful, people were healthy and the population increased. For a thousand years, the Hawaiians lived in delicate harmony with the elements. It wasn't until the West entered the realm, transforming everything, that the fragile balance was destroyed. But that is another story entirely.

Because of its unique history and isolated geography, Hawaii is truly a cultural melting pot. It's one of the few states in the union in which white people are a minority group. Whites, or haoles as they're called in the islands, comprise only about 33 percent of Hawaii's 1.1 million population. Japanese constitute 22 percent, Filipinos 15 percent, Hawaiians and part-Hawaiians account for 12 percent, Chinese about 6 percent and other racial groups 12 percent. The population of Maui is a little more than 100,000 and the ethnic mix is similar to that in the rest of the islands.

PEOPLE

It's a very young, vital society. More than half the community is under thirty-five and over one-quarter of the people were born of racially mixed parents. Three out of every four residents live on the island of Oahu, and almost half of those live in the city of Honolulu.

One trait characterizing many of these people is Hawaii's famous spirit of aloha, a genuine friendliness, an openness to strangers, a willingness to give freely. Undoubtedly, it is one of the finest qualities any people has ever demonstrated. Aloha originated with the Polynesians and played an important role in ancient Hawaiian civilization. When Western colonialists arrived, however, they viewed it not as a Hawaiian form of graciousness, but rather as the naivete of a primitive culture. They turned aloha into a tool for exploiting the Hawaiians, taking practically everything they owned.

Today, unfortunately, the descendants of the colonialists are being repaid in kind. The aloha spirit is still present in the islands, but another social force has arisen—racial hatred. There is growing resentment toward white people and other mainlanders in Hawaii.

Sometimes this hatred spills into ripoffs and violence. Therefore, mainland visitors must be very careful, particularly when traveling in heavily touristed areas. Try not to leave items in your car; if you absolutely must, lock them in the trunk. Don't leave valuable gear unattended in a campsite. And try not to antagonize the islands' young people.

It's exciting to meet folks, and I highly recommend that you mix with local residents, but do it with forethought and consideration. A lot of locals are eager to make new acquaintances; others can be extremely hostile. So choose the situation. If a local group looks bent on trouble, mind your own business. They don't need you, and you don't need them. For most encounters, I'd follow this general rule—be friendly, but be careful.

CUISINE   Nowhere is the influence of Hawaii's melting pot population stronger than in the kitchen. While on Maui, you'll probably eat not only with a fork, but with chopsticks and fingers, as well. You'll sample a wonderfully varied cuisine. In addition to standard American fare, hundreds of restaurants serve Hawaiian, Japanese, Chinese, Korean, Portuguese and Filipino dishes. There are also fresh fruits aplenty—pineapples, papayas, mangoes, bananas and tangerines—plus native fish such as mahimahi, marlin and snapper.

The prime Hawaiian dish is poi, made from crushed taro root and served as a pasty purple liquid. It's pretty bland fare, but it does make a good side dish with roast pork or tripe stew. You should also try *laulau*, a combination of fish, pork and taro leaves wrapped in a *ti* leaf and steamed. And don't neglect to taste baked *ulu* (breadfruit) and *opihi* (limpets).

Among the other Hawaiian culinary traditions are *kalua* pig, a shredded pork dish baked in an *imu*; *lomilomi* salmon, which is salted and mixed with onions and tomatoes; and chicken *laulau*, prepared in taro leaves and coconut milk.

A good way to try all these dishes at one sitting is to attend a luau. This Hawaiian tradition is maintained by community organizations, which advertise the events in the newspaper, and, in a manner of speaking, by major resorts, who sponsor splashy shows.

I suggest that you take in the local color at a neighborhood feast. If you decide instead on one of the commercial events, consider the **Old Lahaina Luau**. It's a small event, staged on the waterfront in a historic region favored by Hawaiian monarchs. Cast members arrive by outrigger canoe and offer a succession of entertaining traditional Hawaiian dances. The *lomilomi* salmon is first rate. Daily. ~ 505 Front Street, Lahaina; 667-1998.

The Hotel Hana Maui's **Hamoa Beach Luau** combines the amenities of a major resort with a warm community atmosphere. Staged at a site James Michener called "the most perfect crescent beach in the Pacific," the event includes local families and a number of the hotel's employees. Tuesday. ~ 248-8211.

Japanese dishes include sushi, sukiyaki, teriyaki and tempura, plus an island favorite—sashimi, or raw fish. On most any menu, including McDonald's, you'll find *saimin*, a noodle soup filled with meat, vegetables and *kamaboko* (fishcake).

You can count on the Koreans for *kim chi*, a spicy salad of pickled cabbage, and *kun koki*, barbecued meat prepared with soy and sesame oil. The Portuguese serve up some delicious sweets including *malasadas* (donuts minus the holes) and *pao doce*, or sweet bread. For Filipino fare, I recommend *adobo*, a pork or chicken dish spiced with garlic and vinegar, and *pochero*, a meat entrée cooked with bananas and several vegetables. In addition to a host of dinner dishes, the Chinese have contributed some less common treats such as *manapua* (a steamed bun filled with barbecued pork) and oxtail soup. They also introduced crack seed to the islands. Made from dried and preserved fruit, it provides a treat as sweet as candy.

As the Hawaiians say, *"Hele mai ai."* Come and eat!

The language common to all Hawaii is English, but because of its **LANGUAGE** diverse cultural heritage, the archipelago also supports several other tongues. Foremost among these are Hawaiian and pidgin.

Hawaiian, closely related to other Polynesian languages, is one of the most fluid and melodious languages in the world. It's composed of only 12 letters: five vowels—*a, e, i, o, u* and seven consonants—*h, k, l, m, n, p, w*.

At first glance, the language appears formidable: how the hell do you pronounce *humuhumunukunukuapuaa*? But actually it's quite simple. After you've mastered a few rules of pronunciation, you can take on any word in the language.

The first thing to remember is that every syllable ends with a vowel, and the next to last syllable receives the accent.

The next rule to keep in mind is that all the letters in Hawaiian are pronounced. Consonants are pronounced the same as in English (except for the *w*, which is pronounced as a *v* when it introduces the last syllable of a word—as in *ewa* or *awa*). Vowels are pronounced the same as in Latin or Spanish: *a* as in *among*, *e* as in *they*, *i* as in *machine*, *o* as in *no* and *u* as in *too*. Hawaiian has four vowel combinations or diphthongs: *au*, pronounced *ow*, *ae* and *ai*, which sound like *eye*, and *ei*, pronounced *ay*.

By now, you're probably wondering what I could possibly have meant when I said Hawaiian was simple. I think the glossary that follows will simplify everything while helping you pronounce common words and place names. Just go through the list, starting with words like *aloha* and *luau* that you already know. After you've practiced pronouncing familiar words, the rules will become second nature; you'll practically be a *kamaaina*.

Just when you start to speak with a swagger, cocky about having learned a new language, some young Hawaiian will start talking at you in a tongue that breaks all the rules you've so carefully mastered. That's pidgin. It started in the 19th century as a lingua franca among Hawaii's many races. Pidgin speakers mix English and Hawaiian with several other tongues to produce a spicy creole. It's a fascinating language with its own vocabulary, a unique syntax and a rising inflection that's hard to mimic.

Pidgin is definitely the hip way to talk in Hawaii. A lot of young Hawaiians use it among themselves as a private language. At times they may start talking pidgin to you, acting as though they don't speak English; then if they decide you're okay, they'll break into English. When that happens, you be one *da kine brah*.

So *brah*, I take *da kine* pidgin words, put 'em together with Hawaiian, make one big list. Savvy?

aa (**ah**-ah)—a type of rough lava
ae (eye)—yes
aikane (eye-**kah**-nay)—friend
akamai (ah-**kah**-my)—wise
alii (ah-**lee**-ee)—chief
aloha (ah-**lo**-ha)—hello; greetings; love
aole (ah-**oh**-lay)—no
auwe (ow-**way**)—ouch!
brah (bra)—friend; brother; bro'
bumby (**bum**-bye)—after a while; by and by
dah makule guys (da mah-**kuh**-lay guys)—senior citizens
da kine (da kyne)—whatdyacallit; thingamajig; that way
diamondhead—in an easterly direction
duh uddah time (duh **uh**-duh time)—once before
ewa (**eh**-vah)—in a westerly direction
hale (**hah**-lay)—house
haole (**how**-lee)—Caucasian; white person
hapa (**hah**-pa)—half
hapa-haole (**hah**-pa **how**-lee)—half-Caucasian
heiau (hey-ee-**ow**)—temple
hele on (**hey**-lay own)—hip; with it
holo holo (**ho**-low **ho**-low)—to visit
howzit? (hows-it)—how you doing? what's happening?
hukilau (**who**-key-lau)—community fishing party
hula (**who**-la)—Hawaiian dance
imu (**ee**-moo)—underground oven
ipo (**ee**-po)—sweetheart
jag up (jag up)—drunk
kahuna (kah-**who**-nah)—priest
kai (kye)—ocean
kaka-roach (**kah**-kah roach)—ripoff; theft
kamaaina (kah-mah-**eye**-nah)—a longtime island resident
kane (kah-**nay**)—man
kapu (**kah**-poo)—taboo; forbidden

kaukau (cow-cow)—food

keiki (**kay**-key)—child

kiawe (key-**ah**-vay)—mesquite tree

kokua (ko-**coo**-ah)—help

kona winds (**ko**-nah winds)—winds that blow against the trades

lanai (lah-**nye**)—porch; also island name

lauhala (lau-**hah**-lah) or *hala* (**hah**-lah)—a tree whose leaves are used in weaving

lei (lay)—flower garland

lolo (low-low)—stupid

lomilomi (**low**-me-**low**-me)—massage; also raw salmon

luau (**loo**-ow)—feast

mahalo (mah-**hah**-low)—thank you

mahalo nui loa (mah-**ha**-low **new**-ee **low**-ah)—thank you very much

mahu (**mah**-who)—gay; homosexual

makai (mah-**kye**)—toward the sea

malihini (mah-lee-**hee**-nee)—newcomer; stranger

mauka (**mau**-kah)—toward the mountains

nani (**nah**-nee)—beautiful

ohana (oh-**hah**-nah)—family

okole (oh-**ko**-lay)—rear; ass

okolemaluna (oh-ko-lay-mah-**loo**-nah)—a toast: bottoms up!

ono (**oh**-no)—tastes good

pahoehoe (pah-**hoy**-hoy)—ropy lava

pakalolo (pah-kah-**low**-low)—marijuana

pakiki head (pah-**key**-key head)—stubborn

pali (**pah**-lee)—cliff

paniolo (pah-nee-**oh**-low)—cowboy

pau (pow)—finished; done

pilikia (pee-lee-**key**-ah)—trouble

puka (**poo**-kah)—hole

pupus (**poo**-poos)—hors d'oeuvres

shaka (**shah**-kah)—great; perfect

swell head—angry

tapa (**tap**-ah)—tree bark which is used as a fabric

wahine (wah-**hee**-nay)—woman

wikiwiki (**wee**-key-**wee**-key)—quickly; in a hurry

you get stink ear—you don't listen well

MUSIC

Music has long been an integral part of Hawaiian life. Most families keep musical instruments in their homes, gathering to play at impromptu livingroom or backyard jam sessions. Hawaiian folk tunes are passed down from generation to generation. In the earliest days, it was the sound of rhythm instruments and chants that filled the air. Drums were fashioned from hollowed-out gourds, coconut shells and breadfruit logs, then covered with sharkskin.

Gourds and coconuts, adorned with tapa cloth and feathers, were also filled with shells or pebbles to produce a rattling sound. Other instruments included the nose flute, a piece of bamboo similar to a mouth flute, but played by exhaling through the nostril; the bamboo organ; and *puili*, pieces of bamboo split into strips, which were struck rhythmically against the body.

Tune in to KPOA-FM 93.5 and 102.7 for island sounds and Hawaiian music.

Western musical scales and instruments were introduced by explorers and missionaries. As ancient Hawaiian music involved a completely different musical system, Hawaiians had to completely re-adapt. Actually, western music caught on quickly, and the hymns brought by missionaries fostered a popular musical style—the *himeni*, or Hawaiian church music.

Strangely enough, a Prussian bandmaster named Henry Berger had a major influence on contemporary Hawaiian music. Brought over by King Kalakaua to lead the Royal Hawaiian Band, Berger helped Hawaiians make the transition to western instruments.

Hawaii has been the birthplace of several different musical instruments and styles. The ukulele, modeled on a Portuguese guitar, quickly became the most popular Hawaiian instrument. Its small size made it easy to carry, and with just four strings, it was simple to play. During the early 1900s, the steel guitar was exported to the mainland. Common in country-and-western music today, it was invented by a young man who experimented by sliding a steel bar across guitar strings.

The slack-key style of guitar playing also comes from Hawaii. In tuning, the six strings are loosened and then played in a variety of ways, from plucking or slapping the strings to sliding along them. A number of different tunings exist, and many have been passed down through families for generations.

During the late 19th century, "*hapa*-haole" songs became the rage. The ukelele was instrumental in contributing to this Hawaiian fad. Written primarily in English with pseudo-Hawaiian themes, songs like "Tiny Bubbles" and "Lovely Hula Hands" were later introduced to the world via Hollywood.

The Hawaiian craze continued on the mainland with radio and television shows such as "Hawaii Calls" and "The Harry Owens Show." In the 1950s, little mainland girls donned plastic hula skirts and danced along with Hilo Hattie and Ray Kinney.

It was not until the 1970s that both the hula and music of old Hawaii made a comeback. Groups such as the Sons of Hawaii and the Makaha Sons of Niihau, along with Auntie Genoa Keawe and the late Gabby Pahinui, became popular. Before long, a new form of Hawaiian music was being heard, a combination of ancient chants and contemporary sounds, performed by such islanders as Cecelio and Kapono, Kalapana, Olomana, the Beamer Brothers, Karen Keawehawaii, the Peter Moon Band and the Brothers Cazimero.

Today many of these groups, along with other notables such as Hapa, the Kaau Crater Boys, Palani Vaughn, Brother Nolan, Ohta San, Willie K and Butch Helemano, bring both innovation to the Hawaiian music scene and contribute to the preservation of an ancient tradition.

Along with palm trees, the hula—swaying hips, grass skirts, colorful leis—is linked forever in people's minds with the Hawaiian Islands. This western idea of hula is very different from what the dance has traditionally meant to native Hawaiians.

Hula is an old dance form, its origin shrouded in mystery. The ancient hula, *kahiko*, was more concerned with religion and spirituality than entertainment. Originally performed only by men, it was used in rituals to communicate with a deity—a connection to nature and the gods. Accompanied by drums and chants, *kahiko* expressed the islands' culture, mythology and history in hand and body movements. It later evolved from a strictly religious rite to a method of communicating stories and legends. Over the years, women were allowed to study the rituals and eventually became the primary dancers.

When westerners arrived, the *kahiko* hula began another transformation. Explorers and sailors were more interested in its erotic element, ignoring the cultural significance. Missionaries simply found it scandalous and set out to destroy the tradition. They dressed Hawaiians in western garb and outlawed the *kahiko* hula.

The hula tradition was resurrected by King David Kalakaua. Known by the moniker "Merrie Monarch," Kalakaua loved music and dance. For his coronation in 1883, he called together the kingdom's best dancers to perform the chants and hulas once again. He was also instrumental in the development of the contemporary hula, the *auwana* hula, which added new steps and movements and was accompanied by ukeleles and guitars rather than drums.

By the 1920s, modern hula had been popularized by Hollywood, westernized and introduced as kitschy tropicana. Real grass skirts gave way to cellophane versions, plastic leis replaced fragrant island garlands, and exaggerated gyrations supplanted the hypnotic movements of the traditional dance.

Fortunately, with the resurgence of Hawaiian pride in recent decades, Polynesian culture has been reclaimed and *kahiko* hula and chants have made a welcome comeback.

FOUR

Lahaina

Maui's top tourist destination is a waterfront enclave that stretches for over two miles along a natural harbor, but measures only a couple of blocks deep. Simultaneously chic and funky, Lahaina has gained an international reputation for its art galleries, false-front stores and waterfront restaurants.

It also happens to be one of Hawaii's most historic towns. A royal seat since the 16th century, Lahaina was long a playground for the alii. The royal surfing grounds lay just south of today's town center, and in 1802, Kamehameha I established his headquarters here, taking up residence in the Brick Palace, the first Western-style building in Hawaii.

It was in Lahaina that the first high school and first printing press west of the Rockies were established in 1831. From Lahaina, Kamehameha III promulgated Hawaii's first constitution in 1840, and established a legislative body that met in town until the capital was eventually moved to Honolulu.

During the 1820s, this quaint port also became a vital watering place for whaling ships and evolved into the whaling capital of the world. At its peak in the mid-1840s, the whaling trade brought over 400 ships a year into the harbor.

To the raffish sailors who favored it for its superb anchorage, grog shops and uninhibited women, Lahaina was heaven itself. To the stiff-collared missionaries who arrived in 1823, the town was a hellhole—a place of sin, abomination and vile degradation. Some of Lahaina's most colorful history was written when the Congregationalists prevented naked women from swimming out to meet the whalers. Their belligerent brethren anchored in the harbor replied by cannon-balling mission homes and rioting along the waterfront.

The town declined with the loss of the whaling trade in the 1860s, and was transformed into a quiet sugar plantation town, serving the Pioneer Sugar Mill that opened during the same decade. Not until developers began building resorts in nearby Kaanapali a century later did it fully revive. During the 1960s, Lahaina was designated a national historic landmark and restoration of many important sites was begun. By the 1970s, the place was a gathering spot not only for the jet set but the ultra hip as well. Clubs like the Blue Max made Lahaina a hot nightspot where famous musicians came to vacation and jam.

Today Lahaina retains much of its old charm in the ramshackle storefronts that line the water along Front Street. Most points of interest lie within a half-mile of the old sea wall that protects this narrow thoroughfare from the ocean, so the best way to explore the town is on foot.

Start at **Lahaina Harbor**, located on Wharf Street, and take a stroll along the docks. In addition to tour boats, pleasure craft from around the world put in here or cast anchor in the Lahaina Roads just offshore. During the heyday of the whaling industry in the 1840s, the Auau Channel between Lahaina and Lanai was a forest of masts.

Carthaginian II, the steel-hulled brig at dock's end, preserves those days in a shipboard museum. Actually a turn-of-the-century brig that was converted into a replica of an old square-rigged sailing ship, this floating display case features videotapes on whales and intriguing artifacts from days of yore. Admission. ~ 661-3262.

Across Wharf Street sits the **Pioneer Inn**, a rambling hostelry built in 1901. With its second-story veranda and landscaped garden, this aging woodframe hotel is a great place to bend an elbow and breathe in the salt air. ~ 658 Wharf Street; 661-3636.

Just north of here a Hawaii Visitors Bureau sign points out the chair-shaped **Hauola Stone**, a source of healing power for ancient Hawaiians, who sat in the natural formation and let the waves wash over them.

◆◆

ROYAL HAWAIIAN HOLIDAYS

Although the Hawaiian capital moved to Honolulu in 1850, Lahaina remained a favorite vacation spot for several kings, including Kamehameha III, IV and V, and Queen Liliuokalani. All had second homes in the area and returned often to indulge in those favorite Hawaiian pastimes, rest and relaxation.

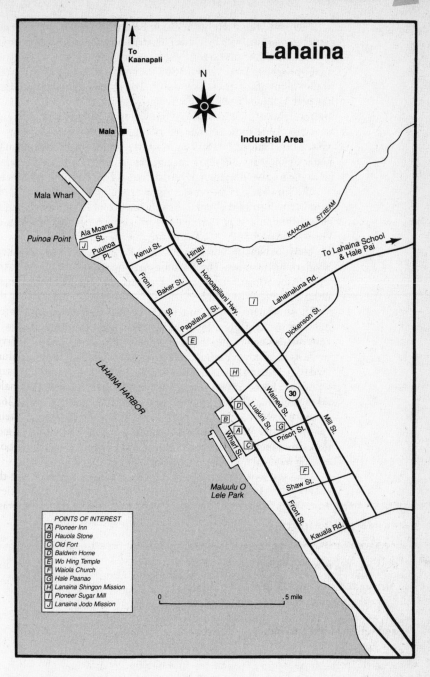

Lahaina

To Kaanapali

N

Mala

Mala Wharf

Puinoa Point

Industrial Area

Ala Moana St.

Puunoa Pl.

J

KAHOMA STREAM

To Lahaina School & Hale Pai

Kenui St.

Hinau St.

Front St.

Baker St.

Honoapiiliani Hwy.

Lahainaluna Rd.

Papalaua St.

I

Dickenson St.

E

LAHAINA HARBOR

H

Wainee St.

30

D

Luakini St.

B

G

Mill St.

A

Prison St.

Wharf St.

C

F

Maluulu O
Lele Park

Shaw St.

Front St.

Kauala Rd.

POINTS OF INTEREST
A Pioneer Inn
B Hauola Stone
C Old Fort
D Baldwin Home
E Wo Hing Temple
F Waiola Church
G Hale Paanao
H Lanaina Shingon Mission
I Pioneer Sugar Mill
J Lanaina Jodo Mission

0   .5 mile

There is nothing left of the **Brick Palace**, the two-story structure commissioned in 1798 by Kamehameha I. Located just inshore from the Hauola Stone and built by an English convict, the palace was used by the king in 1802 and 1803 (although some say he preferred to stay in his grass shack next door). Today the original foundation has been outlined with brick paving.

To the south, a 120-year-old **banyan tree**, among the oldest and largest in the islands, extends its rooting branches across almost an entire acre. Planted in 1873 to mark the advent of Protestant missionaries in Maui 50 years earlier, this shady canopy is a resting place for tourists and mynah birds alike. ~ Front and Hotel streets.

The sprawling giant presses right to the **Old Courthouse** door. Built in 1859 from the remains of the palace of King Kamehameha III, the building was fashioned from coral blocks. The **Lahaina Visitors Center** (667-9175) is located in the courthouse. Here you can pick up maps and brochures. The **Old Jail** in the basement now incongruously houses **The Lahaina Art Society** (661-0111), a non-profit association of local artists. Exhibits at the gallery here are rotating collections of member artists.

Those stone ruins on either side of the courthouse are the remains of the **Old Fort**, built during the 1830s to protect Lahaina from the sins and cannonballs of lawless sailors. The original structure was torn down two decades later to build a jail, but during its heyday the fortress guarded the waterfront with 47 cannons.

Across Front Street you'll find the **Baldwin Home**, Lahaina's oldest building. Constructed of coral and stone in the early 1830s, the place sheltered the family of Reverend Dwight Baldwin, a medical missionary. Today the house contains period pieces and family heirlooms, including some of the good doctor's rather fiendish-looking medical implements. Beneath the hand-hewn ceiling beams rests the Baldwin's Steinway piano; the dining room includes the

LAHAINA EXPERIENCES

- Shop **Front Street**, where the woodframe stores harken back to Lahaina's days as a 19th century whaling port. (p. 83)
- Sample the Hawaiian regional cuisine at **Avalon Restaurant**, where you'll be greeted by the owners who double as chef and hostess. (p. 82)
- Tour the **Baldwin Home**, an 1830s coral-and-stone house originally occupied by a missionary who always wore woolen clothes. (p. 76)
- Go snorkeling along the **Olowalu beaches**, where you'll share the coral reefs with a number of green sea turtles. (p. 86)
- Stay at the turn-of-the century **Pioneer Inn** and hunker down over a glass of rum amid the harpoons and figureheads in the saloon. (p. 79)

family's china, a fragile cargo that made the voyage around Cape Horn; and in the master bedroom stands a four-poster bed fashioned from native *koa*. Admission. ~ 661-3262.

The **Master's Reading Room** next door, an 1834 storehouse and library, is home to the Lahaina Restoration Foundation and not open to the public.

The **Wo Hing Temple**, a Chinese gathering place that dates to 1912, has been lovingly restored. While the temple has been converted into a small museum, the old cookhouse adjacent is used to show films of the islands made by Thomas Edison in 1898 and 1906 during the early days of motion pictures. Admission. ~ 858 Front Street; 661-3262.

The **Holy Innocents Episcopal Church** is a small structure dating from 1927. Very simple in design, the sanctuary is filled with beautiful paintings. The Hawaiian madonna on the altar and the tropical themes of the paintings are noteworthy features. ~ 561 Front Street; 661-4202.

Several other historic spots lie along Wainee Street, which parallels Front Street. **Waiola Cemetery**, with its overgrown lawn and eroded tombstones, contains graves dating to 1829. Queen Keopuolani, the wife of Kamehameha I and the mother of Hawaii's next two kings, is buried here. So is her daughter, Princess Nahienaena, and Governor Hoapali, who ruled Hawaii from 1823 to 1840. Surrounded by blossoming plumeria trees, there are also the graves of early missionaries and Hawaiian commoners.

Maui's first Christian services were performed in 1823 on the grounds of **Waiola Church** next door. Today's chapel, built in 1953, occupies the spot where Wainee Church was constructed in 1832. The earlier structure, Hawaii's first stone church, seated 3000 parishioners and played a vital role in the conversion of the local population to Christianity and Western ways. ~ 661-4349.

A little farther north on Wainee Street sits the **Lahaina Hongwanji Temple** with its three distinctive turrets. The building dates from 1927, but the Buddhist Hongwanji sect has been meeting at this site since 1910.

On the corner of Prison and Wainee streets rise the menacing walls of old **Hale Paahao**, a prison built by convicts in 1854 and used to house rowdy sailors as well as more hardened types. The coral blocks used to build this local hoosegow were taken from the Old Fort on Front Street.

Just north of the jail along Wainee Street sits the **Episcopal Cemetery** and **Hale Aloha**. Walter Murray Gibson, a controversial figure in 19th-century Hawaii politics who eventually became an adviser to King David Kalakaua, is buried here. Hale Aloha, completed in 1858 and restored several years ago, served as a church meetinghouse.

Nearby on Wainee and Dickenson streets, **Maria Lanakila Church** is a lovely white-washed building with interior pillars that was built in 1928 to replace a 19th-century chapel. Adjacent is the **Seamen's Cemetery**, a poorly maintained ground where early sailors were laid to rest.

The **Lahaina Shingon Mission**, a simple plantation-era structure with an ornately gilded altar, was built in 1902 by a Japanese monk and his followers. It now represents another gathering place for Maui's Buddhists. ~ 682 Luakini Street between Hale and Dickenson streets; 661-0466.

The proverbial kids-from-eight-to-eighty set will love the **Sugar Cane Train**, a reconstructed 1890-era steam train. Operating around the West Maui resort area, the Lahaina-Kaanapali & Pacific Railroad engine and passenger cars chug along a six-mile route midway between the mountains and ocean. Various package tours are available with the train rides, including a ride on a semisubmersible vessel in Lahaina, admission to three of Lahaina's museums, and a viewing of the film *Hawaii: Islands of the Gods*, shown on the 180-degree screen at the Omni Theatre. Admission. ~ The main station is off Hinau Street in Lahaina; 661-0089.

Oceanic adventurers should take an opportunity to stop in at **Atlantis Submarines** and reserve an underwater tour. The voyage takes you aboard a 46-passenger submersible down to depths of 150 feet. En route you may see close-up views of technicolor coral reefs and outlandish lava formations. A trip to the depths requires deep pockets; these two-hour excursions aren't cheap. If the tour doesn't interest you, there is a small museum adjacent to the Atlantis office that chronicles submarine history. ~ 665 Front Street, in the Pioneer Inn; 667-2224.

And don't miss **Lahaina Jodo Mission**, a Buddhist enclave one-half mile north of Lahaina on Ala Moana Street. There's a temple and a three-tiered pagoda here, as well as the largest ceremonial bell in Hawaii. The giant bronze Buddha, with the West Maui Mountains in the background, is a sight to behold. It rests amid stone walkways and flowering oleander bushes in a park-like setting. ~ 12 Ala Moana Street; 661-4304.

For a splendid view of Lahaina, head uphill along Lahainaluna Road to **Lahainaluna School**. Established by missionaries in 1831, it is one of the country's oldest high schools. Today this historic facility serves as a public high school for the Lahaina area. On the way uphill you will pass **Pioneer Sugar Mill**, a sugar company tracing back to 1860.

Hale Pai, a printing house dating to 1836, is located nearby. Here early textbooks and Hawaii's first newspaper were printed. Having played a key role in the development of Hawaiian as a written language, Hale Pai is now a fascinating museum devoted to printing. Open Monday–Friday.

To fully capture the spirit of Lahaina, there's only one place to stay—the **Pioneer Inn**. Located smack on Lahaina's waterfront, this wooden hostelry is the center of the area's action. On one side, sloops, ketches and glass-bottom boats are berthed; on the other side lies bustling Front Street with its falsefront shops. The Inn is noisy, vibrant and crowded with tenants and tourists. On the ground floor, you can hunker down over a glass of grog at the saloon, or stroll through the Inn's lushly planted courtyard. You can no longer book a room above the bar, but there are accommodations in the renovated section overlooking the courtyard. These are small and plainly decorated, with telephones, overhead fans and lanais. ~ 658 Wharf Street; 661-3636, 800-457-5457, fax 667-5708. DELUXE.

LODGING

While the building is actually quite modern, the **Plantation Inn** possesses the look and ambience of a turn-of-the-century hostelry. Modeled after the plantation architecture of an earlier era, it features 19 rooms individually decorated in period furniture. Each is adorned with either poster, brass or canopy bed, stained-glass windows and tile bathrooms. Combining the atmosphere of the past with the amenities of the present, guest rooms also feature televisions, refrigerators and air conditioning, as well as VCRs on request. There's a pool with a shaded pavilion and jacuzzi on the premises. Continental breakfast. ~ 174 Lahainaluna Road; 667-9225, 800-433-6815, fax 667-9293. DELUXE.

The Oscar for most original inn goes to the **Lahaina Hotel**. Constructed earlier this century, this 12-room beauty was fully restored and appointed in Gay Nineties finery. Each room is wall to ceiling with gorgeous antiques—leaded glass lamps, mirrored armoires, original oil paintings, cast-iron beds and brass locks. Attention to detail is a way of life: the place simply exudes the aura of another era. If you don't stay here, stop by and visit. ~ 127 Lahainaluna Road; 661-0577, 800-669-3444, fax 667-9480. DELUXE.

The **Maui Islander Hotel** is a warren of woodframe buildings spread across lushly landscaped grounds. The ambience is an odd combination of tropical retreat and motel atmosphere. It features 358 trimly decorated rooms, some of which are small studios (with kitchens) and one-bedroom efficiencies. Swimming pool, laundry, tennis court, picnic area. ~ 660 Wainee Street; 667-9766, 800-367-5226, fax 661-3733. DELUXE.

Perhaps the nicest place to stay on this side of the island is **Puamana**, a 28-acre retreat located about a mile southeast of Lahaina. This townhouse complex, a 1920s-era sugar plantation, rests along a rock-strewn beach. The oceanfront clubhouse, open to guests, was once the plantation manager's house, and the landscaped grounds are still given over to mango, plumeria and torch ginger trees. Guests stay in low-slung plantation-style buildings that sport

CONDOS

◄ *HIDDEN*

shake-shingle roofs and house from two to six units. Prices begin in the deluxe range for one-bedroom facilities that contain kitchens and sleep up to four people, and end in the ultra-deluxe range for two- and three-bedroom efficiencies that sleep up to six and eight, respectively. To round out the amenities there are three pools and a tennis court. Three-night minimum that increases to seven nights during the Christmas season. ~ 34 Pualima Place; 667-2551, 800-628-6731, fax 661-5875. DELUXE TO ULTRA-DELUXE.

Though it's more expensive than many others, **Lahaina Shores Hotel** has the advantage of a beachfront location in Lahaina. This sprawling condominium complex offers studio apartments beginning at $110, while one-bedroom units start at $175. With a swimming pool, jacuzzi and the nearby beach, it's quite convenient. ~ 475 Front Street; 661-4835, 800-628-6699, fax 661-1025. DELUXE TO ULTRA-DELUXE.

DINING

One of my favorite light-food stops is a devil-may-care place called the **Sunrise Café**. Set in a tiny clapboard house with a fresh, airy look, it serves salads, sandwiches and espresso, plus such entrées as smoked *kalua* pork, *laulau*, grilled chicken breast and mahimahi. ~ Located around back at 693 Front Street; 661-8558. BUDGET.

In the Lahaina Shopping Center, the **Thai Chef Restaurant** is a cozy place with an inviting assortment of Southeast Asian dishes. Try the Korean papaya salad, sautéed chili chicken, or seafood with red curry sauce. ~ Wainee Street; 667-2814. MODERATE.

Lani's Gekko serves standard American breakfasts and Japanese lunch and dinner including sushi, tempura, udon and teriyaki. ~ The Wharf Mall, 658 Front Street; 661-0955. BUDGET TO MODERATE.

Also try **Local Food**, a takeout stand that sells—what else?— local food (in the form of plate lunches). ~ 888 Wainee Street; 667-2882. BUDGET.

In keeping with the old hostelry upstairs, the **Pioneer Inn Restaurant** brings back the Lahaina of old. The main dining room is a cozy anchorage dotted with nautical fixtures and specializing in regional fare. The emphasis is on the "bounty of Hawaii"; in other words, fresh fish, upcountry produce and local herbs. Select one of the day's fresh fish specials and you can't go wrong. ~ 658 Wharf Street; 661-3636. DELUXE.

Across the lobby from the Pioneer Inn Restaurant, the **Pioneer Grill and Bar** offers similar but less formal fare and boasts a view of Lahaina Harbor. Portuguese bean soup is a specialty of both eateries and both fire their dishes on a *kiawe* grill. ~ 658 Wharf Street; 661-3636. MODERATE TO DELUXE.

I can't say much for the nomenclature, but the prices are worth note at **Cheeseburgers in Paradise**. This is a rare catch indeed—an inexpensive restaurant smack on the Lahaina waterfront. Granted, you won't find much on the menu other than hamburgers, salads and sandwiches. But if some couples can live on love, why can't the rest of us live on ocean views? ~ 811 Front Street; 661-4855. BUDGET TO MODERATE.

Oceanfront dining was never so cheap as at **Aloha Cantina Maui**. The menu spans the spectrum from ceviche and fajitas to chile rellenos and fish tacos. The margaritas are icy and the salsa is hot. Dining is on two decks overlooking the water. ~ 839 Front Street; 661-8788. BUDGET.

Hawaii's first phone line was installed from Lahaina to Haiku in 1877.

For a taste of the Orient, I'd head to the **Golden Palace Chinese Restaurant**. Boldly decorated with Chinese reliefs, this dimly lit establishment has an extensive Cantonese menu. There are beef, fowl, pork and seafood dishes, as well as chop suey. In the afternoon, the Palace combines sweet-and-sour ribs, roast pork and shrimp and rice chow mein. ~ In the Lahaina Shopping Center on Wainee Street between Papalua Street and Lahainaluna Road; 661-3126. BUDGET TO MODERATE.

Nearby, also in the Lahaina Shopping Center, is **Yakiniku Tropicana**. Specializing in Japanese and Korean food, it has a sushi bar and table seating. ~ Wainee Street between Papalua Street and Lahaina Road; 667-4646. MODERATE TO DELUXE.

Offering a partial view of the water is **Il Bucaniere**, an open-air trattoria. Although this balcony restaurant is on the wrong side of Front Street, it does provide an easy, you-can-sit-at-the-bar-or-take-a-table atmosphere. Wherever you rest your *okole*, you can dine on linguine primavera, chicken with rosemary, Italian baked pork chops or penne with gorgonzola cheese sauce. They also offer pizzas and salads. ~ 666 Front Street; 661-3966. MODERATE.

If you've seen one **Hard Rock Café**, you know about the line for the T-shirt window, the line for a table and the line for the bar. What a formula: just get yourself a show car from the '50s, a few surfboards, guitars and Buddy Holly posters, throw in an exposed-beam ceiling and circular bar and you've got the Maui branch of this popular empire. The menu runs from beef, turkey and veggie burgers to lime barbecue chicken, marinated top sirloin and fajitas. ~ 900 Front Street; 667-7400. MODERATE.

Light, bright and airy, **Compadres** is a great place to sip a margarita or enjoy a Mexican meal with an island flair. The tropical ambience is as appealing as the steaming dishes served here. Especially popular are the fajitas and pork carnitas, but the menu also offers burgers, salads and vegetarian dishes. ~ In the Lahaina Cannery Mall on Front and Kapunakea streets; 661-7189. MODERATE.

The preferred style of dining in Lahaina is steak and seafood at one of the waterfront restaurants along Front Street. And the common denominator is the ever-popular, usually crowded **Kimo's**, where you can enjoy all the tropical amenities while dining on seafood fettuccine, lobster or prime rib. ~ 845 Front Street; 661-4811. MODERATE TO DELUXE.

At **Lahaina Broiler** you can experience the same open-air atmosphere, though lately the place has looked slightly run down. There's always a fresh fish special, as well as an assortment of beef and chicken entrées. ~ 889 Front Street; 661-3111. MODERATE TO DELUXE.

Slightly (I said *slightly*) off the tourist track but still offering a classic Lahaina-dinner-on-the-water-with-sunset-view experience is the **Old Lahaina Café and Luau**. Overhead fans, oceanfront location, nautical feel—it's all here. The menu matches the occasion with fresh island fish, jumbo prawns (prepared five different ways) and a special Hawaiian sampler. Also open for breakfast and lunch. ~ 505 Front Street; 661-3303. MODERATE TO DELUXE.

At **Longhi's**, a European-style café that specializes in Italian dishes, informality is the password. The menu changes daily and is never written down; the waiter simply tells you the day's offerings. Usually there'll be several pasta dishes, sautéed vegetables, salads, a shellfish creation, steak, a wine-soaked chicken or veal dish and perhaps eggplant parmigiana. Longhi's prepares all of its own bread and pasta, buys Maui-grown produce and imports many cheeses from New York. The dinners reflect this diligence. Breakfasts and lunches are cooked with the same care. Definitely recommended, especially for vegetarians, who can choose from many of the dishes offered. ~ 888 Front Street; 667-2288. DELUXE TO ULTRA-DELUXE.

Hawaiian regional cuisine is the order of the day at **Avalon Restaurant & Bar**, an open-air establishment in Mariner's Alley. Adorned with the work of local artists, it is owned by Mark and Judy Ellman. Mark is the master chef—preparing wok-fried *opakapaka* in black bean sauce, Chinese duck with plum sauce and other delectables—while Judy greets the folks out front. Try it for lunch or dinner. ~ 844 Front Street; 667-5559. DELUXE.

David Paul's Lahaina Grill, headlining New American cuisine (with a Southwestern accent), is an intimate dining room with a personalized touch. According to owner/chef David Paul, the menu represents "a gathering of technique, flavors and skills from around the world, utilizing local ingredients to translate each dish into an exceptional dining experience." Order the tequila shrimp and fire cracker rice, soft-shell crabs, Kona coffee-roasted rack of lamb or macadamia-smoked tenderloin and decide for yourself whether he carries it off. ~ 127 Lahainaluna Road; 667-5117. DELUXE TO ULTRA-DELUXE.

A defining experience in Lahaina dining is **Gerard's Restaurant**. Here you'll encounter a French restaurant in a colonial setting with tropical surroundings. Housed in the Plantation Inn, a bed and breakfast reminiscent of early New Orleans, Gerard's provides a chandelier-and-pattern-wallpaper dining room as well as a veranda complete with overhead fans and whitewashed balustrade. The chef prepares fresh fish, rack of lamb, calf veal liver, *confit* of duck and puff pastry with shiitake mushrooms. Of course, that is after having started off with ahi steak tartar or crab bisque. ~ 174 Lahainaluna Road; 661-8939. ULTRA-DELUXE.

Overlooking the Mala Wharf, **The Chart House** looks as indigenous as a Hawaiian sunset. With its shake roof, lava walls and *koa* decor, this veranda-style restaurant is perfect for a drink or dinner. Dine on sirloin, teriyaki beef kabobs or fresh fish. There's also a handy children's menu. Offering views of Lanai and Molokai, the restaurant is a good retreat after a hard day of surfing or sunning. ~ 1450 Front Street; 661-0937. DELUXE.

Near the top of the cognoscenti's list of gourmet establishments is an unlikely looking French restaurant in Olowalu called **Chez Paul**. The place is several miles outside Lahaina in a renovated building that also houses Olowalu's funky general store. But for years this little hideaway has had a reputation far transcending its surroundings. You'll probably drive right past the place at first, but when you do find it, you'll discover a menu featuring such delicacies as *tournedos*, duck *à l'orange*, veal prepared with apples, scampi and several other tempting entrées. While the tab is ethereal, the rave reviews this prim dining room receives make it worth every franc. Closed Sunday in summer. ~ Honoapiilani Highway; 661-3843. ULTRA-DELUXE.

◄ *HIDDEN*

GROCERIES

Lahaina features two supermarkets. **Foodland** is open daily from 6 a.m. to midnight. ~ Lahaina Square Shopping Center on Wainee Street; 661-0975. You can shop at **Nagasako Supermarket** from 7 a.m. until 9 p.m. every day except Sunday (until 8 p.m.). ~ Lahaina Shopping Center on Wainee Street; 661-0985.

For health-food items, stop by **Westside Natural Food**. Open from 7:30 a.m. to 9 p.m. Monday to Saturday and 8:30 a.m. to 8 p.m. on Sunday. ~ 193 Lahanaluna Road; 667-2855.

South of Lahaina, along Honoapiilani Highway in Olowalu, the **Olowalu General Store** has a limited supply of grocery items. ~ 661-3774.

SHOPPING

Lahaina's a great place to combine shopping with sightseeing. Most shops are right on Front Street in the historic wooden buildings facing the water. For a walking tour of the stores and waterfront, start from the Pioneer Inn at the south end of the strip and walk north on the *makai* or ocean side. Then come back along the *mauka*, or mountain, side of the street.

One of the first shops you will encounter on this consumer's tour of Lahaina will be **Sgt. Leisure Resort Patrol**, which has an array of imaginative T-shirts. ~ 701 Front Street; 667-0661.

The Gecko Store, the only shop I've seen with a sand floor, also stocks inexpensive beachwear, as well as T-shirts and toys. ~ 703 Front Street; 661-1078.

The **Endangered Species Store,** which features a multitude of conservation-minded items such as oils and lotions from the rainforest, is a worthy stop. You will also find chimes, statues and a healthy supply of T-shirts and stuffed animals. ~ 707 Front Street; 661-0208.

Past the sea wall, in an overgrown cottage set back from the street, lie several shops including **Pacific Vision**, with its hand-etched glass and crystal pieces. ~ 819 Front Street; 661-0188.

There are just a few more street numbers before this shopper's promenade ends. Then if you cross the road and walk back in the opposite direction, with the sea to your right, you'll pass **South Seas Trading Post,** where you can barter greenbacks for Nepali wedding necklaces, Chinese porcelain opium pillows or New Guinea masks. ~ 780 Front Street; 661-3168.

The oldest American school west of the Rockies is Lahainaluna, founded by missionaries in Lahaina in 1831.

Lahaina Galleries is of special note not only for the contemporary artworks but also because of the imaginative ways in which they're displayed. Even if you're not just dying to write that five-figure check, stop by for a viewing. ~ 728 Front Street; 667-2152.

The Gallery has jade and pearl pieces among its inventory of exotic jewelry. You'll also find Asian antiques, artwork and a ship model gallery at this unusual shop. ~ 716 Front Street; 661-0696.

Nearby at **The Wharf Cinema Center** mall, there's a maze of stores. One shop worth a look is **Seegerpeople**. Essentially a portrait studio, this store adds a twist to an otherwise traditional craft. Instead of being framed, the pictures are mounted on quarter-inch-thick Lucite, cut out in the shape of the subject and placed on a base. The result is a freestanding "photosculpture" and humorous keepsake. ~ 658 Front Street; 661-1084.

Village Gallery features paintings by modern Hawaiian artists. Amid the tourist schlock is some brilliant artwork. ~ 120 Dickenson Street; 661-4402.

Also stop in at the Lahaina Art Society's **Banyan Tree Gallery**. This is a great place if you're in the market for local artwork; on display are pieces by a number of Maui artists. ~ 649 Wharf Street, first floor of the Old Courthouse; 661-0111.

The **Lahaina Cannery Mall,** a massive complex of stores housed in an old canning factory, is the area's most ambitious project. **Lahaina Printsellers** (667-7843), one of my favorite Maui shops, has an astounding collection of ancient maps and engravings from Polynesia and other parts of the world. **Kite Fantasy** (661-4766) is the place to pick up stunt and sport kites including diamond, box and bird designs. Here you'll also find wind socks, mobiles, boomerangs, kaleidoscopes, games and a wide array of toys. Complete flying instructions, including tips on where to launch your kite, are provided by the helpful staff. ~ 1221 Honoapiilani Highway.

Those are just a couple ideas to provide you with a jump start. Propel yourself through this place and you'll find a dozen more reasons that make it a favorite among Lahaina residents. Like the **Guy Buffet Collection**, a shop specializing in the work of one of Hawaii's finest (and funniest) folk artists. ~ 661-1119.

On the corner of Front and Papalana streets, **Lahaina Center** is another shopping mall, a sprawling complex of theaters, stores and restaurants.

Among the shops here is one where everything is **Made in Hawaii**. That includes historic photographs, jewelry, featherwork, T-shirts and ceramics. They also have two larger but equally home-grown establishments, **Liberty House** (661-4451), the Hawaiian department store, and **Hilo Hattie Fashion Center** (667-7911), specializing in the tackiest alohawear imaginable. ~ Lahaina Center, 900 Front Street; 661-5883.

Built to resemble a New England fishing village, **505 Front Street** is an attractive woodframe mall. Situated south of central Lahaina at 505 Front Street, it is home to almost two dozen shops, including galleries, boutiques and jewelry stores.

Most glamorous of all the stores here is **New York–Paris Gallery**, a trendy showcase for the artistic work of several musicians, including John Lennon, Miles Davis and the Rolling Stones' Ronnie Wood. They also have album cover art and pieces signed by the Beatles and the Stones. ~ 505 Front Street; 667-0727.

NIGHTLIFE

Front Street's the strip in Lahaina—a dilapidated row of buildings from which stream some of the freshest sounds around.

At the **Pioneer Bar and Grill**, there is nightly piano music. Tucked into a corner of the Pioneer Inn, this spot features a seagoing motif complete with harpoons, figureheads and other historical nautical decor. Usually packed to the bulkheads with a lively crew, it's a great place to enjoy a tall cold one. ~ 658 Wharf Street; 661-3636.

Moose McGillycuddy's is a hot club offering a large dancefloor and a variety of live music acts. The house is congenial and the drinks imaginatively mixed; for contemporary sounds with dinner, arrive before 10 p.m. Cover. ~ 844 Front Street; 667-7758.

There's always an ocean view at **Aloha Cantina Maui**. And on Thursday, Friday and Sunday nights, add to that live music. The sound is contemporary and the source is generally a solo performer or a duo. ~ 839 Front Street; 661-8788.

Better yet, check out **World Café**, where they have pool tables and live bands. There's something going on every night, whether it be free pool for ladies, drink specials or a local band wailing away. ~ 900 Front Street; 661-1515. Cover.

At **Il Bucaniere**, an open-air dining room overlooking the Front Street action, there's a guitarist nightly. ~ 666 Front Street; 661-3966.

Lahaina's favorite pastime is watching the sun set over the ocean while sipping a tropical concoction at a waterfront watering place. A prime place for this very rewarding activity is **Kimo's**, which also features a range of live music. ~ 845 Front Street; 661-4811.

Or try the **Lahaina Broiler**. After the sun finishes performing, the Lahaina Broiler features do-it-yourself karaoke entertainment. ~ 889 Front Street; 661-3111.

Blue Tropix is one of Maui's most popular nightclubs, featuring a musical showcase that starts the evening with big band tunes and then accelerates through the decades to the 1990s. This high-tech Los Angeles–style club is done in basic black and chrome and features two circular bars and a planetarium ceiling. If that's not enough, you'll also find a huge dancefloor and 11 video screens. Most of the music emanates from a deejay, but live rock bands appear on some nights. Come check out the in crowd. There's a cover charge after 9 p.m. Closed Tuesday and Wednesday. ~ 900 Front Street; 667-5309.

If it's Friday, you can also browse the art galleries of Lahaina, which sponsor a special **Art Night** every week.

For an awe-inspiring glimpse into Hawaii's past, watch the 40-minute film at the **Omni Theatre/Hawaii Experience**. Offering a three-dimensional perspective of the state's cultural and natural history, this film is shown on a huge domed 180-degree screen. Admission. ~ 824 Front Street; 661-8314.

BEACHES & PARKS

PAPALAUA WAYSIDE PARK *Kiawe* trees and scrub vegetation spread right to the shoreline along Papalaua Wayside Park. There are sandy patches between the trees large enough to spread a towel, but I prefer sunbathing at beaches closer to Lahaina. Bounded on one side by Honoapiilani Highway, this narrow beach extends for a mile to join a nicer, lawn-fringed park; then it stretches on toward Olowalu for several more miles. If you want to be alone, just head down the shore. Swimming is good, snorkeling is okay out past the surf break and surfing is excellent at Thousand Peaks breaks and also very good several miles east in Maalaea Bay. There's an outhouse and picnic area at the state wayside and picnic facilities at the grassy park. ~ Located on Honoapiilani Highway about ten miles south of Lahaina.

OLOWALU BEACHES Both to the north and south of Olowalu General Store lie narrow corridors of white sand. This is an excellent area to hunt for Maui diamonds. Swimming is very good, and south of the general store, where road and water meet, you'll find an excellent coral reef for snorkeling. There is also a growing green sea turtle population that can be seen by snorkelers at the 14-mile marker. Surfers will find good breaks with right and left slides about a half-mile north of the general store. Ulua are often caught from Olowalu landing. There are no facilities, but there is a market nearby. ~ To get there, go south from Lahaina on Honoapiilani Highway for about six miles.

LAUNIUPOKO WAYSIDE PARK 🏊 🤽 🏄 There's a seaside lawn shaded by palm trees and a sandy beach. A rock seawall slopes gently for entering swimmers, but offers little to sunbathers. It's located near the West Maui Mountains, with great views of Kahoolawe and Lanai. When the tide is high, it's a good place to take children to swim safely and comfortably in the tidal pool on the other side of the seawall. Otherwise, swimming and snorkeling are mediocre. There is good surf-casting from the seawall and south for three miles. The park has a picnic area, restrooms and showers. ~ Located three miles south of Lahaina on Honoapiilani Highway.

PUAMANA STATE WAYSIDE PARK 🏊 🤽 🏄 A grass-covered strip and narrow beach wedged between Honoapiilani Highway and the ocean, Puamana Park is dotted with ironwood trees. The excellent views make this a choice spot for an enjoyable picnic. ~ Located on Honoapiilani Highway, about two miles south of Lahaina.

ARMORY PARK 🏊 🤽 🏄 The one thing going for this park is its convenient location in Lahaina. Otherwise, it's heavily littered, shadowed by a mall and sometimes crowded. If you do stop by, try to forget all that and concentrate on the sandy beach, lawn and truly startling view of Lanai directly across the Auau Channel. Swimming is okay, snorkeling good past the reef and, for surfing, there are breaks in the summer near the seawall in Lahaina Harbor. This surfing spot is not for beginners! Threadfin and *ulua* are common catches here. Restrooms and tennis courts are across the street at Maluuluolele Park near the playing field. ~ Located right on Front Street next to the 505 Front Street mall.

BABY BEACH 🏊 🤽 This curving stretch of white sand is the best beach in Lahaina. It lacks privacy but certainly not beauty. From here you can look back to Lahaina town and the West Maui Mountains or out over the ocean to Kahoolawe, Lanai and Molokai. Or just close your eyes and soak up the sun. Swimming is good and well protected, if shallow. Snorkeling is only fair. In summer there are breaks nearby at Mala Wharf; left slide. Threadfin is often caught. There are restrooms and showers at the beach. ~ Take Front Street north from Lahaina for about a half-mile. Turn left on Puunoa Place and follow it to the beach.

WAHIKULI WAYSIDE PARK 🏊 🤽 This narrow stretch of beach and lawn, just off the road between Lahaina and Kaanapali, faces Lanai and Molokai. There are facilities aplenty, which might be why this pretty spot is so popular and crowded. Swimming is very good, but snorkeling is only fair. (There's a better spot just north of here near the Lahaina Canoe Club.) The most common catches here are *ulua* and threadfin. Facilities include picnic areas and restrooms; there are tennis courts up the street at the Civic Center. ~ Located on Honoapiilani Highway between Lahaina and Kaanapali.

HANAKAOO BEACH PARK Conveniently located beside Kaanapali Beach Resort, this long and narrow park features a white-sand beach and grassy picnic ground, and is referred to by locals as Canoe Beach. On Saturday during the summer season, this is the place to watch Hawaiian canoe racing. The road is nearby, but the views of Lanai are outstanding. Swimming is good, snorkeling fair, but surfing poor. Common catches include *ulua* and threadfin. There are picnic areas, restrooms and showers. ~ Located on Honoapiilani Highway between Lahaina and Kaanapali.

FIVE

Kaanapali-Kapalua Area

Even in the case of Maui's notorious land developers, there is method to the madness. The stretch of coastline extending for six miles along Maui's western shore, crowded to the extreme with hotels and condominiums, is anchored by two planned resorts. Like handsome bookends supporting an uneven array of dog-eared paperbacks, Kaanapali and Kapalua add class to the arrangement.

Supporting the south end, **Kaanapali** is a 500-acre enclave that extends along three miles of sandy beach and includes six hotels, a half-dozen condominiums, two golf courses and an attractive shopping mall. Back in the 19th century it was a dry and barren segment of the sugar plantation that operated from Lahaina. Raw sugar was hauled by train from the mill out to Black Rock, a dramatic outcropping along Kaanapali Beach, where the produce was loaded onto waiting ships.

In 1963, Kaanapali's first resort opened near Black Rock and development soon spread in both directions. Important to developers, who built the Sheraton Maui hotel around it, **Black Rock** (Puu Kekaa) is a volcanic cinder cone from which ancient Hawaiians believed that the dead departed the earth in their journey to the spirit world. According to legend, the great 18th-century Maui chief Kahekili proved his bravery by leaping from the rock to the ocean below.

Kaanapali's modern-day contribution to Pacific culture is the **Whalers Village Museum**. A three-part facility comprising an outdoor pavilion and two buildings connected by a sky-bridge, the museum details Lahaina's history of whaling and explains the physiology of Hawaii's beloved humpback. Outdoors, you'll find a 30-foot-long whale skeleton and a whaling longboat on display. The "golden era of whaling" is also portrayed in scrimshaw exhibits, a scale model whaling ship, harpoons and other artifacts from the days when Lahaina was one of the world's great whaling ports. ~ Whalers Village, 2435 Kaanapali Parkway; 661-5992.

An earlier chief, Piilani, built a road through the area in the 16th century and gave his name to modern-day Route 30, the Hono-apiilani Highway. Translated as "the bays of Piilani," the road passes several inlets located north of Kaanapali that have been de-veloped in haphazard fashion. Honokowai, Kahana and Napili form a continuous wall of condominiums that sprawls north to Kapalua Bay and offers West Maui's best lodging bargains.

Kapalua, the bookend holding the north side in place, is a for-mer pineapple plantation that was converted into a luxurious 1500-acre resort. Here two major hotels, three golf courses and sev-eral villa-style communities blanket the hillside from the white sands of Kapalua Bay to the deep green foothills of the West Maui Mountains. Like the entire strip along Maui's western flank, Kapalua enjoys otherworldly sunsets and dramatic views of Lanai and Molokai.

LODGING

In the Kaanapali area the modestly priced hotel is not an endan-gered species, it's totally extinct! So prepare yourself for steep tar-iffs. The **Kaanapali Beach Hotel** is a 430-room hostelry that sits right on the beach and sports many restaurants and a large lobby. Guest rooms enjoy private lanais and guests lounge around a grassy courtyard and a swimming pool. ~ 2525 Kaanapali Parkway, Kaanapali; 661-0011, 800-262-8450, fax 667-5978. ULTRA-DELUXE.

Or check out, and check in to, the **Royal Lahaina Resort.** Spreading across 27 acres, it encompasses 542 rooms, 11 tennis courts, 3 swimming pools, 2 restaurants, a coffee shop and a white-sand beach that extends for a half-mile. Rooms in the highrise hotel price in the ultra-deluxe category, while the prices for the nicest ac-commodations, the multiplex cottages that dot the landscaped grounds, head for the sky. ~ 2780 Kekaa Drive, Kaanapali; 661-3611, 800-447-6925, fax 661-6150. ULTRA-DELUXE.

In the realm of luxury hotels, the **Hyatt Regency Maui** is one of the better addresses in Hawaii. Built in 1980, its atrium lobby, Asian artwork and freeform swimming pool have set the standard for resorts ever since. Unlike more recent hotels, in which the size of guest rooms is sacrificed for the sake of lavish grounds, the Hyatt Regency maintains an ideal balance between public and private areas. If you're seeking beautiful surroundings, friendly service and beachfront location, this 812-room extravaganza is the ticket. ~ 200 Nohea Kai Drive, Kaanapali; 661-1234, 800-233-1234, fax 667-4499. ULTRA-DELUXE.

At Black Rock, the sacred lava promontory where cliff divers plunged into the Pacific, the ancient tradition is re-enacted as part of a nightly torch-lighting ceremony at the **Sheraton Maui Kaanapali Beach Resort.** Here 495 rooms and suites are spread across spacious grounds that hold three six-story towers and an Ocean Lanai wing.

The hotel's distinctive architecture—it is partially built atop the rock—places some rooms near the water's edge. Views of the neighbor islands and the West Maui Mountains are breathtaking. Decorated with rattan furniture, tropical prints and seashell-patterned bedspreads, all the rooms are trim and comfortable. You can watch the sunset from several restaurants and lounges, swim in your choice of pools or enjoy snorkeling along Black Rock. (The Sheraton Maui is closed for renovation until November 1996.) ~ 2605 Kaanapali Parkway, Kaanapali; 800-325-3535. ULTRA-DELUXE.

A waterfall plunges down the side of one of the three atrium towers at **Embassy Suites Resort**. Not impressed? How about enough macaws, hooded mergansers and triton sulphur-crested cockatoos to make you think you have checked into an aviary rather than an all-suite hotel. Hop aboard a glass-walled elevator and luxuriate in one of the 413 units. Each one is spacious, attractive and equipped with candy-striped sofas, oak cabinets and Casablanca fans. You'll have a lanai and large bath of your own, and to share with other guests there is a 24-foot waterslide and gazebo pavilion, carp ponds and waterways galore. Besides that, breakfast is free and you're invited to a daily cocktail reception. ~ 104 Kaanapali Shores Place, Kaanapali; 661-2000, 800-602-6284, fax 667-5821. ULTRA-DELUXE.

A subtle architectural style gives the **Kapalua Bay Hotel** a low profile. But don't be misled. Part of a 23,000-acre plantation, this relatively small hotel, with 194 rooms and suites, is the hub of one of Maui's most appealing and romantic resorts. A hillside setting overlooking a white-sand crescent beach means that nearly all the rooms have spectacular ocean views. The accommodations are luxurious and tasteful and include rattan- and wicker-furnished sitting areas, marble baths with sunken tubs, and vanity areas. Floor-to-ceiling french doors open onto spacious lanais. Rock-lined ponds, tropical gardens, three golf courses, restaurants, shops and a tennis facility add to Kapalua's charm. ~ 1 Bay Drive, Kapalua; 669-5656, 800-367-8000, fax 669-4690. ULTRA-DELUXE.

CONDOS

Most condominiums in this area are on the beach or just across the road from it. They are ideally situated for swimming or sunbathing; the major drawback, ironically, is that there are so many other condos around.

Kaanapali Alii ranks as one of Maui's better buys. Here the immense 1500- to 1900-square-foot suites can easily be shared by two couples or a family. All 210 condo units have large living and dining rooms, full kitchens, sitting areas and two baths. Fully carpeted and furnished with rattan, contemporary artwork and potted palms, these units start at $235 and top out at $475. Room service comes from the adjacent Maui Marriott. The contemporary highrise facil-

Kaanapali-Kapalua

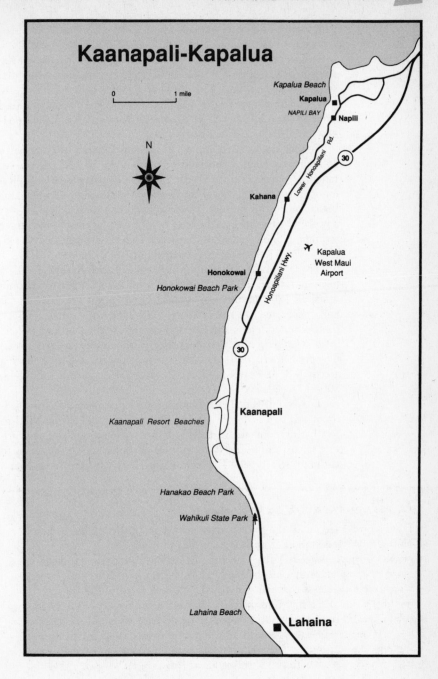

0 _____ 1 mile

N

Kapalua Beach

Kapalua ■

NAPILI BAY   ■ **Napili**

(30)

Kahana ■

✈ Kapalua
West Maui
Airport

Honokowai ■
Honokowai Beach Park

Lower Honoapiilani Rd.

Honoapiilani Hwy.

(30)

Kaanapali ■

Kaanapali Resort Beaches

Hanakao Beach Park

Wahikuli State Park ▲

Lahaina Beach   ■ **Lahaina**

ity rests along the beach and has a pool and tennis court. ~ 50 Nohea Kai Drive, Kaanapali; 667-1400, 800-642-6284, fax 661-1025.

Adjacent to the shops of Whalers Village, **The Whaler on Kaanapali Beach** offers spacious units with *koa* parquet floors and some rattan furniture. With its twin 12-story towers, this ocean-front condominium boasts marble baths and has 150 units priced from $180 to $450. ~ 2481 Kaanapali Parkway, Kaanapali; 661-4861, 800-367-7052, fax 661-8315.

For its 204 condominium units, **Maui Eldorado Resort** has a golf-course setting a short distance from the beach. The rooms, ranging from $135 to $259 per day, are decorated with a tropical motif, furnished in wicker and bamboo and equipped with large baths, lanais and vanities. Low-rise buildings in the complex offer a peaceful alternative to the busy hotel scene. Residents enjoy three swimming pools and a private beach club on the sands of Kaanapali. ~ 2661 Kekaa Drive, Kaanapali; 661-0021, fax 667-7039.

The lava rock–walled units at **Papakea Beach Resort** provide a pleasant retreat. Ranging from $125 studios to $255 two-bedroom units, all 120 condos come with spacious lanais. Though individually decorated, all the units are appointed with tropical prints, pastel-colored lamps and oak and rattan furniture. Although there is no swimming beach on the property, this resort has two attractive pool areas, two spas, three tennis courts and two putting greens. ~ 3543 Lower Honoapiilani Road, Honokowai; 669-4848, 800-367-7052, fax 669-0061.

The **Napili Kai Beach Club** has 162 units—studios, one-bedroom and two-bedroom affairs—that range in price from $155 to $450. Most come with kitchens. All are fully carpeted and have private lanais, rattan furniture, picture windows and direct access to an impressive beach. This resort is perfectly situated for golf and

KAANAPALI-KAPALUA EXPERIENCES

- Try the blackened ahi or the roast banana pork loin amid the gallery-like setting of **Roy's Kahana Bar and Grill**. (p. 99)
- Browse through **Whalers Village**, a shopping mall that seconds as a whaling museum complete with a 30-foot-long whale skeleton. (p. 100)
- Watch the sunset pass through as many themes and variations as the tinkling piano at the **Bay Club** on the beach in Kapalua. (p. 103)
- Follow the dirt road down to **Kahakuloa**, an old farming village where clapboard houses sit beneath a lonely headland on a deep blue bay. (p. 106)
- Surf the 15-foot tubes at **Honolua Bay** or catch the entire spectacle with a bird's eye view from the surrounding cliffs. (p. 107)

snorkeling. ~ 5900 Honoapiilani Road, Napili Bay; 669-6271, 800-367-5030, fax 669-5740.

Aston Kaanapali Shores has hotel room–style accommodations for $119 including refrigerator and microwave; studios from $169 double ($129 from April 1 to December 21) with a balcony and full kitchen; and one-bedroom units with a garden view and full kitchen for $205. They may be large and expensive, but these units are right at the entrance to Honokowai Beach and have two pools, a jacuzzi, tennis courts, fitness center, restaurant and shops. They also have a year-round activities program for children three to ten. ~ 3445 Lower Honoapiilani Road, Honokowai; 667-2211, 800-922-7866, fax 661-0836.

Providing an excellent deal, **Kapalua Villas** are situated on a 1500-acre resort with three golf courses and offer prices that start at $159 ($179 in the peak winter season). The setting is tranquil and the views sweep past the mountains, Oneloa Bay and neighbor islands. The units are low-rise structures with sunken tubs, large lanais and rattan and wicker furniture. Individually decorated, the accommodations provide direct access to swimming, golf and tennis. Oceanview and oceanfront villas range from $229 to $279; two-bedroom units run from $239 to $379. ~ 500 Office Road, Kapalua; 669-8088, 800-545-0018, fax 669-5234.

The following are additional facilities. They are more economical, but I think you'll find that they meet basic requirements for comfort and convenience.

Maui Sands. One-bedroom apartments begin at $80 single or double; two bedrooms run $100 for one to four people. There is a seven-night minimum. Beachfront. ~ 3600 Lower Honoapiilani Road, Kaanapali; 669-1902, 800-367-5037, fax 669-8790.

Paki Maui. One-bedroom apartments start at $159, depending on the view, and sleep one to four people; two-bedroom units start at $219, accommodating up to six people. Swimming pool with jet spa. Oceanfront. ~ 3615 Lower Honoapiilani Road, Kaanapali; 669-8235, 800-535-0085, fax 669-7987.

Aston Maui Park. Studios from $89 ($79 from April 1 to December 21). Across the street from the beach. ~ 3626 Lower Honoapiilani Road, Honokowai; 669-6622, 800-922-7866, fax 669-9647.

Honokowai Palms. One-bedroom apartments (up to four people) with lanai and ocean view run $65 double. Two-bedroom units without lanai are $75 for one to six people. Located right across the street from the ocean. ~ 3666 Lower Honoapiilani Road, Honokowai; 669-6130, 800-669-6284, fax 661-5875.

Hale Maui has one-bedroom condos for $65 double. On the waterfront; no pool. ~ 3711 Lower Honoapiilani Road, Honokowai; 669-6312, fax 669-1302.

Kaleialoha. One-bedroom apartments are $90 double; $7.50 each additional person. Oceanfront. ~ 3785 Lower Honoapiilani Road, Honokowai; 669-8197, 800-222-8688, fax 669-2502.

Hale Ono Loa offers one-bedroom units from $85 to $95 for up to four people. Oceanfront but no beach. ~ 3823 Lower Honoapiilani Road, Honokowai; 669-9680, 800-367-5637, fax 669-0751.

Polynesian Shores. One-bedroom apartments start at $95 double; two-bedroom units, $120 double; three-bedroom apartments, $160 double. All units have ocean view. ~ 3975 Lower Honoapiilani Road, Honokowai; 669-6065, 800-433-6284, fax 669-0909.

Mahina Surf. One-bedroom units start at $110 double ($85 from April 15 to December 14); two-bedroom accommodations are $130 and $105, respectively. Oceanfront on a lava-rock beach. ~ 4057 Lower Honoapiilani Road, Kahana; 669-6068, 800-367-6086, fax 669-4534.

Kahana Reef. Studio apartments, $85 single or double; one-bedroom apartments are $95 single or double; $15 more from December 19 to Easter. All units are oceanfront and have daily maid service. ~ 4471 Lower Honoapiilani Road, Kahana; 669-6491, 800-253-3773, fax 669-2192.

Napili Point Resort. One-bedroom condos are $164 for up to four people ($144 from April 20 to December 21). Here sliding doors lead out to ocean-view patios. Located on a lava rock beach, the resort is a short walk from sandy Napili Bay beach. ~ 5295 Lower Honoapiilani Road, Napili; 669-9222, 800-669-6252, fax 669-7984.

Outrigger's Napili Shores is a beautifully landscaped low-rise resort with studios and one-bedrooms running from $135 to $185. The units are appointed with rattan and oak pieces and the complex is graced by gardens of plumeria and hibiscus. The pool and beach areas are idyllic. ~ 5315 Lower Honoapiilani Road, Napili; 669-8061, 800-688-7444, fax 669-5407.

The Napili Bay. Studio apartments are $75 double for garden views, $85 for partial ocean views and $95 for oceanfront. ~ 33 Hui Road, Napili; 661-5200.

DINING   **Luigi's Pasta & Pizzeria** is located near the entrance to Kaanapali Beach Resort. A patio restaurant overlooking a golf course, it's a pretty place to dine on pizza, pasta and other Italian favorites. Open for dinner only, the restaurant features a menu that includes veal marsala, chicken parmesan and shrimp scampi. ~ 2991 Kaanapali Parkway; 661-3160. MODERATE.

The **Kaanapali Beach Hotel Koffee Shop** serves an all-you-can-eat buffet at a price that is surprisingly out of place for this expensive hotel. But don't expect too much for so little. The menu is limited to scrambled eggs, pancakes, French toast and some side dishes at breakfast, sandwiches and a few entrées for lunch and dinner. ~ Kaanapali Beach Hotel; 661-0011. BUDGET TO MODERATE.

Another way to eat at a reasonable price is by stopping at the take-out stands on the lower level of Whalers Village. There are tables inside or out in the courtyard. **Yakiniku Hahn** has Korean dishes. ~ 661-9798. At **Pizza Paradiso** they serve an assortment of pies (including by the slice) plus spaghetti and meatballs and salads. ~ 667-0333. **Kawara Sobe Takase Restaurant** has noodle dishes, onigiri (rice balls wrapped with seaweed) and tempura. BUDGET.

Spats II is an elegant Italian restaurant featuring regional cuisine. Candle-lit tables, antique armchairs and brass chandeliers are just some of the decorations, which are augmented by a menu of decadent dishes such as lobster on ribbon pasta covered with an herb cream sauce. ~ Hyatt Regency Maui, Kaanapali Beach Resort; 661-1234. DELUXE TO ULTRA-DELUXE.

Peter Merriman, the chef extraordinaire who earned his reputation with a restaurant on the Big Island, transported his brand of Hawaii regional cuisine across the Alenuihaha Channel to open **Hula Grill** on the beach in Kaanapali. Specializing in seafood, this 1930s-era beach house has wok-charred ahi, seafood dim sum dishes and an array of entrées that includes Hawaiian seafood gumbo, *opakapaka* in parchment, firecracker mahimahi and teriyaki ahi. For landlubbers there's New York steak, Thai beef curry and goat cheese pizza. Lunch and dinner. ~ Whalers Village; 667-6636. DELUXE.

Overlooking serene Japanese gardens, the open-air **Swan Court** defines the ultimate Maui experience. Guests enter this upscale restaurant in the Hyatt Regency Maui via a grand staircase to the classical strains of the resident pianist. With a waterfall and gliding swans in the background, you can choose from a variety of daily-changing entrées such as Hunan marinated lamb chops, grilled lobster satay with coconut and lemongrass, island-style bouillabaisse with macadamia sambal and sautéed *ono* with marinated shrimp won tons. For dessert, there's a daily soufflé selection and dessert

ABOVE MAUI

High atop the Hyatt Regency Maui's Lahaina Tower, a 16-inch reflecting telescope probes deep space five nights a week, taking tourists on a trip through the planets and galaxies. **The Tour of the Stars** is a one-hour program managed by the hotel's director of astronomy and designed for the public. It allows guests to look through stationary eyepieces while the computer-driven telescope searches the heavens. Reservations are required. Admission ~ 200 Nohea Kai Drive, Kaanapali; 661-1234.

sampler. ~ 200 Nohea Kai Drive, Kaanapali Beach; 661-1234. ULTRA-DELUXE.

Chico's Cantina is one of those tacky theme restaurants that prove either entertaining or annoying, depending on your disposition and mood. There is a car in the middle of the restaurant with surfboards on top of it, piñatas on the walls—that sort of thing. If you manage to get as far as the food, you'll find fajitas, chimichangas, burritos and other Mexican dishes. ~ Whalers Village; 667-2777. BUDGET TO MODERATE.

You can dine by the water at **Leilani's On The Beach**. The sunsets are otherworldly at this breezy veranda-style dining room. Trimmed in dark woods and lava rock, it's dominated by an outrigger canoe that hangs suspended from the ceiling. On the menu you'll find Malaysian shrimp, spinach and cheese ravioli, Cajun-style fresh fish, ginger chicken and teriyaki steak. Touristy but appealing. ~ Whalers Village; 661-4495. MODERATE TO DELUXE.

Beachcomber, a dinner-only dining room at the Royal Lahaina Resort, has a menu that covers the entire Pacific Rim. You'll find wicker chairs, shell lamps, decorative fans and dragons' heads providing the atmosphere. This is one of Kaanapali's better values. ~ 2780 Kekaa Drive, Kaanapali; 661-3611. MODERATE.

If **Lokelani** were located on a trendy corner in Lahaina, there's no doubt that this fresh-fish house would have people lined up waiting for a table. Instead, you'll find it in the Maui Marriott serving specialties such as pan-seared *opakapaka* marinated in *ponzu* then sautéed with lemongrass or seafood pasta prepared with fresh shrimp, scallops, and Hawaiian fish. Other favorites include rack of lamb with berry compote and five-spice sauce and salad of Kula greens and Roma tomatoes with fried Maui onions. Ask for an outside table overlooking the herb garden where you can enjoy the fresh flowers that add to the tropical ambience. ~ 100 Nohea Kai Drive, Kaanapali; 667-1200. DELUXE TO ULTRA-DELUXE.

SCRIMSHAW TREASURES

Perhaps the best place in Whaler's Village to discover the whaling tradition is **Lahaina Scrimshaw**. During their long journeys, sailors once whiled away the hours by etching and engraving on ivory, creating beautiful articles of scrimshaw. The sale of ivory from animals taken by hunters is banned, but the fossilized remains of ancient mammoths and walruses have kept this art alive. Using ivory that is thousands of years old, artists create a wide array of functional and decorative pieces, many of which are traded by aficionados of this art form. ~ 661-4034.

Located in the Maui Marriott, **Nikko** is a traditional Japanese restaurant that is decorated with woodblock prints and features tableside teppanyaki cooking. Specialties are filet mignon, chicken, shrimp, lobster and a vegetarian stir-fry. You can also enjoy sushi and tempura dishes for appetizers. ~ 100 Nohea Kai Drive, Kaanapali; 667-1200. DELUXE.

From the ship's rigging, captain's chairs and marlin trophies, you could never guess what they serve at **Erik's Seafood Grotto.** What a surprise to discover a menu filled with crabmeat-stuffed prawns, lobster-stuffed chicken breast, Hawaiian salmon and wahoo. Early-bird specials. ~ 4242 Lower Honoapiilani Road, Kahana; 669-4806. MODERATE TO DELUXE.

Dollie's Pub and Café offers lasagna, fettuccine alfredo, chicken parmesan, pizza and sandwiches. This is a sports-on-the-television bar with a small kitchen and dining room adjacent. During football season there is an omelette bar on Sunday mornings. ~ 4310 Lower Honoapiilani Road, Kahana; 669-0266. BUDGET TO MODERATE.

There's not much of an ocean view at **Kahana Keyes Restaurant,** but the wood-trimmed dining room is attractive. The bill of fare is pretty standard—steak and seafood; and the decor is comforting if uninspired. Check out the early-bird specials from 5 to 7 p.m. ~ 4327 Lower Honoapiilani Road, Kahana; 669-8071. MODERATE.

In addition to its namesake, **Maui Tacos** has chimichangas, tostadas, burritos, quesadillas and enchiladas. Nothing fancy, just a few formica booths and tables with molded plastic chairs. But the salsa's fresh daily, the beans are prepared without lard and the chips are made with cholesterol-free vegetable oil. ~ Napili Plaza, Napilihau Street, Napili; 665-0222. BUDGET.

One of Maui's leading restaurants, **Roy's Kahana Bar and Grill** eschews the waterfalls, swans, tinkling pianists and other accoutrements of the island's top dining rooms. Instead, this spacious second-story establishment looks like a gallery with its exposed-beam ceiling, track lighting and paintings. The open kitchen serves up such creations as fresh seared lemongrass *shutome* with Thai basil peanut sauce, island-style roasted banana pork loin with Chinese black bean *hoisin* sauce, sake soy grilled half chicken with Asian honey-mustard sauce and blackened ahi with soy-mustard butter. Reservations are a must! ~ Kahana Gateway Shopping Center, 4405 Honoapiilani Highway, Kahana; 669-6999. DELUXE TO ULTRA-DELUXE.

For Mongolian beef, Peking duck or hot Szechuan bean curd, try **China Boat**. At this family-style restaurant, you can ease into a lacquered seat and take in the Japanese *ukiyoe* prints that adorn the place. Adding to the ambience are lava walls that showcase beautiful Chinese ceramic pieces. Patio dining is also available. ~ 4474 Lower Honoapiilani Road, Kahana; 669-5089. MODERATE.

At the **Orient Express,** they feature a variety of Thai and Chinese dishes including shrimp saté, clay-pot seafood dishes, sour shrimp soup, red curry beef and Thai noodles stir-fried with pork, egg and crushed peanuts. Part of the Napili Shores Resort, this lava-walled restaurant has a shocking-pink-and-purple color scheme. ~ 5315 Lower Honoapiilani Road, Napili; 669-8077. MODERATE.

Maui aficionados agree that **The Plantation House Restaurant** is among the island's best. Capturing their accolades is a spacious establishment with panoramic views of the Kapalua region and a decor that mixes mahogany and wicker with orchids and a roaring fire. Not to be upstaged by the surroundings, the chef prepares fresh island fish five different ways. The most popular is the "taste of the rich forest"—the fish is pressed with wild mushrooms and roasted, then served on spinach with garlic mashed potatoes and Maui onion meunière sauce. For lighter appetites there are salads, pastas, honey guava scallops, and for lunch a wide range of soups and sandwiches. ~ 2000 Plantation Club Drive, Kapalua; 669-6299. DELUXE TO ULTRA-DELUXE.

There's little doubt that Hawaii's finest sunsets occur off the southwest coast of Maui. One of the best spots to catch the spectacle is **The Bay Club** at the Kapalua Bay Hotel, an oceanfront dining room that looks out on Molokai and Lanai. More than just a feast for the eyes, this open-air restaurant offers a gourmet menu at lunch and dinner. You can watch the sky melt from deep blue to flaming red while dining on bouillabaisse, seared sea scallops, Pacific lobster tail, rack of lamb or filet mignon with Maui onion rings. A rough life indeed. Dress code: no shorts, jeans, open-toed shoes or T-shirts. ~ 1 Bay Drive, Kapalua; 669-5656. ULTRA-DELUXE.

For something less expensive, consider **The Market Café**. It's located in the Kapalua Shops adjacent to the Kapalua Bay Hotel. Comfortably equipped with wooden booths and bentwood chairs, the dining area presents fresh fish, steak teriyaki, chicken tetrazzini and several other Italian specialties. ~ 115 Bay Drive, Kapalua; 669-4888. MODERATE.

GROCERIES Out in the Kaanapali area, the best place to shop is **The Food Pantry**, a small supermarket that's open from 6:30 a.m. to 11 p.m. every day. ~ Lower Honoapiilani Road in Honokowai; 669-6208.

Toward Kapalua, try the **Napili Market**, a well-stocked supermarket that's open from 6:30 a.m. to 11 p.m. every day. ~ Napili Plaza on Honoapiilani Highway; 669-1600

SHOPPING Worthy of mention is **Whalers Village** in the Kaanapali Beach Resort on Route 30. This sprawling complex combines a shopping mall with an outdoor museum. Numbered among the stores you'll find gift emporia featuring coral and shells, a shirt store with wild island designs, other stores offering fine men's and women's fashions and a **Waldenbooks** bookstore. ~ 661-8638.

Several shops in this split-level complex should not be missed. **The Secret Jungle** specializes in the cloisonné jewelry and silk-screened fabrics of Laurel Burch. ~ 661-8651. Around the corner at **Lahaina Printsellers Ltd.**, they purvey "fine antique maps and prints." ~ 667-7617. At **Blue Ginger Designs** original styles in women's and children's clothing are featured. ~ 667-5793. **Silks Kaanapali** is the place to find hand-painted silk and rayon dresses and sarongs. Belts, hats, jewelry and other accessories are also sold here. ~ 667-7133. Another store worth visiting here is **Endangered Species**, a preservationist shop selling photos, sculptures and paintings of sharks, whales and rainforests. Through sales of these products it also helps support many environmental causes. ~ 661-1139.

With the continuing influx of Japanese tourists who arrive with a yen for shopping and a strong yen in their purses, the upper tier of Whalers Village has gone stratospheric. Among the shops representing this shift to the chic is **Chanel Boutique**, which displays fine jewelry and designer threads. Chanel also has a line of purses guaranteed to put a hole in your wallet. ~ 661-1555.

And then, to help make shopping the grand adventure it should be, there are the displays. Within this mazework mall you'll discover blunderbusses, intricate scrimshaw pieces, the skeletal remains of leviathans and whaling boats with iron harpoons splayed from the bow. Practically everything, in fact, that a whaler (or a cruising shopper) could desire.

Ever wonder where travel writers shop for kitsch? Members of that dissolute group have been known to frequent **O'Rourke's Tourist Trap**. Under one large roof are glass pineapples, gecko pins, plastic leis, cultured coral pieces and hundreds of other mementos of the islands. ~ 4405 Lower Honoapiilani Highway, Kahana; 669-1406.

For serious shoppers, ready to spend money or be damned, there is nothing to compare with the neighboring hotels. Set like gems within this tourist cluster are several world-class hotels, each hosting numerous elegant shops.

Foremost is the **Hyatt Regency Maui,** along whose wood-paneled lobby are stores that might well be deemed mini-museums. One, called **Elephant Walk**, displays *koa* wood furniture, baskets and Niihau shell jewelry. There are art galleries, a fabric shop, clothing stores, jewelry stores and more—set in an open-air lobby that is filled with rare statuary and exotic birds. ~ 210 Nohea Kai Drive; Kaanapali; 667-2848.

Another favorite Hyatt Regency shop is **Rhonda's Quilts**, where you'll find wallhangings, Thai silk pillows and needlepoint supplies as well as an array of quilts. Many of the quilts are designed by local artists. ~ 210 Nohea Kai Drive, Kaanapali; 661-1234.

La Bareda is an excellent place to find inexpensive Hawaiian souvenirs such as sarongs, straw hats, jewelry and T-shirts. This shop in the Maui Marriott hotel is also knee-deep in key chains, pennants and ceramic pineapples. ~ 100 Nohea Kai Drive, Kaanapali; 667-8226.

Located at 1 Bay Drive, the **Kapalua Bay Hotel** sports another upscale shopping annex. Among the temptations is **Mandalay**, specializing in silks and cottons from Asia. There are blouses and jackets for women as well as a small collection of artfully crafted jewelry. ~ 669-6170. Also stop by **South Seas of Kapalua**, which has native masks from New Guinea and other artwork from Oceania. ~ 669-1249. If you're traveling with young ones or looking for a souvenir for those you left behind, stop by **Kapalua Kids**. Here you can buy children's books on Hawaii as well as soft toys and an array of clothing. ~ 669-0033.

At the **Plantation Course Golf Shop** you'll find an impressive collection of jackets, shirts, sweaters, sweatshirts and shorts, many with a tropical flair. This is also a good place to look for the work of signature designers. ~ 300 Plantation Club Drive, Kapalua; 669-8877.

NIGHTLIFE Possibly the prettiest place in these parts to enjoy a drink 'neath the tropic moon is the bar at **Hula Grill**. Located in the Whalers Village mall, this beach house–style gathering place is decorated with original Hawaiian outrigger canoes. It features Hawaiian music and hula nightly until nine o'clock. The place is located right on the water, so you can listen to a slow set, then stroll the beach. ~ Whalers Village; 667-6636.

A solo pianist performs nightly at the Hyatt Regency Maui in the elegant waterfront **Swan Court**. For contemporary Hawaiian and guitar music, head over to the **Weeping Banyan**, an open-air lounge. ~ 200 Nohea Kai Drive; 661-1234.

There's music and Hawaiian entertainment at the Westin Maui in the **Villa Restaurant**. At the hotel's **Sound of the Falls**, a classical pianist plays nightly, except Sunday. ~ 2365 Kaanapali Parkway; 667-2525.

At the Maui Marriott, the **Makai Bar** cooks every night with a solo or duo performing Hawaiian and pop numbers. If you'd rather get up there and perform yourself, you can join the hostess in a karaoke-style sing-along at the **Lobby Bar** on Thursday, Friday or Saturday. On Sunday night a standup comedian will take your place. ~ 100 Nohea Kai Drive; 667-1200.

The Sheraton Maui is a prime nightspot both early and later in the evening. Just before sunset you can watch the torchlighting and cliff-diving ceremony from the **Sundowner Bar**. Then adjourn to **On The Rocks** for karaoke. (The Sheraton Maui is closed for renovation until November 1996.) ~ Kaanapali Parkway; 661-0031.

There's Hawaiian-style entertainment nightly at the **Royal Ocean Terrace Lounge**, a beachfront watering hole on the grounds of the Royal Lahaina Resort. Arrive early and you can watch the sunset between Lanai and Molokai followed by the ubiquitous torch-lighting ceremony. ~ 2780 Kekaa Drive; 661-3611.

For soft entertainment in a relaxed setting, try the **Bay Club** at the Kapalua Bay Hotel. This open-air lounge with nightly pianist is set in a lovely restaurant overlooking the water. The melodies are as serene and relaxing as the views of neighboring Molokai. ~ 1 Bay Drive; 669-8008.

At **The Bay Lounge**, in the lobby of the Kapalua Bay Hotel, you can enjoy live Hawaiian music and a nightly hula show over cocktails and great views of the Pacific. ~ 1 Bay Drive; 367-8000.

A Hawaiian duo plays in the evenings at **The Lobby Lounge and Library** at the Ritz-Carlton Kapalua. At the **Anuenue Lounge** you can enjoy a pianist. ~ 1 Ritz-Carlton Drive, Kapalua; 669-6200.

KAANAPALI RESORT BEACHES The sprawling complex of Kaanapali hotels sits astride a beautiful white-sand beach that extends for three miles. Looking out on Lanai and Molokai, this is a classic palm-fringed strand. The entire area is heavily developed and crowded with tourists glistening in coconut oil. But it is an extraordinarily fine beach where the swimming is very good and the skindiving excellent around Black Rock at the Sheraton Maui. The beach has no facilities, but there are restaurants nearby. ~ To get there, take the public right-of-way to the beach from any of the Kaanapali resort hotels.

BEACHES & PARKS

HONOKOWAI BEACH PARK Compared to the beaches fronting Kaanapali's nearby resorts, this is a bit disappointing. The large lawn is pleasant enough, but the beach itself is small, with a reef that projects right to the shoreline. On the other hand, the view of Molokai is awesome. In the shallow reef waters the swimming and snorkeling are fair; surfing is nonexistent. Threadfin and *ulua*

PUEONE O HONOKAHUA

The Kapalua area includes one of Maui's most important cultural zones, Pueone O Honokahua. This 14-acre preserve, near the Ritz-Carlton Kapalua, was the site of fishing shrines and *heiaus* where the ancient Hawaiians worshipped their gods and made astronomical observations. Today you can see a burial ground dating back to 950 A.D. and portions of the King's Highway, a 16th-century stone road around Maui. Also extant are the outlines of terraced taro patches farmed by early inhabitants. Although this land has been claimed in turn by King Kamehameha III, the sugar king, H. P. Baldwin, and lastly the Maui Land and Pineapple Company, the state now protects and preserves it as a native Hawaiian sanctuary.

are among the most frequent catches. Picnic tables, restrooms and showers are available and directly across the street is a supermarket. ~ The beach is on Lower Honoapiilani Road (which is the oceanfront section of Route 30) north of Kaanapali in Honokowai.

NAPILI BAY You'll find wall-to-wall condominiums along the small cove. There's a crowded but beautiful white-sand beach studded with palm trees and looking out on Molokai. Swimming and snorkeling are delightful and the surfing here is particularly good for beginners. ~ Located several miles north of Kaanapali, with rights-of-way to the beach from Lower Honoapiilani Road via Napili Place or Hui Drive.

KAPALUA BEACH This is the next cove over from Napili Bay. It's equally beautiful, but not as heavily developed. The crescent of white sand that lines Kapalua Bay is bounded on either end by rocky points and backdropped by a line of coconut trees and the Kapalua Bay Hotel. Swimming and snorkeling are excellent. ~ There's a right-of-way to the beach from Lower Honoapiilani Road near the Napili Kai Beach Club.

D. T. FLEMING PARK One of Maui's nicest beach parks, D. T. Fleming has a spacious white-sand beach and a rolling lawn shaded with palm and ironwood trees. Unfortunately, a major resort resides just uphill from the beach. Sometimes windy, the park is plagued by rough and dangerous surf during the winter. Use caution! There's a nice view of Molokai's rugged East End. You'll find good swimming and bodysurfing and fair snorkeling here. There are also good breaks nearby at Little Makaha, named after the famous Oahu beach. For anglers the prime catches here are *ulua* and *papio*. There are restrooms, a picnic area and showers. ~ Located just off Honoapiilani Highway, about seven miles north of Kaanapali.

Northwest Maui To escape from the crowds and commotion of the Kaanapali-Kapalua area and travel north on the Honoapiilani Highway is to journey from the ridiculous to the sublime. As you curve along the edge of the West Maui Mountains, en route around the side of the island to Kahului and Wailuku, you'll pass several hidden beaches that lie along an exotic and undeveloped shore. This is a region of the Valley Isle rarely ever seen by visitors.

Near the rocky beach and lush valley at **Honokohau Bay**, the Honoapiilani Highway (Route 30) becomes the Kahekili Highway (Route 340). This macadam track snakes high above the ocean, hugging the coastline. From the highway rises a series of multihued **sandstone cliffs** that seems alien to this volcanic region and creates a picturesque backdrop to the rocky shore.

As the road continues, the scenery is some of the most magnificent on Maui. Down a dirt side road sits the rustic village of

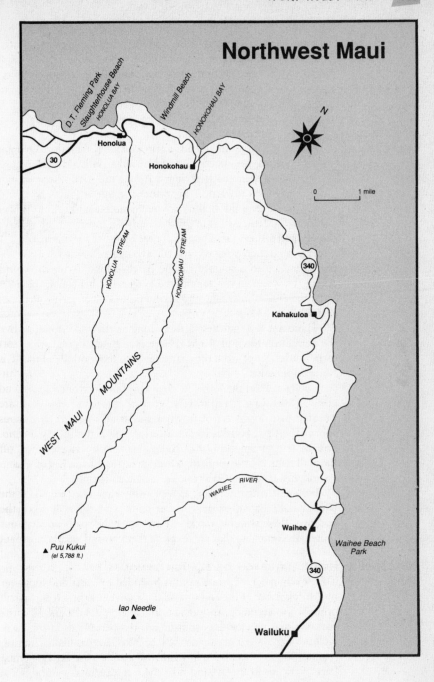

Northwest Maui

D.T. Fleming Park
Slaughterhouse Beach
HONOLUA BAY
Windmill Beach
HONOKOHAU BAY

Honolua

Honokohau

30

0   1 mile

HONOLUA STREAM

HONOKOHAU STREAM

340

Kahakuloa

WEST MAUI MOUNTAINS

WAIHEE RIVER

Waihee

Waihee Beach
Park

Puu Kukui
(el 5,788 ft.)

340

Iao Needle

Wailuku

HIDDEN ► **Kahakuloa.** Nestled in an overgrown valley beside a deep blue bay, the community is protected by a solitary headland rising directly from the sea. Woodframe houses and churches, which appear ready to fall to the next gusting wind, are spotted throughout this enchanting area. Kahakuloa is cattle country, and you'll find that the villagers live and farm much as their forefathers did back when most of Maui was unclaimed terrain.

It was from the shoreline near Kahakuloa that the Polynesian canoe *Hokulea* left on its famous voyage.

The road ascends again outside Kahakuloa. Opening below you, one valley after another falls seaward in a series of spine-backed ridges. Above the road, the mountain range rises toward its 5788-foot summit at Puu Kukui.

Six miles beyond Kahakuloa, you'll stumble upon **Aina Anuhea Tropical Gardens,** which in this heavenly environment represents a further ascent into the ethereal. Its six acres of curving paths lead along a mountain stream, through a Japanese garden, past a waterfall and up to a solitary gazebo perched high above the world. Along the way you can take in the ginger and heliconia, the maile and lokelani. Admission. ~ Kahekili Highway, between Kahakuloa and Waihee; 244-0689.

There are lush gulches farther along as the road descends into the plantation town of **Waihee.** Here cane fields, dotted with small farm houses, slope from the roadside up to the foothills of the West Maui Mountains.

You're still on the Kahekili Highway, but now once again it really is a highway, a well-traveled road that leads toward Kahului. Located just northwest of town, a side road leads to two sacred spots. The first, **Halekii Heiau,** overlooking Kahului Bay and Iao Stream, dates from the 1700s. Today this temple, once as large as a football field, is little more than a stone heap. **Pihana Kalani Heiau,** a short distance away, was once a sacrificial temple.

Before driving this route, as well as the back road from Hana to Ulupalakua, remember that the car rental agencies will not insure you over these winding tracks. Many cover the roads anyway, and I highly recommend that you explore them both if weather permits.

BEACHES & PARKS

MOKULEIA BEACH OR SLAUGHTERHOUSE BEACH
This lovely patch of white sand is bounded by cliffs and looks out on Molokai. Set at the end of a shallow cove, the beach is partially protected. Swimming, snorkeling and surfing are all good. This is part of a marine sanctuary so fishing is not permitted. There are no facilities here. ~ To get to the beach, take Honoapiilani Highway (Route 30) for exactly eight-tenths of a mile past D. T. Fleming Park. Park on Route 30 and take the steep path down about 100 yards to the beach.

HIDDEN ►

HONOLUA BAY 🏊 🤿 🏄 🛶 A rocky beach makes this cliff-rimmed bay unappealing for sunbathers, but there are rich coral deposits offshore and beautiful trees growing near the water. In winter you're likely to find crowds along the top of the cliff watching surfers work some of the finest breaks in all Hawaii: perfect tubes up to 15 feet. Swimming is good, but the bottom is rocky. Snorkeling is excellent, particularly on the west side of the bay. No fishing is allowed; this is part of a marine sanctuary. There are no facilities (and usually very few people) here. ~ To reach Honolua Bay, take Honoapiilani Highway (Route 30) for about one-and-a-third miles north from D. T. Fleming Park. The dirt road to the beach is open only to cars with boats in tow. Park with the other cars along Route 30 and follow the paths to the beach. ◄ HIDDEN

PUNALAU OR WINDMILL BEACH 🏊 🤿 🏄 🛶 A white-sand beach studded with rocks, Punalau is surrounded by cliffs and intriguing rock formations. Very secluded. The swimming is okay and when the water is calm snorkeling is excellent. A fascinating reef extends along the coast all through this area. Surfing is fine, peaking in winter; left and right slides. Leatherback, *papio*, milkfish, *moano* and big-eyed scad are the primary catches for anglers. ~ It is just three-and-a-half miles north from D. T. Fleming Park on Honoapiilani Highway (Route 30). Turn left onto the dirt road and follow it a short distance to the beach. ◄ HIDDEN

▲ For those interested in pitching a camp here, a permit is required from Maui Pineapple Co., Honolua Division, 4900 Honoapiilani Highway, Lahaina (669-6201) and must be obtained in person. There is a three-day limit and a $5 day-use fee, but no facilities.

HONOKOHAU BAY 🏊 🤿 🏄 🛶 This rocky beach is surrounded by cliffs. To the interior, a lush valley rises steadily into the folds of the West Maui Mountains. When the water is calm, swimming and snorkeling are good. The surf offers rugged, two- to twelve-foot breaks. Keep in mind the changeable nature of this wave action, since it can vary quickly from the gentle to the dangerous. Milkfish, *papio*, leatherback, *moano* and big-eyed scad are the principal species caught in these waters. ~ To get there, follow Honoapiilani Highway (Route 30) about six miles north of D. T. Fleming Park.

▲ Camping is allowed here, but the place is very rocky, and there are no facilities.

SIX

Kihei-Wailea Area

Stretching from Maalaea Bay to Makena is a nearly continuous succession of beautiful beaches that make Kihei and Wailea favored resort destinations. Second only to the Lahaina-Kaanapali area in popularity, this seaside enclave rests in the rainshadow of Haleakala, which looms in the background. Maui's southeastern shore receives only ten inches of rain a year, making it the driest, sunniest spot on the island. It also experiences heavy winds, particularly in the afternoon, which sweep across the island's isthmus.

Since the 1970s, this long, lean stretch of coast has become a developer's playground. Kihei in particular, lacking a master plan, has grown by accretion from a small local community into a haphazard collection of condominiums and minimalls. It's an unattractive, six-mile strip lined by a golden beach.

Situated strategically along this beachfront are cement **pillboxes**, reminders of World War II's threatened Japanese invasion. Placed along Kihei Road just north of town, they are not far from **Kealia Pond Bird Sanctuary**, a 300-acre reserve frequented by migratory waterfowl as well as Hawaiian stilts and Hawaiian coots.

To the south lies Wailea, an urbane answer to the random growth patterns of its scruffy neighbor. Wailea is a planned resort, all 1450 manicured acres of it. Here *kiawe* scrubland has been transformed into a flowering oasis that is home to five top-class hotels and six condominiums, as well as the required retinue of golf courses, tennis courts and overpriced shops. Like Kihei, it is blessed with beautiful beaches.

Home to some of Maui's most luxurious resorts, Wailea is the place to find Picasso originals, 50,000-square-foot spas and villas designed to keep a smile on the face of a high roller. Mediterranean- and plantation-style architecture, accented by polished limestone tile and granite boulders imported from Mount Fuji, make this swank resort area an international retreat.

Connected by a mile-and-a-half-long ocean walk, and lining five crescent beaches, the resort's luxury properties comprise a self-contained retreat. Spread across a region three times the size of Waikiki, Wailea is the Valley Isle's fastest growing resort destination.

You'll have to go well past Wailea, to where the coast road becomes narrower, to escape the tourist complexes. I highly recommend visiting **Makena Beach,** located along Makena Alanui Road about four miles beyond Wailea. Although development has struck here, too, Makena is still one of Maui's finest strands. A hippie hangout in the 1960s and early 1970s, it still retains a freewheeling atmosphere, especially at nearby "Little Makena," Maui's most famous nude beach.

Past here the road gets rough as it presses south to **Ahihi-Kinau Natural Area Reserve.** Encompassing over 2000 acres of land and ocean bottom, this preserve harbors an amazing array of marine life and contains the remains of an early Hawaiian fishing village. Almost 100 larval fish species and about two dozen species of stony coral have been found in this ecologically rich reserve.

The road continues on, bisecting the **1790 lava flow,** which resulted from Haleakala's last eruption. The flow created Cape Kinau, a thumb-shaped peninsula dividing Ahihi Bay and **La Perouse Bay.** When I drove this route recently in a compact rental car, I reached La Perouse Bay before being forced by poor road conditions to turn back. The bay is named for the ill-starred French navigator, Jean-François de la Pérouse, who anchored here in 1786, the first Westerner to visit Maui. After a brief sojourn in this enchanting spot, he sailed off and was later lost at sea.

HIDDEN ►

Anywhere along this coastline you can gaze out at **Molokini,** a crescent-shaped islet that is a favorite spot among skindivers. Resting in the Alalakeihi Channel three miles west of Maui, it measures a scant 19 acres in area and rises 165 feet above sea level. The island is actually a tuff cone created by volcanic eruptions deep underwater that solidified into a hard substance called tuff. Black coral divers harvested the surrounding waters until the 1970s. According to Hawaiian legend, Molokini was created when the volcano goddess Pele cut a rival lover—a lizard—in two, turning the tail into Molokini and the head into the cinder cone near Makena Beach.

LODGING

Like Kaanapali, this oceanfront strip features condominiums, but there are a couple of hotels that I would recommend. The **Nona Lani Cottages** tops the list, with eight quaint wooden cottages situated across busy Kihei Road from a white-sand beach. Each is a one-bedroom unit with lanai, all-electric kitchen and a living room capable of housing one or two extra sleepers. There's wall-to-wall carpeting and a shower-tub combination, plus television, but no phone or air conditioner. Like most cottages in Hawaii, these are

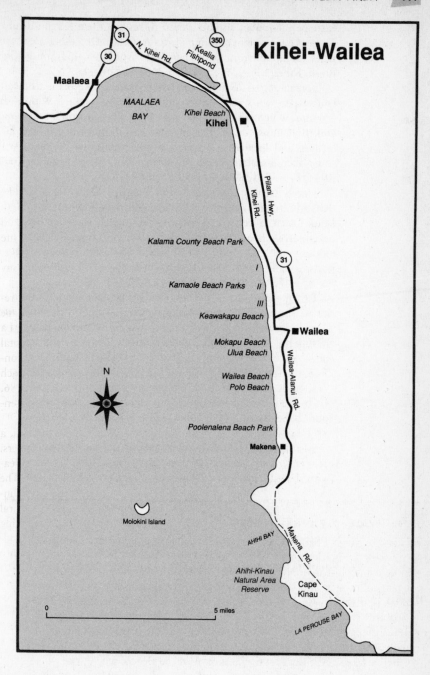

Kihei-Wailea

31
30
350

Maalaea

N. Kihei Rd.
Kealia
Fishpond

MAALAEA
BAY

Kihei Beach
Kihei

Piilani Hwy.

Kihei Rd.

31

Kalama County Beach Park

I

Kamaole Beach Parks   II

III

Keawakapu Beach

Wailea

Mokapu Beach
Ulua Beach

Wailea-Alanui Rd.

Wailea Beach
Polo Beach

N

Poolenalena Beach Park

Makena

Molokini Island

AHIHI BAY

Makena Rd.

Ahihi-Kinau
Natural Area
Reserve

Cape
Kinau

0   5 miles

LA PEROUSE BAY

extremely popular, so you'll need to reserve them far in advance. There is a four-night minimum from April 1 to December 15; seven-night minimum from December 16 to April 1. ~ 455 South Kihei Road, Kihei; 879-2497, 800-733-2688. MODERATE.

Spread across 28 acres, the **Aston Maui Lu Resort** is tropically landscaped with palm trees and flowering plants. Within the grounds, which are across the street from a beach, you'll find a pool and two tennis courts. The guest rooms are furnished in standard fashion and located in a series of interconnecting buildings with some accommodations on the beach. ~ 575 South Kihei Road, Kihei; 879-5881, 800-922-7866, fax 879-4627. DELUXE.

Hotels are rare in Kihei. And in Wailea, a hotel in anything less than an ultra-deluxe price range is a contradiction in terms. So the **Maui Coast Hotel**, a 260-room facility across the street from the beach, provides a little (very little, I grant you) relief. It's light, airy, modern and has a pool, tennis courts and cluster of nearby restaurants. ~ 2259 South Kihei Road, Kihei; 874-6284, 800-426-0670, fax 875-4731. DELUXE TO ULTRA-DELUXE.

Down the road at the **Maui Oceanfront Hotel** you'll find a series of six buildings designed in mock-Hawaiian style and sandwiched between the highway and a white-sand beach. The rooms are tiny but attractively decorated with carpeting, air conditioning, television and refrigerator. ~ 2980 South Kihei Road, Kihei; 879-7744, 800-367-5004, fax 800-477-2329. MODERATE TO DELUXE.

Kihei is home to **Hale O'Wahine**, a women-only bed and breakfast that consists of four units, one right on Sugar Beach. ~ 2777 South Kihei Road B-105, Kihei; 874-5148, fax 572-0403. MODERATE TO DELUXE.

Also here is **Triple Lei**, an exclusively gay and lesbian bed and breakfast. This tropical contemporary home offers three rooms (with shared bath) and a 700-square-foot suite complete with a dry

KIHEI-WAILEA EXPERIENCES

- Hike the **King's Highway**, an ancient Hawaiian trail along the ocean that traverses the black domain of a 1790 lava flow. (p. 44)
- Skindive **Ahihi-Kinau Natural Area Reserve** amid two dozen types of technicolor coral and 100 species of equally dazzling fish. (p. 110)
- Book reservations for one of the eight cozy accommodations at **Nona Lani Cottages** and explore a nearby beach that extends for miles. (p. 110)
- Tuck yourself into a leather chair, gaze out over the ocean and splurge with a gourmet dinner at **Seasons** restaurant. (p. 117)
- Catch a wave and check out the scene at **Makena Beach**, where rock stars jammed during the hippie days of the late '60s. (p. 121)

sauna and a private bath. There's a pool on the grounds but Little Makena beach is only five minutes away. ~ P.O. Box 959, Kihei, HI 96753; phone/fax 874-8645. MODERATE TO DELUXE.

The lushly landscaped **Four Seasons Resort Maui at Wailea** is the ultimate among ultimate destinations. The only Maui resort we know to feature a trompe l'oeil artwork in the lobby, it's a wind-swept, Hawaiian palace–style complex set on a luxurious beach. Furnished with wicker and rattan, most of the 380 plantation-style rooms offer ocean views. Casablanca fans, tropical plants and marbletop vanities add to the comfort. Louvered doors open onto spacious lanais. Reflecting pools, waterfalls and fountains give the public areas an elegant tropical air. ~ 3900 Wailea Alanui, Wailea; 874-8000, 800-334-6284, fax 874-2222. ULTRA-DELUXE.

The all-suite **Kea Lani Hotel** is a 22-acre resort done in south-ern Mediterranean style. Turning its back on Hawaiian royalty, the Eurocentric lobby would look familiar to Louis XIV. Seven water-falls, four fountains and a swim-up bar create attractions decadent enough for the Sun King himself. Among the accommodations are 413 suites and 37 oceanfront villas, each appointed with oak fix-tures, floral prints and mirrored doors. The Roman-style baths fea-ture Italian marble (of course) and all the two-story villas come with their own plunge pool. ~ 4100 Wailea Alanui, Wailea; 875-4100, 800-659-4100, fax 875-1200. ULTRA-DELUXE.

Its remote location makes the **Makena Resort Maui Prince Hotel** an unusual find. Built around a courtyard adorned with lush tropical gardens and lily ponds, the 304-room establishment re-wards those willing to drive a few extra minutes to Maui's southern-most retreat. Here you're likely to be lulled to sleep by the sound of the surf. Decorated with heliconia and bougainvillea, the rooms and suites open onto lanais. This V-shaped hotel is next door to two of Maui's top golf courses. ~ 5400 Makena Alanui, Makena; 874-1111, 800-321-6284, fax 879-8763. ULTRA-DELUXE.

CONDOS

Leilani Kai. This cozy nine-unit apartment hotel is right on the beach. Studio apartments are $75 double ($60 during the off-season, May 1 to November 30); one-bedroom units are $100 double ($75 off-season); two bedrooms will run you $125 for one to four peo-ple ($90 off-season). ~ 1226 Uluniu Street, Kihei; 879-2606, 800-367-5234, fax 242-1845.

Kihei Kai. Oceanside one-bedroom apartments are $85 to $105 double ($75 to $90 from mid-April to mid-December). Each has television, full kitchen and lanai. ~ 61 North Kihei Road, Kihei; 879-2357, 800-735-2357.

Sunseeker Resort. A small, personalized place where studios with kitchenettes go for $60 double and one-bedrooms for $70 double. Add $6 for each additional person. ~ 551 South Kihei Road, Kihei; 879-1261, 800-532-6284, fax 874-3877.

Mana Kai Maui Resort. This highrise condominium has "hotel units" that consist of the extra bedroom and bath from a two-bedroom apartment, renting for $100 ($115 from December 17 through April 15). One-bedroom units with kitchens start at $155 ($185 in winter). The condo has a beachfront location, plus an adjoining restaurant and bar. ~ 2960 South Kihei Road, Kihei; 879-1561, 800-525-2025, fax 874-5042.

Lihi Kai. This establishment has nine beach cottages with full kitchens, all renting for $59 single or double. Rates are lower for a seven-night stay. To be sure of getting a cottage, you'd best make reservations far in advance. There is a three-night minimum. ~ 2121 Iliili Road, Kihei; 879-2335, 800-544-4524.

Kamaole Beach Royale. A six-story condo across the street from a beach park, this has one-bedroom apartments for $65 double; two-bedroom units, $75 double. From December to April, the rates increase to $90 and $100, respectively. ~ 2385 South Kihei Road, Kihei; 879-3131, 800-421-3661, fax 879-9163.

Kapulanikai. A cozy place with only 12 apartments, all of which overlook the ocean and a grassy, park-like setting. One-bedroom apartments rent for $80 single or double ($65 from April to mid-December). ~ 73 Kapu Place, Kihei; 879-1607, fax 879-3329.

DINING

Now that condominiums have mushroomed from its white sands, Kihei is no longer a poor person's paradise. Yet there are still several short-order griddles like **Suda's Store and Snack Shop** around. ~ 61 South Kihei Road, Kihei; 879-2668. BUDGET.

You'll find another take-out window at **Azeka's Market Snack Shop** in nearby Azeka Place Shopping Center. For atmosphere there's a parking lot, but for food there's a fair choice, with hamburgers and plate lunches priced low. ~ 1278 South Kihei Road, Kihei; 879-0611. BUDGET.

Surfside Spirits and Deli has a takeout delicatessen serving sandwiches, salads and slaw. ~ 1993 South Kihei Road, Kihei; 879-1385. BUDGET.

At **Canton Chef**, on the other hand, the cuisine ranges from roast duck to beef with oyster sauce. This traditional Chinese restaurant offers almost 100 different choices including a selection of spicy Szechuan dishes. ~ 2463 South Kihei Road, Kihei; 879-1988. BUDGET TO MODERATE.

Margarita's Beach Cantina is one of those big brassy Mexican restaurants that are ever more present along the beaches. The kind that have live sports on big-screen television and a buzzing night scene. What sells this place is the oceanside dining and happy-hour margarita specials. The menu covers lunch and dinner, featuring carnitas, tacos and chimichangas, as well as hamburgers, chicken sandwiches, peel-and-eat shrimp and oyster shooters. ~ 101 North Kihei Road, Kihei; 879-5311. MODERATE.

For inexpensive Korean food, there's **The Kal Bi House**. Squeezed into a corner of Kihei Center and furnished with molded-plastic seats, it's not much on atmosphere. But it's hard to beat their cheap barbecued ribs, grilled chicken and beef marinated in Korean sauce, *katsu* chicken or Korean soups. A good place for a takeout meal. ~ 1215 South Kihei Road, Kihei; 874-8454. BUDGET.

Parked in the same complex is **Stella Blues Café & Delicatessen**. Here you can dine indoors or outside beneath a sidewalk umbrella. The bill of fare includes vegetarian dishes, pastas and sandwiches. ~ 1215 South Kihei Road, Kihei; 874-3779. MODERATE.

Speaking of pasta, that's the specialty at **La Pastaria**, a contemporary restaurant that features dinner shows on Wednesday night. On any evening you can order gourmet pizza, calzone, baked lasagna or spaghetti, or just sit back and enjoy a cappuccino. ~ Lipoa Center, 41 East Lipoa Street, Kihei; 879-9001. MODERATE.

> Morning is the best time to go to the beach in Wailea and especially in Kihei. Later in the day, the wind picks up.

There are inexpensive Japanese dishes a few doors down at **Kaipuni Restaurant**. You can order sushi, donburi, tempura or noodles at the counter and sit at one of the tables placed indoors and outside. Closed Sunday. ~ Lipoa Center, 41 East Lipoa Street, Kihei; 879-3854. BUDGET.

If you prefer something from Southeast Asia, **Royal Thai Cuisine** sits across the street in yet another shopping mall. Here the chairs are wood, the menu includes *dozens* of selections, such as crab legs, chili shrimp, cashew chicken or seafood combinations. ~ Azeka Place Shopping Center, 1280 South Kihei Road, Kihei; 874-0813. BUDGET TO MODERATE.

Did you say Greek? No problem. Just a few malls away (this one is called Kai Nani Village) is the **Greek Bistro** with a full selection of Mediterranean dishes such as gyros, moussaka, souvlaki, lamb kebabs and dolmas. ~ 2511 South Kihei Road, Kihei; 879-9330. MODERATE.

Or forget the ethnic food and head next door to the **Kihei Prime Rib and Seafood House**. A reliable if undistinguished dining room, it offers a good salad bar and numerous beef and fresh fish dishes. There are views across the road overlooking the ocean. Early-bird specials. ~ 2511 South Kihei Road, Kihei; 879-1954. DELUXE TO ULTRA-DELUXE.

The **Ukulele Grill** at the Maui Lu Resort is a cavernous hall with bandstand and sunken dining room. You'll sometimes be serenaded at dinner by one of the resident musicians. The menu here is a medley of Asian, American and island dishes that includes salmon *katsu* wrapped in *nori*, stir-fried seafood, New York steak, duck confit and *imu*-roasted beef. They also serve breakfast, but you won't be serenaded over your eggs benedict. ~ 575 South Kihei Road, Kihei; 879-5881. MODERATE TO DELUXE.

The tab at **A Pacific Café Maui** will fluctuate dramatically depending on whether you order an inexpensive pizza or one of the dishes specially prepared on the wood-burning grill. A sister to the famous gourmet restaurant on Kauai, the Maui sibling is beautifully designed with a bolted-beam ceiling, bright pastel walls and a heart-shaped bar. From that smoky grill they serve up ahi steak, Chilean sea bass and Mongolian rack of lamb. Or how about roast duck with garlic mashed potatoes or scallops in polenta crust? ~ Azeka II, 1279 South Kihei Road, Kihei; 879-0069. DELUXE.

Why do celebrities such as Richard Dreyfuss, Harry Hamlin and Debra Winger book reservations at **Carelli's On The Beach**? Perhaps it's the imaginative Italian menu at this Keawakapu Beach establishment. Specialties include steamed clams in garlic, interesting pastas and fire-roasted rack of lamb. The open-air dining room, with its murals of Venice and the chic Mangia bar, adds to the allure. ~ 2980 South Kihei Road, Kihei; 875-0001. DELUXE.

Billed as "Wailea's alternative to high-priced dining," **Sandcastle at Wailea** is a welcome change. Bentwood chairs, brass fixtures and plastic tablecloths create a comfortable although uncreative atmosphere. The menu consists of middle-of-the-road American entrées with pizzas and pastas to round things off. ~ Wailea Shopping Village, Wailea; 879-0606. MODERATE.

All those *Travel/Holiday Magazine* awards at the entrance to **Raffles** signify that this is Renaissance Wailea Beach Resort's signature restaurant and one of the most highly respected dining rooms on the island. The ambience is elegant Singapore-style. The cuisine, however, is island classic: rack of lamb with papaya chutney, crisp whole fish with coconut curry, broiled filet of beef with shiitake mushrooms and daily fresh fish selections. Dinner only. Closed Sunday and Monday. ~ 3550 Wailea Alanui, Wailea; 879-4900. ULTRA-DELUXE.

From the day his ship docked in 1924 until his death four decades later, the writer Don Blanding lured visitors to the islands with more than a dozen books. An exhibition of this haole poet laureate's work is found at the Aston Wailea Resort restaurant named for one of his best-known volumes, **Hula Moons**. The open-air establishment is like a small museum appointed with art pieces, ceramic plates and aloha shirts that Blanding designed, as well as his books, poems and sheet music. The menu includes Szechuan roasted New Zealand lamb chops, South Pacific shellfish bouillabaisse and vegetarian entrées. Fresh berries in wine sauce with ice cream highlight the dessert list. ~ 3700 Wailea Alanui Drive, Wailea; 879-1922. DELUXE TO ULTRA-DELUXE.

At **Hana Gion** you can choose between tableside *teppanyaki* cooking or a private booth. Built in Japan, broken down and shipped to Maui for reassembly, this beautiful restaurant in the Renaissance Wailea Beach Resort was created with the guidance of one of Kyoto's leading restaurant-owning families. Specialties such as tempura, *yosenabe*, *shabu-shabu*, sukiyaki and chicken *mizutaki* are served by kimono-clad waitresses. There's also a popular sushi bar on the premises. ~ 3550 Wailea Alanui, Wailea; 879-4900. DELUXE TO ULTRA-DELUXE.

Seasons, the signature restaurant at the Four Seasons Resort Wailea, gained a vaunted reputation soon after it opened in 1990. Marble trim, chairs upholstered in leather and knockout ocean views create the suitable ambience that is accented with a dancefloor. But it is the cuisine for which the dining room is particularly known. Specializing in fresh fish and locally grown produce prepared in a contemporary American style, it is one of Maui's top restaurants. ~ 3900 Wailea Alanui, Wailea; 874-8000. ULTRA-DELUXE.

Café Kula at the Grand Wailea Resort has a terrace dining area that offers light, healthy breakfast and lunch choices. Start the day with a breakfast burrito, vegetable quiche, muesli or pastries. For lunch consider the garden burger, herb ricotta lasagna or garden salad served with chicken and a pineapple vinaigrette. ~ 3850 Wailea Alanui, Wailea; 875-1234. BUDGET TO MODERATE.

Consider the *kiawe*-grilled hamburgers, the giant onion rings or the salads at the Kea Lani Hotel's **Polo Beach Grille and Bar**. This poolside dining spot is also a great place for a cool drink. ~ 4100 Wailea Alanui, Wailea; 808-875-4100. MODERATE TO DELUXE.

A tranquil oceanfront setting makes the **Prince Court** the place to enjoy Hawaiian regional cuisine. At this signature restaurant in the Maui Prince Hotel, you can choose from a menu that begins with volcano-spiced ahi sashimi with wasabi caviar, duet of fresh Dungeness crab cakes and Maui onion soup. The bill of fare continues with *kiawe*-grilled swordfish on Kula tomato salad and medallions of veal on caramelized Maui onion mashed potatoes. Wicker furniture and tropical foliage add to the elegance. ~ 5400 Makena Alanui, Makena; 874-1111. DELUXE TO ULTRA-DELUXE.

Hakone is the kind of restaurant you'd expect to find at any self-respecting Japanese-owned resort. The shoji screens, Japanese fans and a sushi bar are authentic; the ocean views are entirely Hawaiian. Start with tempura or miso soup. Entrées include sashimi, sukiyaki and New York steak with mushrooms and Kula onions. ~ Maui Prince Hotel, 5400 Makena Alanui, Makena; 874-1111. ULTRA-DELUXE.

GROCERIES

Foodland is a large supermarket open 24 hours a day. ~ Kihei Town Center on South Kihei Road; 879-9350.

Star Market, also open 24 hours a day, has a large selection of groceries. ~ 1310 South Kihei Road; 879-5871.

Azeka's Market up the road is often price-competitive, though. Open Monday through Saturday, from 7:30 a.m. to 5 p.m. ~ 1278 South Kihei Road; 879-0611.

For healthful items, try **Hawaiian Moons Natural Foods**. Open 8 a.m. to 8 p.m. Monday through Saturday and 8 a.m. to 6 p.m. on Sunday. ~ 2411 South Kihei Road, Kihei; 875-4356.

If you're camping at Makena, you'll find **Whaler's General Store** in Wailea fairly convenient, but I'm afraid you'll pay for the convenience. This small store, situated in the posh Wailea Shopping Village, is painfully overpriced. Open every day from 7:30 a.m. to 9:30 p.m. ~ 3750 Wailea Alanui; 879-3044.

SHOPPING   Shopping in Kihei is centered in the malls and doesn't hold a lot of promise. You'll find swimwear shops and an assortment of other clothing outlets, but nothing with style and panache. Foremost among the malls is **Azeka Place Shopping Center**, which stretches along the 1200 South block of Kihei Road.

Kukui Mall just down the road has that most wonderful of inventions—a bookstore: a **Waldenbooks** bookstore to be exact. ~ 874-3688.

Kihei Kalama Village, an open-air market with about 20 vendors, is a funky counterpoint to Kihei's other shopping spots. Here you'll find T-shirts, jewelry, and souvenirs sold at cut-rate prices by local people. ~ 1941 South Kihei Road, Kihei.

If you don't find what you're searching for at any of these addresses, there are countless other strip malls along Kihei Road.

Or, if you prefer more sophisticated shops, continue on to Wailea. The elite counterpart to Kihei, this resort complex features two dozen different stores in **Wailea Shopping Village**.

Tropicana sells pearls and custom accessories made by leading Maui artisans. In the Aston Wailea Resort, this shop is a good place to find original designs in rings, necklaces and pendants. ~ 3700 Wailea Alanui, Wailea; 879-1922.

Much of the $30 million art collection in the Grand Wailea Resort and Spa comes from the personal holdings of the owner, Takeshi Sekiguchi. At the hotel's **Napua Gallery**, you can see some of his best Picasso lithographs, including *Les Deux Femmes Nues*. This series focuses on Picasso's longtime companion, Françoise Gilot, and demonstrates the artist's personal evolution. Also available for purchase are paintings, mixed media works and sculpture by leading contemporary artists. ~ 3850 Wailea Alanui, Wailea; 875-1234.

The **Dolphin Gallery** in the same hotel is the place to look for sculpture, art and jewelry with an emphasis on marine mammals. ~ 3850 Wailea Alanui, Wailea; 875-1234.

In an imaginative blend of local and European fashion designs, antique aloha shirts, Balinese sarongs, hippie dresses and Panama hats are just some of the attractions at the Kea Lani Hotel's **Mango Club**. ~ 4100 Wailea Alanui Drive, Wailea; 875-4100.

At **Mandalay Imports** you'll find Thai silk, designer dresses, lacquer chests, Chinese opera coats, beaded belts and Balinese art. This shop in the Four Seasons Resort Wailea also sells innovative necklaces and ceramic vases. ~ 3900 Wailea Alanui, Wailea; 874-5111.

The Maui Lu Resort's **Ukulele Grill** features Hawaiian contemporary music nightly. They also stage special concert events in their spacious facility. ~ 575 South Kihei Road, Kihei; 879-5881.

NIGHTLIFE

Down the road apiece, there's a piano bar at **La Pastaria**, an Italian restaurant that also features dinner theater. ~ Lipoa Center, 41 East Lipoa Street, Kihei; 879-9001.

The **Sunset Terrace Lounge** is a pleasant spot to see live Hawaiian entertainment as day turns to night. It's located at the Renaissance Wailea Beach Resort, where you can also enjoy a quiet drink to the sound of a piano at Raffles. ~ 3550 Wailea Alanui, Wailea; 879-4900.

Live Hawaiian entertainment is a nightly feature at the Aston Wailea Resort in **Hula Moons**. Come for dinner or have a drink as you enjoy an appealing island show. ~ Wailea Alanui, Wailea; 879-1922.

Leave it to the Grand Wailea Resort Hotel and Spa—the accent's on Grand—to have Maui's most elaborate high-tech nightclub. **Tsunami** cost $4 million to build and has 20 video monitors and a 14-foot-wide karaoke screen. Cover on the weekend. ~ 3850 Wailea Alanui, Wailea; 875-1234.

A trio plays contemporary classics on the terrace of **Seasons**. A second venue here at the Four Seasons Resort Wailea is the **Cabana Café**, where live Hawaiian music and dancing is perfectly timed for a sunset drink. ~ 3900 Wailea Alanui, Wailea; 874-8000.

There is Hawaiian entertainment nightly at the **Molokini Lounge** over in Makena at the Maui Prince Hotel. ~ 5400 Makena Alanui; 874-1111.

KIHEI BEACH This narrow, palm-fringed beach that runs from Maalaea Bay to Kihei can be seen from several points along Kihei Road and is accessible from the highway. The entire stretch is dotted with small parks and picnic areas and doesn't actually go by a specific name. There are buildings and numerous condominiums along this strip, but few large crowds on the beach. Beach joggers take note: You can run for miles along this unbroken strand, but watch for heavy winds in the afternoon. Shallow weed-ridden waters make for poor swimming and only fair snorkeling (you'll find better at Kamaole beaches). For those anglers in the crowd, bonefish, *papio*, mullet, goatfish, *ulua*, *moano* and mountain bass are all caught here. There are picnic tables and restrooms at Kihei Memorial Park, which is midway along the beach.

BEACHES & PARKS

KALAMA COUNTY BEACH PARK This is a long, broad park that has an ample lawn but very little beach. Rather than lapping along the sand, waves wash up against a stone seawall. Backdropped by Haleakala, Kalama has stunning views of West Maui, Lanai and Kahoolawe. This is an excellent place for a picnic but, before you pack your lunch, remember that the park, like all Kihei's beaches, is swept by afternoon winds. For surfers there are summer breaks over a coral reef; left and right slides. Snorkeling and fishing are fair; swimming is poor. There are picnic areas, restrooms, a shower and tennis courts. ~ Located on South Kihei Road, across from Kihei Town Center.

KAMAOLE BEACH PARKS (I, II AND III) Strung like beads along the Kihei shore are these three beautiful beaches. Their white sands are fringed with grass and studded with trees. With Haleakala in the background, they all offer magnificent views of the West Maui Mountains, Lanai and Kahoolawe—and all are windswept in the afternoon. Each has picnic areas, restrooms, lifeguard and showers. Kamaole III also has a playground. Swimming is very good on all three beaches. The best snorkeling is near the rocks ringing Kamaole III. Goatfish is the main catch. ~ The parks are on South Kihei Road near Kihei Town Center.

KEAWAKAPU BEACH Ho hum, yet another beautiful white-sand beach . . . Like other nearby parks, Keawakapu has marvelous views of the West Maui Mountains and Lanai, but is plagued by afternoon winds. The half-mile-long beach is bordered on both ends by lava points. The swimming is good, but Keawakapu is not as well protected as the Kamaole beaches. Snorkelers, try the area around the rocks. The fishing is excellent. There are no facilities except showers, but it is only a short distance to the markets and restaurants of Kihei and Wailea. ~ Located on South Kihei Road between Kihei and Wailea.

MOKAPU AND ULUA These are two crescent-shaped beaches fringed with palms and looking out toward Lanai and Kahoolawe. Much of their natural beauty has been spoiled by the nearby hotels and condominiums The beaches have landscaped miniparks and are popular with bodysurfers. Swimming and snorkeling are both good; restrooms and a shower are available. ~ To get there, follow the signs near Renaissance Wailea Beach Resort.

WAILEA BEACH Another lovely white-sand strip, once fringed with *kiawe* trees, is now dominated by two very large, very upscale resorts, part of the ultramodern Wailea development here. Swimming is good (the beach is popular with bodysurfers) and so is snorkeling. Restrooms and showers are available. ~ The beach is adjacent to the Four Seasons Wailea Resort just a half-mile south of Wailea Shopping Village.

POLO BEACH 🏄 🐟 Though not quite as attractive as Wailea Beach, it still has a lot to offer. There's a bountiful stretch of white sand and great views of Kahoolawe and Molokini. The beach has a landscaped minipark with picnic tables, restrooms and showers and is popular with bodysurfers. Swimming is good here and the snorkeling is excellent. ~ You'll find it about one mile south of Wailea Shopping Village.

POOLENALENA (OR PAIPU) BEACH PARK 🏄 🐟 ⛵ Also known by locals as Chang's Beach, this is a lovely white-sand beach that has been transformed into an attractive little facility frequented by people from throughout the area. After Makena, it is the prettiest beach in the Kihei-Wailea region. The beach has no permanent facilities, but there are portable toilets and it is only two miles from the market in Wailea. Swimming is good, snorkeling fair and fishing very good—many species are caught here. ~ Located on Makena Alanui about 1.7 miles south of Wailea Shopping Village.

▲ There is unofficial tent camping here under the *kiawe* trees that front the beach but it is illegal and you can be arrested.

BLACK SANDS BEACH OR ONEULI BEACH 🏄 🐟 ⛵ This is a ◄ *HIDDEN* long, narrow, salt-and-pepper beach located just north of Red Hill, a shoreline cinder cone. Fringed with *kiawe* trees, this stretch of beach is less attractive but more secluded than Makena. Facilities are nonexistent and it's four miles to the market in Wailea. Swimming and snorkeling are both fair, but the fishing is very good, many species being caught here. ~ To reach it, follow Makena Alanui south from Wailea Shopping Village for three-and-three-quarters miles. Turn right on the dirt road at the north end of Red Hill, then bear right to the beach.

▲ There is unofficial camping but, again, it is illegal and not recommended.

MAKENA (OR ONELOA) BEACH   Much more than a beach, Makena is an institution. For over a decade, it's been a countercultural

◆◆

MAKENA LANDING

Now a peaceful cove, Makena Landing was once a port as busy as Lahaina. During the California gold rush, prevailing winds prompted many San Francisco–bound ships coming up from Cape Horn to resupply here. Fresh fruits and vegetables, badly needed by the would-be miners, were traded in abundance. Later local ranchers delivered their cattle to market by tethering them to longboats and swimming the animals out to steamers waiting just offshore from Makena Landing.

gathering place. There are even stories about rock stars jamming here during Makena's heyday in the early 1970s. Once a hideaway for hippies, the beach today is increasingly popular with mainstream tourists. So far this long, wide corridor of white sand curving south from Red Hill is still the most beautiful beach on Maui, but it is slated for mondo-condo development. ~ From Wailea Shopping Village, go about four-and-one-half miles south on Makena-Alanui Drive. Turn right into the parking lot.

HIDDEN ►   **LITTLE BEACH (PUU OLAI BEACH)** 🏊 🤿 🎣 This pretty stretch of white sand next to Makena Beach, just across Red Hill, is a nude beach. It's also popular with the island's gay crowd. But if you go nude here or at Makena, watch out for police; they regularly bust nudists. Swimming is good (bodysurfing is especially good at Little Makena) and you can snorkel near the rocks at the north end of the beach. The fishing is fair. There are no facilities. ~ To get there, follow Makena Alanui for about four-and-one-half miles south from Wailea Shopping Village. Watch for Red Hill, the large cinder cone on your right. Just past Red Hill, turn right into the parking lot for Makena Beach. From here a path leads over Red Hill to Little Beach.

▲ Camping though unofficial is very popular here, but beware of thieves.

SEVEN

Kahului-Wailuku Area

The island's commercial and civic centers, as well as the greatest concentration of Maui residents, are located in the adjoining cities of Kahului and Wailuku. With no clear dividing place, these two municipalities seem at first glance to be "twin towns." They drift into one another as you climb uphill from Kahului Harbor toward the mountains. Kahului is significantly younger than its neighbor, however, and focuses its daily life around commerce. Maui's main airport is here, together with a skein of shopping malls and a few hotels lining a blue-collar waterfront. Wailuku presents a more rolling terrain and is the seat of government for Maui County.

Kahului, with its bustling harbor and busy shopping complexes, offers little to the sightseer. The piers along the waterfront, lined with container-cargo ships and weekly cruise ships, are the embarkation point for Maui's sugar and pineapple crops. Established as a sugar town more than a century ago, Kahului has a commercial feel about it.

Coming from the airport along Kaahumanu Avenue (Route 32), you can wander through **Kanaha Pond Wildlife Sanctuary**. Once a royal fishpond, this is now an important bird refuge, especially for the rare Hawaiian stilt and Hawaiian coot.

The highway leads uphill to **Wailuku**, Maui's administrative center. Older and more interesting than Kahului, Wailuku sits astride the foothills of the West Maui Mountains. A mix of woodframe plantation houses and suburban homes, it even boasts a multi-story civic building. For a short tour of the aging woodfront quarter, take a right on Market Street and follow it several blocks to **Happy Valley**. This former red-light district still retains the charm, if not the action, of a bygone era. Here you'll discover narrow streets and tinroof houses framed by the sharply rising, deeply creased face of the West Maui Mountains.

The county government buildings reside along High Street. Just across the road rests picturesque **Kaahumanu Church**. Queen Kaahumanu attended services here in 1832 when the church was a grass shack, and requested that the first permanent church be named after her. Now Maui's oldest church, this grand stone-and-plaster structure was constructed in 1876, and has been kept in excellent condition for its many visitors. With a lofty white spire, it is the area's most dramatic manmade landmark. ~ 244-5189.

Kahului, then Maui's largest town, was deliberately destroyed by fire in 1890 to kill rats that were spreading an epidemic of bubonic plague.

Nearby you'll find the **Bailey House Museum**, run by the Maui Historical Society museum. Housed in the home of a former missionary, the displays include 19th-century Hawaiian artifacts, remnants from the early sugarcane industry and period pieces from the missionary years. This stone-and-plaster house (completed in 1850) has walls 20 inches thick and beams fashioned from hand-hewn sandalwood. Together with an adjoining seminary building, it harkens back to Wailuku's days as an early center of western culture. Admission. ~ 2375-A Main Street; 244-3326.

Bounded on both sides by the sharp walls of Iao Valley, **Tropical Gardens of Maui** encompasses four densely planted acres of fruit trees, orchids and flowering plants. Iao Stream rushes through the property, which offers garden paths and a lily pond. Admission. ~ 244-3085.

Up the road at **Kepaniwai County Park**, there's an outdoor cultural showcase to discover. Backdropped by Iao Valley's adze-like peaks, this adult playground features lovely Japanese and Chinese monuments as well as a taro patch. There are arched bridges, a swimming pool and an Oriental garden. The houses of Hawaii's many cultural groups are represented by a Hawaiian grass hut, New England saltbox (complete with white picket fence), Filipino bamboo house and a Portuguese villa. On this site in 1790 Kamehameha's forces overwhelmed the army of a Maui chief in a battle so terrible that the corpses blocking Iao Stream gave Kepaniwai ("damming of the waters") and Wailuku ("bloody river") their names.

Uphill at the **John F. Kennedy Profile** you'll see Hawaii's answer to Mt. Rushmore, chiseled by nature. Ironically, this geologic formation, which bears an uncanny resemblance to the former president, was never noticed until after his assassination.

Iao Valley State Monument, surrounded by those same moss-mantled cliffs, provides an excellent view of **Iao Needle**, a single spire that rises to a point 1200 feet above the valley (and 2250 feet above sea level). With the possible exception of Haleakala Crater, this awesome peak is Maui's most famous landmark. A basalt core that has withstood the ravages of erosion, the "Needle" and mist-filled valley have long been a place of pilgrimage for Hawaiians. (Be

sure to explore the paths from the parking lot that lead across Iao Stream and up to a vista point.)

LODGING   The hotel strip in the harbor town of Kahului lies along the beach on Kahului Bay.

The **Maui Seaside Hotel** consists of two separate complexes sitting beside each other along Kaahumanu Avenue (Route 32). There is a pool, restaurant and lounge. Rooms in the older poolside wing are a bit less expensive: Clean, but lacking in decorative flair, the surroundings are quite adequate. Just a few well-spent dollars more places you in a larger, more attractive room in the newer complex, which has more upscale appointments. Both facilities feature telephones, televisions and air conditioning. Some include kitchenettes. ~ 100 West Kaahumanu Avenue; 877-3311, 800-367-7000, fax 922-0052. MODERATE TO DELUXE.

The nearby **Maui Palms Hotel** has comfortable and spacious rooms with wall-to-wall carpeting, telephone and color television, but lacks decoration. This beachfront facility has a pool tucked between the lobby and the rooms. There's also an Asian-American restaurant on the premises that provides a convenient dining facility for folks staying anywhere along Kahului's hotel row. The grounds are studded with palms; considering the price, the ambience is quite appealing. ~ 170 Kaahumanu Avenue; 877-0071, 800-367-5004, fax 871-5797. MODERATE.

HIDDEN ►   Even by Maui's mellow standards, life at the **Banana Bungalow** is *low* key. When I stopped by there was no one around. The rooms—plain, clean units with shared baths—are among the cheapest on the island. There are shared facilities with two to a room as well as private singles and doubles. A cross between a hotel and a hostel, you'll find Banana Bungalow has an ambience unlike any place else on Maui. Free coffee and tea are available in the morning at the neighboring restaurant. There are a television lounge, laundry facilities and a jacuzzi. ~ 310 North Market Street, Wailuku; 244-5090, 800-846-7835, fax 243-2219. BUDGET.

Northshore Inn is another clean, trim hostel-cum-hotel with shared rooms and private singles or doubles. The lobby/television room is decorated with surfboards, flags and modern art, and the place has an easy, windswept air about it. There are laundry and kitchen facilities; baths are shared. Every room has a refrigerator and overhead fan. ~ 2080 Vineyard Street, Wailuku; 242-8999, fax 244-5004. BUDGET.

DINING   The best place in Kahului for a quick, inexpensive meal is at one of several shopping arcades along Kaahumanu Avenue (Route 32). For common fare, head over to the Maui Mall. Here you can drop in at **Restaurant Matsu** (871-0822), a short-order eatery that features

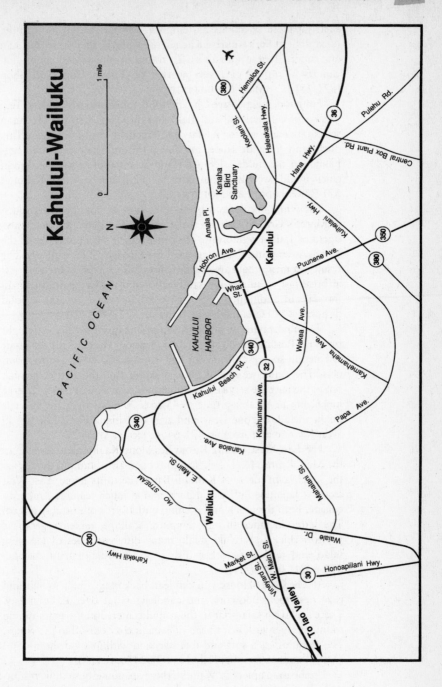

such Japanese selections as tempura, yakitori, sushi and *saimin*. Next door at **Siu's Chinese Kitchen** (871-0828), they serve dim sum and other Chinese specialties. To round off the calorie count, you can try a cup of *guri guri* sherbet at **Tasaka Guri Guri Shop** (871-4513). ~ Maui Mall. BUDGET.

For good, inexpensive Chinese food, join the locals at **Ming Yen**. The decor is functional and plain, but the Cantonese and Szechuan selections make up for it. Favorite Szechuan dishes include crispy duck with fragrant sauce, mu shu pork and spicy Szechuan eggplant. On the milder side are Cantonese standbys such as lemon chicken and sweet and sour pork. ~ 162 Alamaha Street, Kahului; 871-7787. BUDGET TO MODERATE.

The white booths and black-tile tables are an appealing touch at **Marco's Grill & Deli**. So is the attention to detail at this family-operated Italian restaurant. They blend their own coffee, bake the breads, even grind their own meat for sausages and meatballs. The result is a menu that ranges from chocolate cinnamon French toast at breakfast to submarine sandwiches and vodka rigatoni later in the day. In addition to pasta entrées, they serve several seafood dishes. ~ 444 Hana Highway, Kahului; 877-4446. MODERATE.

If you're staying at one of Kahului's bayfront hotels, you might try **Vi's Restaurant** in the Maui Seaside Hotel. This open-air Polynesian-style establishment has seafood and other assorted dinners. The ambience here is quite pleasant, and the staff congenial, but in the past the service has sometimes been slow. Vi doesn't serve lunch, but at breakfast time (6:45 to 9:00 a.m.) the daily specials might include T-bone steak and eggs or banana hot cakes. ~ 100 West Kaahumanu Avenue; 871-6494. MODERATE.

The **East-West Dining Room** lies along Kaahumanu Avenue in the Maui Palms Hotel. This spacious open-air restaurant looks past the hotel lawn out over Kahului Bay. True to its name, East-West serves a Japanese buffet at dinner, and at lunch features American cuisine. Both the lunch and evening buffets are comfortably priced. The latter includes shrimp tempura, scallops, mixed vegetables, yakitori chicken, teriyaki steak, many different types of Japanese salad and a host of other dishes. ~ 170 Kaahumanu Avenue; 877-0071. MODERATE.

At **The Chart House** you can lean back in a captain's chair and gaze past the woodwork and candlelight out over Kahului Bay. There's a lavish salad-bar-in-the-round centered in the main dining room, an open grill just to the side and a cozy bar off in the wings. The menu offers a surf-and-turf selection with many dishes. ~ 500 North Puunene Avenue, Kahului; 877-2476. DELUXE.

Up the road apiece in Wailuku there are numerous ethnic restaurants guaranteed to please both the palate and the purse. **Sam Sato's** features Japanese and American cuisine. Open for breakfast and lunch, it specializes in *manju* (a bean cake pastry), dry *mein* (a noodle dish) and the ubiquitous *saimin*. ~ 1750 Wili Pa Loop; 244-7124. BUDGET.

The nearby **Fujiya** stirs up some similar money belt–tightening Japanese meals. Well worth a visit. ~ 133 Market Street; 244-0206. BUDGET.

Siam Thai Cuisine is always a good choice for Southeast Asian fare. Attractively decorated with posters and artwork from Thailand, this restaurant features a complete menu that includes dozens of delicious dishes. Try the chicken-coconut soup, *tom-yum goong*, Siam chicken, or the *pod-pet*, beef or pork or chicken sautéed with ginger and bamboo shoots. This is a local favorite. No lunch on Sundays. ~ 123 North Market Street, Wailuku; 244-3817. BUDGET.

Local, affordable and attractively decorated—what more can you ask? Well, **Chums** will go one more and add tasty food. Settle into a hardwood booth and order from an island-style menu that includes *saimin*, won ton soup, curry stew, teriyaki pork and mahimahi. Or stay middle-of-the-road with a sandwich or salad. ~ 1900 Main Street, Wailuku; 244-1000. BUDGET.

Saeng's Thai Cuisine sits in a beautifully designed building embellished with fine woodwork and adorned with Asian accoutrements. The menu, which lists six pages of dishes from Thailand, is like an encyclopedia of fine dining. Meals, served in the dining room or out on a windswept veranda, begin with *sateh* and spring rolls, venture on to dishes like the "evil prince" and "tofu delight," and end over tea and tapioca pudding. ~ 2119 Vineyard Street, Wailuku; 244-1567. BUDGET TO MODERATE.

Wailuku is becoming more hip by the month, and the center of "hipdom" is an espresso house with a hand-painted floor, upstairs dining room with ocean views and a pizza/quesadilla/salad/pasta menu. At **Café Kup a Kuppa** you can order scrambled eggs or bagel with lox and cream cheese for breakfast; lunch includes chicken,

KAHULUI-WAILUKU EXPERIENCES

- Cross the arched bridges in **Kepaniwai County Park**, then wander uphill to a profile in the rocks that looks amazingly like John Kennedy. (p. 124)
- Shop Wailuku's funky **North Market Street**, where the woodframe shops have names like Memory Lane and Raiders of the Lost Art. (p. 131)
- Relive Hawaii's colonial history on the grounds of a working plantation at the **Alexander & Baldwin Sugar Museum**. (p. 133)
- Stand watch at **McGregor Point** for the foaming eruption of one of the 2000 humpback whales that visit Maui annually. (p. 133)

turkey, vegetable or tuna sandwiches, and daily specials like quiche. No dinner; closed Saturday and Sunday. ~ 79 Church Street; 244-0500. BUDGET.

As well as being a Maui institution, **Hamburger Mary's** is a center for gays. Imaginatively decorated with surfboards and antique posters, it attracts a mixed clientele with an appealing menu of hamburgers (who would have guessed?), sandwiches, salads and steaks. There's also a hearty breakfast menu. Closed Sundays. ~ 2010 Main Street, Wailuku; 244-7776. MODERATE.

Ramon's is the region's entry in the Mexican food category. Half of this split-level eatery is decorated with sombreros and piñatas; the other part is given over to floral prints. The menu has a single theme, however, and it is spelled out with tacos, tamales and chile rellenos. ~ 2102 Vineyard Street, Wailuku; 244-7243. BUDGET.

Wailuku's low-rent district lies along Lower Main Street, where ethnic restaurants cater almost exclusively to locals. These are informal, family-owned, formica-and-naugahyde-chair cafés that serve good food at down-to-earth prices. You'll find Japanese food at **Tokyo Tei**. ~ 1063 Lower Main Street; 242-9630. BUDGET.

Southeast Asia is represented by **A Touch of Saigon**. On the menu you'll find stir-fried vegetables, curried chicken rice plates, shrimp in clay pot and beef noodle dishes. ~ 1246 Lower Main Street; 244-7845. BUDGET.

GROCERIES Kahului features two sprawling supermarkets. **Foodland** is open every day from 6 a.m. to 11 p.m. ~ Kaahumanu Center, Kaahumanu Avenue; 877-2808. **Star Super Market** is open every day from 6 a.m. to 10 p.m. ~ Maui Mall, Kaahumanu Avenue; 877-3441.

Down to Earth Natural Foods in Wailuku has a complete line of health food items and fresh produce. Add to that a healthy stock of herbs and you have what amounts to a natural food supermarket. This gets my dollar for being the best place on Maui to shop for natural foods. Open every day. ~ 1910 Vineyard Street; 242-6821.

There are also stores in two of the shopping centers lining Kaahumanu Avenue: **Ah Fook's Super Market** (877-3308) in Kahului Shopping Center and **Maui Natural Foods** (877-3018) in the Maui Mall. Both open every day.

Wakamatsu Fish Market in Wailuku has fresh fish daily. ~ 145 Market Street; 244-4111.

Love's Bakery Thrift Shop sells day-old baked goods at old-fashioned prices. ~ 344 Ano Street, Kahului; 877-3160. In Wailuku, **Holsum/Orowheat Thrift Shop** is another place for baked goods. ~ 1380 Lower Main Street; 242-9155.

SHOPPING For everyday shopping needs, you should find the Kahului malls very convenient. Three sprawling centers are strung along Kaahumanu Avenue (Route 32).

Kaahumanu Center is Maui's finest and most contemporary shopping mall, with Liberty House (877-3361) and Sears (877-2221), a photo studio, Waldenbooks (871-6112), boutiques, shoe stores, candy stores, a sundries shop and a jeweler. For Japanese gourmet foods, try Shirokiya (877-5551).

Nearby Maui Mall has a smaller inventory of shops. Sir Wilfred's Tobacconist (877-3711) stocks a connoisseur's selection of tobaccos and coffees, and even has a coffee bar.

You might also try Kahului Shopping Center, though I prefer the other, more convenient malls.

Up in Wailuku, a tumbledown town with a friendly face, you'll find the little shops and solicitous merchants that we have come to associate with small-town America. Along North Market Street you'll discover several imaginative shops operated by low-key entrepreneurs. There's Traders of the Lost Art, with ancestral carvings and art from Africa, Asia and the Pacific, as well as Aloha shirts, Oriental rugs, jewelry and antiques. ~ 62 North Market Street; 242-7753.

Memory Lane features antiques and unusual collectibles. ~ 130 North Market Street; 244-4196.

Brown & Kobayashi, another nearby antique store, specializes in rare pieces from the Orient. ~ 160-A North Market Street, Wailuku; 242-0804.

While in the neighborhood, you might as well stop in at Alii Antiques and round out your visit to this falsefront antique row. ~ 244-8012.

Wailuku Gallery specializes in works by Maui artists. ~ 28 North Market Street; 244-4544.

Some of the island's most reasonably priced souvenirs are found at the Maui Historical Society Museum Gift Shop. Here you'll find an outstanding collection of local history books and art prints. Quilts and koa bookmarks are also popular. ~ 2375-A Main Street, Wailuku; 244-3326.

MAUI'S FAMOUS POTATO CHIPS

Always a favorite with locals, Maui potato chips have now become a worldwide phenomenon. One of the most popular brands is "Kitch'n Cook'd," made at the family-owned and operated Maui Potato Chip Factory. This place has been around since the 1950s, annually increasing in popularity, and it now brings in orders from around the globe. These chips are hard to find in mainland stores, but you can stock up on them here where they're freshly made! Closed Sunday. ~ 295 Lalo Place, off Highway 36, Kahului; 877-3652.

NIGHTLIFE   If Kahului can be said to have an entertainment strip, Kaahumanu Avenue (Route 32) is the place. Here you can enjoy a live band and dancing at the **Maui Palms Hotel** on Saturday night and karaoke on Thursday and Friday nights. ~ 170 Kaahumanu Avenue; 877-0071.

Up in Wailuku, **Aki's** entertains a local crowd almost every night around its bar. Located in Wailuku's Happy Valley section, it's a good place to meet people, or just to sit back and enjoy a tall, cool drink. ~ 309 North Market Street; 244-8122.

The gay nightspot on Maui is **Hamburger Mary's**, an attractive watering hole with overhead fans and a collection of antique wall-hangings worthy of a museum. There's music and dancing nightly. Attracting both gay men and women, Hamburger Mary's also draws a straight crowd, especially on nights when the cruise ship that travels around the island chain is in port. ~ 2010 Main Street, Wailuku; 244-7776.

BEACHES & PARKS   **HOALOHA PARK**   Located next to the Kahului hotels, this is Kahului's only beach, but unfortunately the nearby harbor facilities detract from the natural beauty of its white sands. What with heavy boat traffic on one side and several hotels on the other, the place is not recommended. There are much better beaches in other areas of the island. Swimming and snorkeling are poor; surfers will find good breaks (two to six feet, with a left slide) off the jetty mouth near the north shore of Kahului Harbor. It is, however, a good spot to beachcomb, particularly for Maui diamonds. Picnic tables are available. Goatfish, *papio* and triggerfish can be hooked from the pier; *ulua* and *papio* are often caught along the shore. ~ Located on Kaahumanu Avenue (Route 32).

KEPANIWAI COUNTY PARK   This beautiful park is carefully landscaped and surrounded by sheer cliffs. You'll discover paths over arched bridges and through gardens, plus pagodas, a thatch-roofed hut, a taro patch and banana, papaya and coconut trees. An ideal and romantic spot for picnicking, it has picnic pavilions, restrooms and a swimming pool. ~ Located in Wailuku on the road to Iao Valley.

WAIHEE BEACH PARK   This park is used almost exclusively by local residents. Bordered by a golf course and shaded with ironwood trees and *naupaka* bushes, it has a sandy beach and one of Maui's longest and widest reefs. There's a grassy area perfect for picnicking, established picnic areas and restrooms with showers. Beachcombing, *limu* gathering, fishing, swimming and snorkeling are all good. ~ Located outside Wailuku on the rural road that circles the West Maui Mountains. To get there from Route 340 in Waiehu, turn right on Halewaiu Road and then take the beach access road from Waiehu Golf Course.

Central Maui is defined not by what it is but by what lies to the east and west of it. On one side Haleakala lifts into the clouds; on the other hand loom the West Maui mountains, a folded landscape over 5000 feet in elevation. Between them, at the center of the island, sits an isthmus planted in sugar cane and pineapple. Never rising more than a few hundred feet above sea level, it houses Kahului along its northern edge and serves as the gateway to both the Lahaina–Kaanapali and Kihei–Wailea areas.

Central Maui

Three highways cross the isthmus separating West Maui from the slopes of Haleakala. From Kahului, Mokulele Highway (Route 350) tracks south to Kihei through this rich agricultural area. The Kuihelani Highway (Route 380), running diagonally across sugar cane plantations, joins the Honoapiilani Highway (Route 30) in its course from Wailuku along the West Maui Mountains. The low-lying area that supports this network of roadways was formed by lava flows from Haleakala and the West Maui Mountains.

The **Alexander & Baldwin Sugar Museum**, situated on the grounds of a working plantation, provides a brief introduction to Hawaii's main crop. Tracing the history of sugar cultivation in the islands, its displays portray everything from early life in the cane fields to contemporary methods for producing refined sugar. Closed on Sunday except in July and August. Admission. ~ Puunene Avenue and Hansen Road, Puunene; 871-8058.

The first sugar plantation laborers on Maui began to arrive from China in 1852.

The **Maui Tropical Plantation** is a 120-acre enclave complete with orchards and groves displaying dozens of island fruit plants. Here you'll see avocados, papayas, bananas, pineapples, mangoes and macadamia nuts growing in lush profusion. There's a tropical nursery and a tram that will carry you through this ersatz plantation. Ask about the plantation's Hawaiian country barbecue. On Tuesday, Wednesday and Thursday evenings you can enjoy a guided tour, cocktails, cookout dinner and a Hawaiian-style musical revue for one all-inclusive price. Admission for the tram. ~ 1670 Honoapiilani Highway; 244-7643.

Then, as you pass the small boat harbor at **Maalaea Bay**, the highway hugs the southwest coast. There are excellent lookouts along this elevated roadway, especially near the lighthouse at **McGregor Point**. During whale season you might spy a leviathan from this landlocked crow's nest. Just offshore there are prime whale breeding areas.

Down the road from McGregor Point, you'll see three islands anchored offshore. As you look seaward, the portside islet is **Molokini**, the crescent-shaped remains of a volcanic crater.

Kahoolawe, a barren, desiccated island once used for naval target practice, sits in the center. Located seven miles off Maui's south coast, it is a bald, windblasted place, hot, arid and home to feral goats. Hawaiian activists long demanded an end to the bombing of this sacred isle by the U.S. Navy. After years of demonstrations, their demands were finally acknowledged in 1994 when the island was turned over to the state of Hawaii.

The humpbacked island to starboard is **Lanai.** Lying eight miles across the Kealaikahiki Channel, it is a pear-shaped island boasting a 3370-foot peak and a population of about 2000 people.

As you continue toward Kaanapali, **Molokai** sails into view. Known as the "Friendly Isle," it covers 260 square miles and contains the highest per capita concentration of native Hawaiians of any of the main islands. With a population of 6700 people, it's a sleepy destination ideal for a Maui getaway excursion.

EIGHT

Hana Highway

The Hana Highway (Route 360), a bumpy, tortuous road running between Kahului and Hana, is one of the most beautiful drives in all Hawaii. Following the path of an ancient Hawaiian trail, it may in fact be one of the prettiest drives in the world. The road courses through a rainforest, a luxurious jungle crowded with ferns and African tulip trees, and leads to black sand beaches and rain-drenched hamlets. The vegetation is so thick it seems to be spilling out from the mountainside in a cascade of greenery. You'll be traveling the windward side of Haleakala, hugging its lower slopes en route to a small Hawaiian town that receives 70 inches of rain a year.

There are over 600 twists and turns and 56 one-lane bridges along this adequately maintained paved road. It will take at least three hours to drive the 51 miles to Hana. To make the entire circuit around the south coast, plan either to sleep in Hana or to leave very early and drive all day. If you can, take your time—there's a lot to see.

About seven miles east of Kahului, you'll pass the quaint, weather-beaten town of **Paia**. This old sugar plantation town, now a burgeoning artist colony and windsurfing mecca, has been painted in nursery colors. Along either of Paia's two streets, falsefront buildings have been freshly refurbished.

On the eastern side of town is the **Mantokuji Buddhist Temple**, which celebrates the sunrise and sunset every day by sounding its huge gong 18 times.

Hookipa Beach Park, one of the world's premier windsurfing spots, lies about three miles east of town. Brilliantly colored sails race along the horizon as windsurfers perform amazing acrobatic stunts, cartwheeling across the waves.

Within the next ten miles the roadway is transformed, as your slow, winding adventure begins. You'll drive past sugar cane fields, across verdant gorges, through valleys dotted with tumbledown cottages and along fern-cloaked hillsides.

Route 36 becomes Route 360, beginning a new series of mileage markers that are helpful in locating sites along the way. Near the two-mile marker, a short trail leads to an idyllic swimming hole at **Twin Falls** (the path begins from the west side of the Hoolawa Stream bridge on the right side of the road).

Nearby Huelo, a tiny "rooster town" (so named because nothing ever seems to be stirring except the roosters), is known for the **Kaulanapueo Church**. A coral chapel built in 1853, this New England–style sanctuary strikes a dramatic pose with the sea as a backdrop.

Farther along, on **Waikamoi Ridge**, you'll see picnic areas and a nature trail. Here you can visit a bamboo forest, learn about native vegetation and explore the countryside.

Another picnic area, at **Puohokamoa Falls** (11-mile marker), nestles beside a waterfall and large pool. If you packed a lunch, this is a perfect place to enjoy it. Trails above and below the main pool lead to other waterfalls.

A few zigzags farther, at **Kaumahina State Wayside** (12-mile marker), a tree-studded park overlooks Honomanu Gulch and Keanae Peninsula. From here the road descends the gulch, where a side road leads left to **Honomanu Bay** (14-mile marker) and its black sand beach.

Above Keanae Peninsula, you'll pass the **Keanae Arboretum** (16-mile marker). You can stroll freely through paved trails in these splendid tropical gardens, which feature many native Hawaiian plants including several dozen varieties of taro. Another section of the gardens is devoted to exotic tropical plants and there is a mile-long trail that leads into a natural rainforest.

Just past the arboretum, turn left onto the road to the **Keanae Peninsula** (17-mile marker). This rocky, windswept point offers stunning views of Haleakala. You'll pass rustic houses, a patchwork of garden plots and a coral-and-stone church built around 1860. A picture of serenity and rural perfection, Keanae is inhabited by native Hawaiians who still grow taro and pound poi. Their home is a lush rainforest—a quiltwork of taro plots, banana trees, palms—that runs to the rim of a ragged coastline.

◄ HIDDEN

Another side road descends to **Wailua** (18-mile marker), a Hawaiian agricultural and fishing village. Here is another luxurious checkerboard where taro gardens alternate with banana patches and the landscape is adorned with clapboard houses. The town is known for **St. Gabriel's Church**, a simple structure made completely of sand and coral, dating from 1870.

Back on the main road, there's yet another picnic area and waterfall at **Puaakaa State Wayside** (22-mile marker). The cascade tumbles into a natural pool in a setting framed by eucalyptus and banana trees.

HIDDEN ▶

Past here, another side road bumps three miles through picturesque **Nahiku** (25-mile marker) to a bluff overlooking the sea. The view spreads across three bays all the way back to Wailua. Directly below, the ocean pounds against rock outcroppings, spraying salt mist across a stunning vista. Set in one of the wettest spots along the entire coast, Nahiku village is inundated by rainforest and graced by yet another 19th-century church.

For a close-up of the exquisite plant life you've been passing on the Hana Highway, stop by **Hana Gardenland**. This five-acre preserve has winding paths that curve past a variety of tropical plants and trees. Here are orchids, anthuriums, heliconia and ginger as well as papaya and mango trees. This lush enclave also offers a gallery filled with local arts and crafts plus a café with an emphasis on (surprise, surprise) locally grown foods. ~ Hana Highway, 30-mile marker; 248-8975.

Hana's three police officers report that the region's number one crime is driving without a seatbelt.

Right before the town of Hana, on the right, is **Helani Gardens**, a sprawling oasis of tropical plant life. Only a section of the gardens are currently open to the public, but it's worth a stop as they contain a wealth of flowering plants, trees and vines. You'll also find fruit trees, baobab trees, papyrus, ginger plants and even a carp pond. Visits by appointment only. ~ 248-8274.

Several miles before Hana, be sure to stop at **Waianapanapa State Park**. Here you'll find a black-sand beach and two lava tubes, **Waianapanapa** and **Waiomao caves**. Hawaiian mythology tells of a Hawaiian princess who hid from her cruel husband here, only to be discovered by him and slain. Now every spring the waters hereabouts are said to run red with her blood. Offshore you will also see several sea arches and nearby a blowhole that spouts periodically.

To reach the secluded hamlet of **Hana**, you can take the old Hawaiian shoreline trail (see the "Hiking" section in Chapter Two) or continue on along the highway. This Eden-like town, carpeted with pandanus, taro and banana trees, sits above an inviting bay. Known as "heavenly Hana," it's a ranch town inhabited primarily by part-Hawaiians. Because of its remote location it has changed little over the years. The rain that continually buffets Hana makes it a prime agricultural area and adds to the luxuriant, unsettling beauty of the place.

Because of its strategic location directly across from the Big Island, Hana was an early battleground in the wars between the chiefs of Maui and the Big Island, who conquered, lost and regained the region in a succession of bloody struggles. During the 19th century it became a sugar plantation, employing different ethnic groups who were brought in to work the fields. Then, in 1946, Paul Fagan, a San Francisco industrialist, bought 14,000 acres and created the Hana Ranch, turning the area into grazing land for Hereford cattle and opening the exclusive Hotel Hana Maui.

Head down to **Hana Bay**. Here you can stroll the beach, explore the wharf and take a short path along the water to a plaque that marks the **Birthplace of Kaahumanu**, King Kamehameha I's favorite wife and a key player in the 1819 overthrow of the ancestral Hawaiian religious system. To reach this sacred spot, pick up the trail leading from the boat landing on the right side of the bay. It leads along the base of **Kauiki Hill**, a cinder cone covered with ironwood trees that was the scene of fierce battles between Kahekili, the renowned Maui chief, and the Big Island chief Kalaniopuu.

◄ HIDDEN

Near the Hotel Hana Maui (where you can request a key to open the gate), you can drive or hike up a short road to **Mount Lyons** (that camel-humped hill with the cross on top). From this

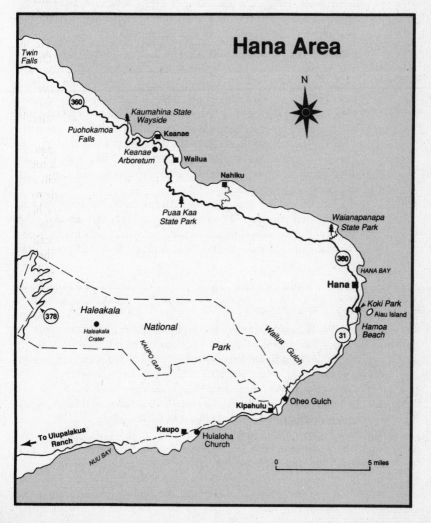

Hana Area

N

Twin Falls

360

Kaumahina State Wayside

Puohokamoa Falls

Keanae

Keanae Arboretum

Wailua

Nahiku

Puaa Kaa State Park

Waianapanapa State Park

360

HANA BAY

Hana

Koki Park

Alau Island

378

Haleakala

Haleakala Crater

National

KAUPO GAP

Park

Wailua Gulch

Hamoa Beach

31

Kipahulu

Oheo Gulch

To Ulupalakua Ranch

Kaupo

Huialoha Church

NUU BAY

0   5 miles

aerie, a memorial to Paul Fagan, there's a fine view of Hana Bay and the surrounding coastline.

The **Hana Cultural Center**, an enticing little museum, displays such artifacts from Hana's past as primitive stone tools, rare shells and Hawaiian games. There are antique photographs and elaborately stitched quilts. ~ 4974 Uakea Street; 248-8622.

Also on the grounds, the old **Court House**, built in 1871, is a modest but appealing structure containing five small benches and the original desk for the judge.

Wananalua Church, a lovely chapel built from coral blocks during the mid-19th century, has been beautifully refurbished. Today, services are conducted in English and Hawaiian. Located atop an ancient *heiau*, stately and imposing in appearance, it is a perfect expression of the days when Christianity was crushing the old Hawaiian beliefs. ~ Hauoli Street and Hana Highway.

FROM HANA TO ULUPALAKUA   The backroad from Hana around the southeast side of Maui is one of the island's great adventures. It leads along the side of Haleakala past dense rainforest and tumbling waterfalls to an arid expanse covered by lava flows, and then opens onto Maui's vaunted Upcountry region. Since a five-mile stretch is unpaved and other sections are punctuated with potholes, car rental companies generally do not permit driving on parts of this route; so check with them in advance or be prepared to take your chances. Also check on road conditions: The road is sometimes closed during periods of heavy rain.

Past Hana, the road, now designated the Piilani Highway and renumbered as Route 31 (with mileage markers that descend in sequence), worsens as it winds toward an overgrown ravine where **Wailua Falls** (45-mile marker) and another waterfall pour down sharp cliff faces.

HANA HIGHWAY EXPERIENCES

- Follow the **Hana–Waianapapa Coastal Trail** to a pair of sea caves that legend tells were once the hiding place of a Hawaiian princess. (p. 44)
- Ride the breezes at **Hookipa Beach Park**, where experts perform airborne acrobats at one of the world's top windsurfing locales. (p. 148)
- Make a pilgrimage through taro farms and banana patches to an 1860 coral-and-stone church on the remote **Keanae Peninsula**. (p. 136)
- Rent a cabin at **Waianapanapa State Park** and wander out your front door past sea arches and lava tubes. (p. 148)
- Choose from four varieties of fresh fish (prepared ten different ways!) at **Mama's Fish House**. (p. 145)

At **Oheo Gulch** in the Kipahulu District of the Haleakala National Park (42-mile marker), a series of waterfalls tumbles into two dozen pools before reaching the sea. The pools are rock-bound, some are bordered by cliffs, and several provide excellent swimming holes. This is an eerie and beautiful place from which you can see up and down the rugged coastline. Used centuries ago by early Hawaiians, they still offer a cool, refreshing experience.

Another special spot, **Charles Lindbergh's grave** (41-mile marker), rests on a promontory overlooking the ocean. The great aviator spent his last days here and lies buried beside Palapala Hoomau Church. The whitewashed chapel and surrounding shade trees create a place of serenity and remarkable beauty. (To find the grave, continue 1.2 miles past Oheo Gulch. Watch for the church through the trees on the left. Turn left onto an unpaved road and drive several hundred yards, paralleling a stone fence. Turn left into the churchyard.)

◄ HIDDEN

Not far from here, in **Kipahulu**, the paved road gives way to dirt. It's five miles to the nearest pavement, so your car should have good shock absorbers; sometimes the weather makes it impassable. The road rises along seaside cliffs, some of which are so steep they jut out to overhang the road. This is wild, uninhabited country, ripe for exploration.

Huialoha Church, built in 1859, rests below the road on a wind-wracked peninsula. The last time I visited this aging worship hall, horses were grazing in the churchyard. Nearby you'll encounter the tinroof town of **Kaupo**, with its funky general store. Located directly above the town is **Kaupo Gap**, through which billowing clouds pour into Haleakala Crater.

◄ HIDDEN

The road bumps inland, then returns seaward to **Nuu Bay's** rocky beach. From here the rustic route climbs into a desolate area scarred by lava and inhabited with scrub vegetation. The sea views are magnificent as the road bisects the **1790 lava flow**. This was the last volcanic eruption on Maui; it left its mark in a torn and terrible landscape that slopes for miles to the sea.

It's several miles farther until you reach **Ulupalakua Ranch**, a lush counterpoint to the lava wasteland behind. With its grassy acres and curving rangeland, the ranch provides a perfect introduction to Maui's Upcountry region.

Along the Hana Highway out in Paia, about seven miles from Kahului, sits **Nalu Kai Lodge**. Tucked behind the Kihata Restaurant near the town hub, this eight-unit resting place is a real sleeper. The last time I was by, only three rooms were available; the others were accommodating permanent residents. If you snag one of the vacant rooms, you'll check into a small, plain cubicle with no carpeting and little decoration. Sound unappealing? Well, even bare walls

LODGING

sometimes look good at the right price. ~ Hana Highway; 579-8009. BUDGET.

A very convenient accommodation located on the Hana Highway in Keanae is the Maui YMCA's **Camp Keanae**. For just $10 a night, both men and women are welcome to roll out their sleeping bags on bunks in the dormitory. Set in a spacious wooden house overlooking the sea, this crash pad comes with hot showers, full-size gym, kitchen and outdoor cooking area. Sorry, the maximum stay here is five nights. ~ Hana Highway; 242-9007. BUDGET.

Aloha Cottages, perched on a hillside above Hana Bay, has two-bedroom cottages that are situated among banana trees and feature hardwood floors and walls fashioned from redwood. The decor is simple, the kitchens are all-electric and many of the furnishings are rattan. Representing one of Hana's best bargains, the cottages have been recommended many times over the years by readers and friends. There are only five units at this small complex, so advance reservations are a good idea. ~ 73 Keawa Place; 248-8420. MODERATE.

You can also consider heading down toward the water to the **Hana Kai Maui Resort**. Located smack on a rocky beach, these two twin-story buildings sit amid lush surroundings. The ornamental pool is a freshwater affair fed by toe-dipping spring water. The location and exotic grounds rate a big plus. Both studio apartments and one-bedroom condominiums are available. ~ 1533 Ukea Road; 248-8426, 800-346-2772, fax 248-7482. DELUXE.

Speaking of scenery, **Heavenly Hana Inn** is blessed indeed. Located about two miles outside Hana, this hostelry offers three suites and is entered through a Japanese gate. On either side, stone lions guard a luxuriant garden. The interior mirrors this elegance. Each two-bedroom suite is decorated in a Japanese style with futon beds, shoji screens and tiled bathrooms with sunken tubs. Continental breakfast provided. ~ Hana Highway; phone/fax 248-8442. ULTRA-DELUXE.

Hana Plantation Houses has everything from homes to cottages to studios. Scattered throughout the Hana area, there are homes with either mountain or ocean views; each unit is fully equipped with kitchens and hot tubs. The wood-paneled accommodations, decorated with tapa-cloth designs and Hawaiian paintings, include a wraparound lanai and interior garden. Most are cooled with ceiling fans and all have outdoor grills perfect for a private luau. Environmentalists will want to check out the solar-powered Waikaloa Beach House. Some facilities are within walking distance of the beach and ancient Hawaiian fishponds. ~ Locations throughout Hana; 248-7868, 800-228-4262, fax 248-8240. MODERATE TO ULTRA-DELUXE.

Hana Alii Holidays offers a similar selection of accommodations—including studios and homes—in several price ranges. Here you can settle into a place on Hana Bay or on an idyllic hillside. Some units sit atop lava-rock bluffs overlooking the ocean, others are found in secluded five-acre settings. All accommodations come with lanais and outdoor barbecues; some have full kitchens. Picture windows, *koa*-wood detailing, ceiling fans and decks add to the ambience. ~ 103 Keawa Place; 248-7742, 800-548-0478. MODERATE TO ULTRA-DELUXE.

One of Hawaii's finest resting places is the **Hotel Hana Maui**, a luxurious retreat on a hillside above the bay. From ocean views to tropical landscape to rolling lawn, this friendly inn is a unique, world-class resort. Spread across the 66-acre grounds are 94 cottages, all elegantly designed and devoid of clocks, radios and televisions. The hotel's health and fitness complex sponsors a variety of hiking excursions and nature walks. The adjacent 25-meter pool, landscaped with lava walls and monkeypod trees, enjoys a spectacular setting. The staff has been here for generations, lending a sense of home to an enchanting locale. Rates for this getaway of getaways are stratospheric, but I highly recommend the Hotel Hana Maui. ~ 248-8211, 800-321-4262, fax 248-7202. ULTRA-DELUXE.

Don't forget the cabins at **Waianapanapa State Park** (for information, refer to the "Beaches & Parks" section later in this chapter).

The road to Hana is also home to several bed and breakfasts that cater to a gay, lesbian and straight clientele. **Golden Bamboo Ranch** has three suites and a cottage amid seven acres of gardens. There are views of the ocean through a horse pasture. ~ 1205 Kaupakalua Road, Haiku; 572-7824. **Halfway to Hana House** is a studio with a mini-kitchen overlooking the ocean. ~ P.O. Box 675, Haiku, HI 96708; 572-1176, fax 572-3609. BUDGET TO MODERATE.

Also serving a similar clientele, **Huelo Point Lookout** is set on two acres and bounded by the ocean on three sides. There's lodging in two cottages and a lookout house suite, each with full kitchen. Hot tub; pool. ~ P.O. Box 117, Paia, HI 96779; phone/fax 573-0914. **Napulani O'Hana** offers spacious but bland accommodations within a few miles of Hana. It's a ranch-style house set on four acres. ~ P.O. Box 118, Hana, HI 96713; 248-8935. Huelo

NOTHING IS SACRED

Every tourist to Maui dreams of visiting the "Seven Sacred Pools" at Oheo Gulch in Hana. In fact, says Mark Tanaka-Sanders, a ranger who helps manage a coastal section of Haleakala National Park, "there are 24 pools in the area." Who's responsible for the miscount? "Blame it on the tourist industry," he says. "It's also important to know that the Hawaiian people do not consider these pools sacred." They refer to them as the pools at Oheo.

Point Lookout is moderate in price; Napulani O'Hana runs in the deluxe to ultra-deluxe range.

DINING   Paia, an artsy little town located just a few miles out on the Hana Highway, has several restaurants to choose from. If you don't select any of them, however, be forewarned—there are no pit stops between here and Hana.

Wunderbar is an uneasy cross between a European dining room and an American bar and grill. You can order a beer at the bar or select from a nouvelle cuisine menu that includes German selections, fresh fish and pasta dishes. They also have full, American-style breakfast and lunch menus. ~ 89 Hana Highway, Paia; 579-8808. MODERATE TO DELUXE.

If you're craving a tasty fish sandwich, the **Paia Fish Market** is the place to go. When you're not in the mood for seafood, this eatery also offers burgers, pasta and Mexican dishes such as fajitas. It's is a casual place with plenty of greenery, and prints of water sports on the walls. ~ Corner of Baldwin Avenue and Hana Highway; 579-8030. BUDGET TO MODERATE.

For box lunches, drop in at **Picnics**. Open for breakfast, lunch and dinner, this light and airy café serves a variety of items including spinach-nut burger and mahimahi sandwiches. The menu also offers patrons basic breakfast selections, deli sandwiches and plain old hamburgers. ~ 30 Baldwin Avenue, Paia; 579-8021. BUDGET.

The Vegan Restaurant is the prime address hereabouts for vegetarian food. Place your order at the counter—there are salads, sandwiches and hot entrées that include Thai specialties. Closed Monday. ~ 115 Baldwin Avenue, Paia; 579-9144. BUDGET.

Bangkok Cuisine promises "authentic Thai food." They certainly sport an authentically attractive look with a dining room decorated with tiles and pastel walls. There's also a patio where you can dine alfresco beneath an umbrella of palm trees. Oh, and the menu—Cornish game hen in a sauce of garlic and black pepper, eggplant beef, evil prince shrimp and crab legs in bean sauce. ~ 120 Hana Highway, Paia; 579-8979. BUDGET TO MODERATE.

Just down the street you'll find **Kihata Restaurant**. This old-style restaurant, with bamboo partitions and a screen door that slams, is another favorite watering place for Paia residents. There's a glistening formica counter up front, and a cluster of tables in back. Dining in this local hangout is definitely casual. And the menu is ethnic: In addition to sushi bar specialties, it includes Japanese noodle dishes, *tonkatsu* (deep-fried pork), teriyaki and tempura. Closed Monday. ~ 115 Hana Highway, Paia; 579-9035. BUDGET.

Or, for masterfully prepared food without the sophisticated trappings, try **Mama's Fish House** outside Paia. Unlike most well-heeled restaurants, this oceanfront nook is simply decorated: shell leis, an old Hawaiian photo here, a painting there, plus potted plants. Elegant simplicity. During lunch, there is a varied menu that includes California cuisine–style dishes and ever-changing specialties. Other than a few steak and poultry dishes, the dinner menu is entirely seafood. The evening entrées include bouillabaisse, scampi and fresh Hawaiian lobster. Another of Mama's treats is fresh fish: There are always at least four varieties, prepared ten different ways. ~ Hana Highway; 579-8488. DELUXE TO ULTRA-DELUXE.

America's first domestic rubber plantation opened in Nahiku in 1905. You can still see a few remaining rubber plants in the area.

If you plan to stay in Hana for any length of time, pack some groceries in with the raingear. You'll find only four restaurants along the entire eastern stretch of the island. Luckily, they cover the gamut from budget to ultra-deluxe.

Tutu's At Hana Bay, located within whistling distance of the water, whips up sandwiches, hamburgers and teriyaki chicken for breakfast and lunch. ~ Hana Bay; 248-8224. BUDGET.

Open for breakfast and lunch, **Hana Gardenland Café** offers patio dining overlooking a tropical nursery. The menu includes such items as quiche, pastas, salads and the restaurant has Hana's only complete espresso bar. If you're headed out on a hike, stop here to pick up a picnic lunch. ~ Hana Highway at Kalo Road; 248-7340. BUDGET.

Hana Ranch Restaurant is a small, spiffy establishment decorated with blond wood and offering great ocean views. There's a flagstone lanai for outdoor dining. Open daily for lunch, they serve dinner every Monday, Friday and Saturday. On Wednesday night they serve pizza. Lunch is buffet style; in the evening they offer fresh fish, chops, steak and baby back ribs. ~ Hana Highway; 248-8255. DELUXE TO ULTRA-DELUXE.

There's also a **takeout stand** serving breakfast and lunch, with picnic tables overlooking the ocean. ~ Hana Bay. BUDGET.

Hana's premier restaurant is the dining room of the **Hotel Hana Maui**. This extraordinary resort, perched on a hillside overlooking the ocean, serves gourmet meals to its guests and the public alike. For lunch the bill of fare includes a variety of salads served in tortilla bowls, fresh fish, hibachi chicken and sashimi. The evening menu features pan-seared veal chops, bamboo-steamed seafood *lau-lau* and baked Hunan-style lamb. The menu changes seasonally. ~ Hana Highway; 248-8211. ULTRA-DELUXE.

GROCERIES

You'd better stock up before coming if you plan to stay very long in this remote region. There are few restaurants and even fewer stores. With a limited stock of grocery items are **Hana Ranch Store**, open daily from 7 a.m. to 7 p.m. ~ Mill Street, Hana; 248-8261; and **Hasegawa General Store**, open Monday through Saturday

from 8 a.m. to 5:30 p.m., and Sunday from 9 a.m. to 4:30 p.m. ~
Hana Highway, Hana; 248-8231.

Over on the Hana Highway in Paia, **Nagata Store** has a small
supply of groceries. Open Monday through Friday 6 a.m. to 7 p.m.,
Saturday 6 a.m. to 6 p.m., and Sunday 6 a.m. to 1 p.m. ~ 579-9252.
If you can't find what you need here, check the **H&P Market &
Seafood.** Open Monday through Friday 7 a.m. to 7 p.m., Saturday
7 a.m. to 6 p.m., and Sunday 7 a.m. to 1 p.m. ~ In the Nagata Store,
Hana Highway (579-9640). You can also try the **Paia General
Store.** Open from 6 a.m. to 9 p.m. during the week, opens at 7 a.m.
on weekends. ~ Hana Highway, Paia; 579-9514.

Mana Foods has a complete stock of health foods and organic
produce. Open from 8 a.m. to 8 p.m. every day. ~ 49 Baldwin Avenue, Paia; 579-8078.

Clear across the island, along the back road from Hana, there's
HIDDEN ► a sleeper called **Kaupo General Store** that's usually open in the afternoon. You'll find it tucked away in the southeast corner of the
island. Selling a limited range of food, drinks and wares, this
70-year-old store fills the gaps on the shelves with curios from its
illustrious history. ~ 248-8054.

SHOPPING Paia, an artist colony seven miles outside Kahului, is my favorite
place to shop on Maui. Many fine artisans live in the Upcountry
area and come down to sell their wares at the small shops lining the
Hana Highway. The town itself is a work of art, with old wooden
buildings that provide a welcome respite from the crowded shores
of Kaanapali and Kihei. I'll mention just the shops I like most.
Browse through town to see for yourself. If you discover places I
missed, please let me know.

On display at the **Maui Crafts Guild** is a range of handmade
items all by local artists. Here you'll find anything from pressed hibiscus flowers to bamboo furniture. There are also fabrics, ceramics, jewelry, baskets and other Maui-made items. ~ 43 Hana
Highway; 579-9697.

Paia Trading Company has a few interesting antiques and a lot
of junk. Among the more noteworthy items: turquoise and silver
jewelry, wooden washboards, apothecary jars and antique glassware. ~ 106 Hana Highway; 579-9472.

Eddie Flotte Watercolors features original artworks by an original character. Flotte's paintings capture the down-home lifestyles
of Upcountry residents. ~ 83 Hana Highway, Paia; 579-9641.

Summerhouse Boutique might be called a chic dress shop. But
they sell everything from jewelry and postcards to porcelain dolls
and natural fiber garments. ~ 83 Hana Highway, Paia; 579-9201.

Around the corner on Baldwin Avenue lies another shop worth
browsing. **Maui Girl and Co.** features a fine selection of women's

fashions, including designer clothing, manufactured designs and locally made styles. They also have '30s and '40s aloha shirts for men, as well as informal beachwear. ~ 12 Baldwin Avenue; 579-9266.

One of my favorite shops in Hana is the **Hana Coast Gallery** in the Hotel Hana Maui. It features native Hawaiian art and artifacts and fine paintings by Maui artists, as well as pieces by the novelist Henry Miller. Also here are beautiful serigraphs, model racing canoes in *koa*, ceremonial objects, feathered leis, fiber collages and painted tapa cloth. ~ Hana Highway; 248-8636.

Also on the grounds of Hotel Hana Maui is **Susan Marie**, a shop specializing in sportswear, embroidered shirts and accessories with a tropical flair. ~ Hana Highway; 248-8211.

For everything you could possibly want or need, drop by the **Hasegawa General Store**. This store stocks everything from groceries, clothing and hardware to placemats, movie rentals, film and gas. The original Hasegawa's burned down years ago, but the name is still famous. ~ 5165 Hana Highway; 248-8231.

Hana Gardenland is a five-acre landscape nursery that seconds as an art gallery. All the orchids, bromeliads and cut flowers can be shipped home. Or you can shop in the gallery for Hawaiian crafts, including a number by artists from the Hana area. ~ Hana Highway at Kalo Road; 248-8975.

The honor system is alive and well at the untended self-serve **coconut stand** near Hana Highway's 48-mile marker.

NIGHTLIFE

Wunderbar usually has live bands on Wednesday, Thursday, Friday and Saturday nights as well as Sunday afternoons. This local bar often draws an Upcountry crowd. Cover. ~ 89 Hana Highway, Paia; 579-8808.

In the early evening, you can enjoy a duo singing Hawaiian music at the Hotel Hana Maui's **Paniolo Bar**. As relaxed as Hana itself, this low-key establishment is always inviting. ~ Hana Highway; 248-8211.

BEACHES & PARKS

H. A. BALDWIN PARK This spacious county park is bordered by a playing field on one side and a crescent-shaped beach on the other. Palm and ironwood trees dot the half-mile-long beach. There's good shell collecting and a great view of West Maui. The swimming is good, as is the bodysurfing, but beware of currents; the snorkeling cannot be recommended. For surfing there are winter breaks, with a right slide. Fishing for threadfin, mountain bass, goatfish and *ulua* is good. Facilities include a picnic area with large pavilion, showers and restrooms. ~ To get there, turn left off Route 360, about seven miles east of Kahului on the Hana Highway.

▲ Tent camping is allowed on a quarter-acre meadow; a county permit is required.

HOOKIPA BEACH PARK 🏄 🏊 For surfers and windsurfers this is one of the best spots on Maui. The beach itself is little more than a narrow rectangle of sand paralleled by a rocky shelf. Offshore, top-ranked windsurfers may be performing airborne stunts. On any day you're likely to see a hundred sails with boards attached skimming the whitecaps. The swimming is good only when the surf is low. There are picnic areas, restrooms and showers. ~ The park is located on the Hana Highway about three miles east of Paia.

HIDDEN ► **HONOMANU BAY** 🏄 A tranquil black-sand-and-rock beach surrounded by pandanus-covered hills and bisected by a stream, Honomanu Bay is a beautiful and secluded spot. There are no facilities, and the water is often too rough for swimming, but it's a favorite with surfers. ~ It is located off of the Hana Highway (Route 360), about 30 miles east of Kahului. Turn off onto the dirt road located east of Kaumahina State Wayside; follow it to the beach.

WAIANAPANAPA STATE PARK 🏄 🐟 ⚓ Set in a heavenly seaside locale, this park is one of Hawaii's prettiest public facilities and is a very popular spot. The entire area is lush with tropical foliage and especially palmy pandanus trees. There's a black-sand beach, sea arches, a blowhole and two legendary caves. But pack your parkas; wind and rain are frequent. Swimming and snorkeling are both good—when the water is calm—and the fishing is good. Facilities here include a picnic area, restrooms and showers. ~ Located just off the Hana Highway (Route 360) about four miles north of the town of Hana.

▲ There are campsites for up to 60 people on a grass-covered bluff overlooking the sea. These are plain but attractive accommodations renting on a sliding scale (starting at $10 single and $14 double up to $30 for six people). Each one contains a small bedroom with two bunk beds, plus a living room that can double as an extra bedroom. All cabins are equipped with bedding and complete kitchen facilities, and some have ocean views. A state permit is required. The cabins are rented through the Division of State Parks. ~ 54 South High Street, Wailuku, Maui, HI 96793; 243-5354.

HANA BEACH PARK 🏄 🐟 🏊 ⚓ Tucked into a well-protected corner of Hana Bay, this park has a large pavilion and a curving stretch of sandy beach. It's a great place to meet local people. Swimming is fine; snorkeling is good near the lighthouse; and surfers will find both summer and winter breaks on the north side of the bay (left slide). Bonefish, *ulua* and *papio* are routinely taken here and *moilii* run in the months of June and July. As well as the picnic area, there are restrooms and showers and there is a snack bar across the street. ~ Located off the Hana Highway at Hana Bay.

HIDDEN ► **RED SAND BEACH** 🏄 🐟 🏃 ⚓ Known to the Hawaiians as Kaiha-lulu ("roaring sea") Beach, this is one of the most exotic and truly secluded beaches in all Hawaii. It is protected by lofty cliffs and can be reached only over a precarious trail. A volcanic cinder beach, the sand is reddish in hue and coarse underfoot. Most dramatic of all is the lava barrier that crosses the mouth of this natural amphitheater, protecting the beach and creating an inshore pool. This is another beach popular with nudists. Swimming, snorkeling and fishing are all good. There are no facilities. ~ This is one place where getting to the beach becomes a grand adventure. It is located on the far side of Kauiki Hill in Hana. Follow Uakea Road to its southern terminus. There is a grassy plot on the left between Hana School and the parking lot for the Hotel Hana Maui's sea ranch cottages. Here you will find a trail leading into the undergrowth. It traverses an overgrown Japanese cemetery and curves around Kauiki Hill, then descends precipitously to the beach. Be careful!

HAMOA BEACH Located at the head of Mokae Cove, this stretch of salt-and-pepper sand with rock outcroppings at each end is a pretty place. Unfortunately, the Hotel Hana Maui uses the beach as a semiprivate preserve. There are restrooms for guests and separate facilities for everybody else and a dining pavilion that is available only to guests, so a sense of segregation pervades the beach. ~ To reach the place, follow the Hana Highway south from Hana for a little over a mile. Turn left on Haneoo Road and follow it for a mile to Hamoa.

KOKI BEACH PARK A sandy plot paralleled by a grassy park, this beach is more welcoming than Hamoa. Backdropped by lofty red cinder cliffs, Koki can be very windy and is plagued by currents. With a small island and sea arch offshore, it is also very pretty. Swimming is good, but exercise caution. ~ Located half a mile back up the Haenoo Road toward the highway.

OHEO GULCH The stream that tumbles down Haleakala through the Oheo Gulch forms several large pools and numerous small ones. The main pools descend from above the Hana Highway to the sea. This is a truly enchanting area swept by frequent wind

SPRING TRAINING, HANA STYLE

In 1946, Hana hosted the only mainland American baseball team ever to conduct spring training in Hawaii. That was the year that financier Paul Fagan brought the Pacific Coast League's San Francisco Seals to the islands. Arriving with the players was a squadron of sportswriters who sent back glowing dispatches on "Heavenly Hana," helping to promote the destination and the Hotel Hana Maui, owned of course by Paul Fagan.

and rain, and shadowed by Haleakala. It overlooks Maui's rugged eastern shore. You can swim in the chilly waters and camp nearby. There are picnic facilities and outhouses; bring your own drinking water. ~ Located in the National Park's Kipahulu section (about ten miles south of Hana).

▲ Primitive, meadow-style camping is available on a bluff above the sea. No permit is required and there are no restrictions on the number of occupants but there is a three-day limit.

NINE

Upcountry and Haleakala

Maui's Upcountry is a verdant mountainous belt that encircles Haleakala along its middle slopes. Situated between coastline and crater rim, it's a region of ample rainfall and sparse population that is ideal for camping, hiking or just wandering. Here the flat fields of sugar cane and pineapples that blanket central Maui give way to open ranchland where curving hills are filled with grazing horses.

Farmers plant tomatoes, cabbages, carrots and the region's famous Maui onions. Proteas, those delicate flowers native to Australia and South Africa, grow in colorful profusion. Hibiscus, jacarandas and other wildflowers sweep along the hillsides like a rainstorm. And on the region's two ranches—20,000-acre Haleakala Ranch and 20,000-acre Ulupalakua Ranch—Angus and Hereford cattle complete a picture far removed from Hawaii's tropical beaches.

Home to *paniolos*, Hawaii's version of the Western cowboy, the Upcountry region lies along the highways that lead to the crest of Haleakala. Route 37, Haleakala Highway, becomes the Kula Highway as it ascends to the Kula uplands. The **Church of the Holy Ghost** (12-mile marker), a unique octagonal chapel, was built here in 1897 for Portuguese immigrants working on Maui's ranches and farms.

This roadway angles southwest through Ulupalakua Ranch to the ruins of the **Makee Sugar Mill**, a once flourishing enterprise built in 1878. A currently flourishing business, **Tedeschi Winery**, sits just across the road. Producing a pineapple wine called Maui Blanc, the winery rests in an old jailhouse built of lava and coral in 1857. Here at Hawaii's first winery you can stop for a taster's tour. ~ 878-6058.

You can also turn up Route 377 to **Kula Botanical Gardens**. An excellent place for picnicking, the landscaped slopes contain an aviary, pond, "Taboo Garden" with poisonous plants and over 40 varieties of protea, the flowering shrub that grows so beautifully in this region. Admission. ~ Kula; 878-1715.

Several farms, including **Sunrise Protea Farm**, devoted primarily to proteas, are located nearby. ~ Haleakala Crater Road; 876-0200.

Another intriguing place is the tiny town of **Makawao**, where battered buildings and falsefront stores create an Old West atmosphere. This is the capital of Maui's cowboy country, similar to Waimea on the Big Island, with a rodeo every Fourth of July.

From Makawao the possibilities for exploring the Upcountry area are many. There are two **loop tours** I particularly recommend. ◄ *HIDDEN*
The first climbs from town along Olinda Road (Route 390) past **Pookela Church** (572-8751), a coral sanctuary built in 1843.

It continues through a frequently rain-drenched region to the **Tree Growth Research Area**, jointly sponsored by state and federal forestry services. You can circle back down toward Makawao on Piiholo Road past the **University of Hawaii Agricultural Station**, where you will see more of the area's richly planted acreage.

The second loop leads down Route 365 to the Hana Highway. Turn left on the highway for several miles to Haiku Road, then head left along this country lane, which leads into overgrown areas, across one-lane bridges, past banana patches and through the tin-roof town of **Haiku**.

A mountain lodge on the road to the summit of Haleakala offers a **LODGING**
cold-air retreat that is well-situated for anyone who wants to catch the sunrise over the valley. For years, **Kula Lodge** has rented Swiss chalets complete with fireplaces, sleeping lofts and sweeping views. The individual chalets are carpeted wall-to-wall and trimmed with stained-wood paneling. The central lodge features a cheery restaurant, bar and stone fireplace. An appealing mountain hideaway. ~ 878-1535, 800-233-1535, fax 878-2518. DELUXE TO ULTRA-DELUXE.

What more could an urban cowpoke ask for than a bed and breakfast with trail rides that begin in the front yard? That's the scene up at **Silver Cloud Ranch**, a nine-acre spread located at 3000- ◄ *HIDDEN*
feet elevation on the slopes of Haleakala. In addition to a broad swath of cattle country, the ranch looks out over several neighboring islands. Accommodations include six bedrooms in a big ranch house, a bunkhouse with five studio units and a private cottage. Full breakfast, pardner. R.R. 2, Box 201, Kula, HI 96790; 878-6101, fax 878-2132. MODERATE.

One of Maui's premier gay retreats is **Camp Kula**, a spacious five-bedroom house that rests on seven acres where "HIV-positive guests are *always* welcome!" Located on the side of Haleakala at the 3000-foot level, it caters exclusively to gay men and women. Guests have full access to the kitchen, the living room and other features of the house. ~ Kula; phone/fax 878-2528. BUDGET TO MODERATE.

Among other gay retreats, **Kailua Maui Gardens**, a gay-owned, mixed-clientele bed and breakfast has everything from a one-room cottage to a three-bedroom house. It's set in a tropical garden with shaded paths and bridges plus a pool and spa. ~ S.R. Box 9, Haiku, HI 96708; 572-9726, 800-258-8588. MODERATE TO DELUXE.

Also with a mixed clientele is **Waipio Bay Lookout**, a two-acre spread in Huelo on a cliff above the ocean. There's a pool, jacuzzi and sundeck at this three-unit facility. ~ P.O. Box 1095, Haiku, HI 96708; 572-4530. MODERATE TO DELUXE.

DINING

There are several good dining spots in Pukalani Terrace Center in Pukalani on the Haleakala Highway. Among them is **Nick's Place**, a breakfast-and-lunch-only cafeteria serving Japanese-Chinese-American fare. Choose from such à la carte items as *chow fun*, tempura, Portuguese sausage, stew or corned-beef hash; together they make a hearty meal. At breakfast, try the eggs with Portuguese sausage. ~ Pukalani Terrace Center; 572-8258. BUDGET.

A good local restaurant for breakfast or lunch is the **Up Country Café**. The theme here is bovine all the way, with the restaurant decked out in everything from cow bells to cow salt-and-pepper shakers. Breakfast is pretty predictable; lunch includes a half-dozen entrées such as prime rib and New York steak, as well as such non-bovine fare as chicken curry with fresh country vegetables, sautéed mahimahi and vegetarian lasagna. Also open for dinner Thursday through Saturday. ~ Haleakala Highway and Aewa Place, Pukalani; 572-2395. BUDGET TO MODERATE.

For something a step more upscale, consider the **Makawao Steak House**. Knotty pine walls and a comfortable lounge lend the place an air of refined rusticity. The menu, popular among the Upcountry gentry, is a mix of surf-and-turf dishes. Dinner only. ~ 3612 Baldwin Avenue, Makawao; 572-8711. DELUXE.

In Makawao, you can go Mediterranean at **Casanova Italian Restaurant & Deli**, a stylish bistro that serves Italian-style seafood and pasta dishes. For something faster, cheaper and more casual, you can try the adjacent deli. The restaurant and the deli are open seven days a week. ~ 1188 Makawao Avenue; 572-0220. MODERATE TO DELUXE.

Or head across the street to **Polli's Mexican Restaurant**. This sombreros-on-the-wall-and-oilcloth-on-the-tables eatery offers a full selection of Mexican dishes. A local gathering place popular with residents throughout Maui's Upcountry region, Polli's has become an institution over the years. It will inevitably be crowded with natives dining on tacos, burritos, tamales and tostadas. ~ 1202 Makawao Avenue, Makawao; 572-7808. BUDGET TO MODERATE.

Upcountry's contribution to the culinary revolution that has been sweeping Hawaii the past few years is **Haliimaile General Store**. A former plantation store that has been converted into a chic gathering place, it puts a creative spin on American cuisine and serves roast

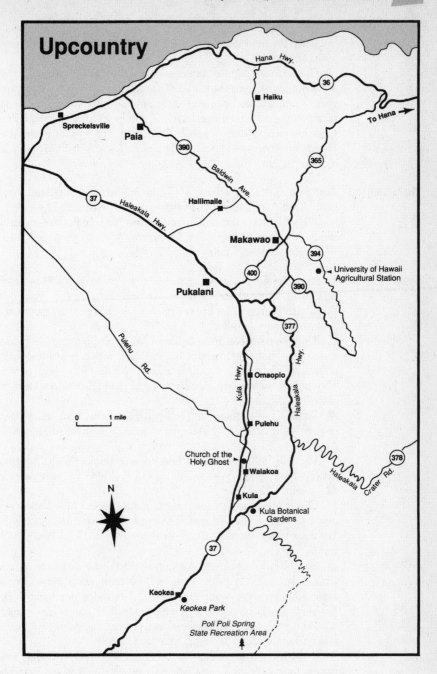

Upcountry

Hana Hwy.

Haiku

36

To Hana →

Spreckelsville

Paia

390

365

Baldwin Ave.

37

Haleakala Hwy.

Haliimaile

Makawao

394

University of Hawaii
Agricultural Station

400

Pukalani

390

Pulehu Rd.

377

Kula Hwy.

Omaopio

Haleakala Hwy.

0   1 mile

Pulehu

378

Church of the
Holy Ghost →

Waiakoa

Haleakala Crater Rd.

N

Kula

Kula Botanical
Gardens

37

Keokea

Keokea Park

Poli Poli Spring
State Recreation Area

duckling, fresh island fish and beef from the Big Island. Dinner only on Saturday and Sunday. ~ 900 Haliimaile Road, Haliimaile; 572-2666. DELUXE.

On the lower slope of Haleakala, **Kula Lodge Restaurant** enjoys a panoramic view of the island. Through picture windows you can gaze out on a landscape that rolls for miles to the sea. The exposed-beam ceiling and stone fireplace lend a homey feel, as do the home-made pastries. Specialties include rack of lamb, pasta dishes and vegetarian entrées. ~ Haleakala Highway, Kula; 878-1535. MODERATE TO DELUXE.

GROCERIES   Along the Haleakala Highway (Route 37) there's a **Foodland**, open from 5 a.m. to midnight. ~ Pukalani Terrace Center; 572-0674.

You can also count on **Down to Earth Natural Foods** for health foods and New Age supplies. Open from 8 a.m. to 8 p.m. ~ 1169 Makawao Avenue, Makawao; 572-1488.

SHOPPING   Baldwin Avenue in the western-style town of Makawao has developed over the years into a prime arts-and-crafts center. Housed in the falsefront stores that line the street you'll find galleries galore and a few boutiques besides.

The Courtyard at 3620 Baldwin Avenue is an attractive wood-frame mall that contains **Hot Island Glass**, with a museum-quality collection of handblown glass pieces. ~ 572-4527. Also here is **Viewpoints Gallery**, which puts many of the higher-priced Lahaina galleries to shame. ~ 572-5979.

Gecko Trading Company is a small shop that features contemporary fashions at reasonable prices. ~ 3621 Baldwin Avenue; 572-0249.

The kids will love **Maui Child Toys & Books** for the puppets, art supplies, wooden toys and music tapes. ~ 3643 Baldwin Avenue, Makawao; 572-2765.

Check out **Goodie's** for the gift items: crystal mobiles, locally made jewelry, picture frames. There are also women's fashions by Upcountry designers. ~ 3633 Baldwin Avenue, Makawao; 572-0288.

HIDDEN ►   On the outskirts of Makawao, the 1917 Mediterranean-style Baldwin mansion is home to the **Hui Noeau Visual Arts Center**. Here you can view rotating educational exhibits, purchase works by Maui artists or take the plunge yourself at one of the regular workshops on painting, printmaking, pottery, sculpture and much, much more. ~ 2841 Baldwin Avenue; 572-6560.

In the Kula Lodge complex, the **Curtis Wilson Cost Gallery** sells prints, limited editions and originals by Curtis Wilson Cost. The emphasis is on local landscapes and ocean scenery. ~ Haleakala Highway; 878-6544.

Proteas of Hawaii is a good place to find Maui's signature plant. They also sell orchids. ~ 210 Mauna Place, Kula; 878-2533.

There are live bands on the weekends and disco music several weeknights at **Casanova Italian Restaurant**. One of Upcountry's only nightspots, it features a range of live acts—from local Mauian to internationally known. There's a drag show every Thursday night. Cover. ~ 1188 Makawao Avenue, Makawao; 572-0220.

POLIPOLI SPRING STATE RECREATION AREA 🚶 Located at 6200-foot elevation on the slopes of Haleakala, this densely forested area is an ideal mountain retreat. Monterey and sugi pine, eucalyptus and Monterey cypress grow in stately profusion; not far from the campground there's a grove of redwoods. From Polipoli's ethereal heights you can look out over Central and West Maui, as well as the islands of Lanai, Molokai and Kahoolawe. Miles of trails, some leading up to the volcano summit, crisscross the park. Polipoli has a picnic area, restrooms and running water. ~ From Kahului, take Haleakala Highway (Route 37) through Pukalani and past Waiakoa to Route 377. Turn left on 377 and follow it a short distance to the road marked for Polipoli. About half of this ten-mile road to the park is paved. The second half of the track is extremely rough and often muddy. It is advisable to take a four-wheel-drive vehicle.

▲ There is meadow-style camping (a state permit is required) for up to 20 people; the cabin houses up to ten people and rents on a sliding scale from $10 single and $14 double up to $50 for ten people. The spacious cabin (three bedrooms) is sparsely furnished and lacks electricity. It does have a wood heating stove, gas cooking stove, gas lanterns, kitchen utensils and bedding. It can be rented from the Division of State Parks. It's recommended to bring in drinking water.

KEOKEA PARK is a pleasant picnic spot on Route 37 in Keokea. There's a rolling lawn with picnic tables and restrooms.

UPCOUNTRY AND HALEAKALA EXPERIENCES

- Bicycle down the 10,000-foot slopes of a volcanic crater with **Cruiser Bob's Haleakala Downhill** and arrive at sea level in time for breakfast. (p. 40)
- Wander over one-lane bridges and through banana patches to the tinroof town of **Haiku**. (p. 152)
- Discover **Polli's Mexican Restaurant** (a favorite among locals looking for a downhome dinner) before it's discovered. (p. 154)
- Camp in the belly of a dormant volcano at **Haleakala National Park**, where your yard is a moonscape of lava flows and cinder cones. (p. 158)

Haleakala National Park

It seems only fitting that the approach to the summit of Haleakala is along one of the world's fastest-climbing roads. From Kahului to the summit rim—a distance of 40 miles along Routes 37, 377 and 378—the macadam road rises from sea level to over 10,000 feet, and the silence is broken only by the sound of ears popping from the ascent.

At the volcano summit, 10,023-feet in elevation, you look out over an awesome expanse—seven miles long, over two miles wide, 21 miles around. This dormant volcano, which last erupted around 1790, is the central feature of a 28,665-acre national park that extends all the way through the Kipahulu Valley to the sea. The crater floor, 3000 feet below the rim, is a multihued wasteland filled with cinder cones, lava flows and mini-craters. It's a legendary place, with a mythic tradition that's as vital as its geologic history. It was from Haleakala ("House of the Sun") that the demigod Maui lassoed the sun and slowed its track across the sky to give his mother more daylight to dry her tapa cloth.

In the afternoon, the volcano's colors are most vivid, but during the morning the crater is more likely to be free of clouds. Before going up Haleakala, call 871-5054 for a weather report. Then you can decide what time of day will be best for your explorations. Remember that it takes an hour-and-a half to two hours to reach the summit from Kahului, longer from the Kaanapali-Kapalua area. Be sure to bring warm clothes since the temperature drop from sea level to 10,000 feet can be 30° or more.

On the way up to the summit you'll pass **Hosmer Grove** (6800-feet), a picnic area and campground surrounded by eucalyptus, spruce, juniper and cedar trees.

National Park Headquarters, located at the 7030-foot elevation, contains an information desk and maps, and makes a good starting point. Be sure to see the Hawaiian state bird, the nene, a rare species of Hawaiian goose, that likes to rest in a pond nearby. ~ 572-9306.

The first crater view comes at **Leleiwi Overlook**, an 8800-foot perch from where you'll be able to see all the way from Hana across the island to Kihei. Here at sunset, under correct meteorological conditions, you can see your shadow projected on the clouds and haloed by a rainbow. To experience this "Specter of the Brocken," stand atop the volcano rim looking toward the cloud-filled crater with the setting sun at your back.

Up the hill, a side road leads to **Kalahaku Overlook**, a 9324-foot aerie that offers a unique view of several cinder cones within the volcano. Just below the parking lot are numerous **silverswords**. Related to sunflowers, these spike-leaved plants grow only on Maui and the Big Island. They remain low bristling plants for 20 years or more before blooming into a flowering stalk. Each plant blossoms once, sometime between May and November, and then dies.

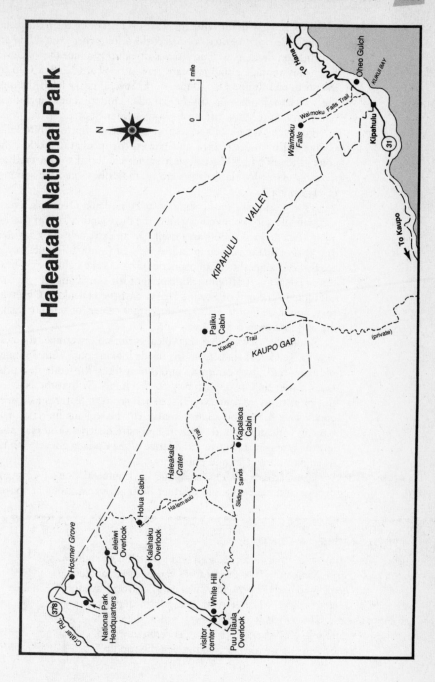

Haleakala National Park

N

0   1 mile

To Hana

Oheo Gulch

KUKUI BAY

Waimoku Falls Trail

Waimoku Falls

Kipahulu

31

KIPAHULU   VALLEY

To Kaupo

Paliku Cabin

Kaupo   Trail

KAUPO GAP

(private)

Kapalaoa Cabin

Haleakala Crater

Trail

Sliding Sands

Holua Cabin

Halemauu

Hosmer Grove

Leleiwi Overlook

Kalahaku Overlook

National Park Headquarters

378

Crater Rd.

White Hill

visitor center

Puu Ulaula Overlook

The best view of the wilderness area is farther up the road at the **Haleakala Visitors Center**, 9745-feet elevation, where you'll find an information desk, as well as a series of exhibits about the volcano. From this vantage point you can gaze out toward Koolau Gap to the north and Kaupo Gap to the south. Several peaks located along the volcano loom out of the clouds; cinder cones, including 600-foot Puu o Maui, rise up from the crater floor.

From the visitors center a short trail heads up to **White Hill**. Composed of andesite lava and named for its characteristic light color, this mound is dotted with stone windbreaks once used as sleeping places by Hawaiians who periodically visited the summit of Haleakala.

It's a short drive to the summit at **Puu Ulaula Overlook**. From the plate-glass lookout you can view the Big Island, Molokai, Lanai, West Maui and wilderness area itself. On an extremely clear day this 360° panorama may even include a view of Oahu, 130 miles away.

Perched high above atmospheric haze and the lights of civilization, Haleakala is also an excellent spot for stargazing. If you can continue to the end of Skyline Drive, past the **Haleakala Observatory**, you'll see that it is also an important center for satellite tracking and television communications.

While the views along the volcano rim are awesome, the best way to see Haleakala is from the inside looking out. With 36 miles of hiking trails, two campsites and three cabins, the wilderness provides a tremendous opportunity for explorers. Within the belly of this monstrous volcano, you'll see such geologic features as cinder cones, lava tubes and spatter vents. The Hawaiians marked their passing with stone altars, shelters and adze quarries. You may also spy the rare nene (a Hawaiian relative of the Canada goose), as well as chukar partridges and pheasants.

HIDDEN ► The **volcano floor** is a unique environment, one of constant change and unpredictable weather. Rainfall varies from 12 inches

LATE SLEEPERS, TAKE NOTE

One of Maui's favorite rituals is a predawn trip to the top of Haleakala to watch the sun rise. Unfortunately, the weather can be foggy and cold. Besides that, getting up early is probably the last thing you want to do on vacation. If so, consider the alternative: Sleep late, take your time getting to the top, and arrive in time for sunset. But, then again, you'll miss a dazzling, almost religious experience. In any case, call 871-5054 to check on the weather before making the trip up!

annually in the southwestern corner to 200 inches at Paliku. Temperatures, usually hovering between 55° and 75° during daylight, may fall below freezing at night. Campers should come prepared with warm clothing and sleeping gear, a tent, poncho, lantern and stove (no open fires are permitted). Don't forget the sunblock, as the elevation on the bottom averages 6700 feet and the ultraviolet radiation is intense.

Within the wilderness area you can explore three main trails. **Sliding Sands Trail**, a steep cinder and ash path, begins near the Haleakala Visitors Center. It descends from the rim along the south wall to Kapalaoa cabin, then on to Paliku cabin. In the course of this ten-mile trek, the trail drops over 3000 feet. From Paliku, the **Kaupo Trail** leaves the crater through Kaupo Gap and descends to the tiny town of Kaupo, eight miles away on Maui's southeast coast. **Halemauu Trail** (8 miles) begins from the road three-and-a-half miles beyond National Park Headquarters and descends 1400 feet to the crater floor. It passes Holua cabin and eventually joins Sliding Sands Trail near the Paliku cabin.

There are campgrounds at **Holua** and **Paliku** that require a permit from National Park Headquarters. Permits are given out on a first-come, first-served basis (not available in advance), so plan accordingly. Camping is limited to two days at one site and three days total at both. The campgrounds have pit toilets and running water. There is also a 12-person cabin at each campsite and at **Kapalaoa**. Equipped with wood stoves, pit toilets, cooking utensils and mattresses, these primitive facilities are extremely popular. So popular, in fact, that guests are chosen by a monthly lottery three months in advance. ~ For more information, write Haleakala National Park, P.O. Box 369, Makawao, Maui, HI 96768, or call 572-9306.

CAMPING

TEN

Lanai

Eight miles from Maui, across the historic whaling anchorage at Lahaina Roads, lies the pear-shaped island of Lanai. The word *lanai*, usually meaning "porch," is more appropriately translated as "swelling" on this humpbacked isle. In profile the island, formed by an extinct volcano, resembles the humpback whales that frequent its waters. It rises in a curved ridge from the south, then gradually tapers to the north. The east side is cut by deep gulches, while the west is bounded by spectacular sea cliffs rising 1500 to 2000 feet. Lanaihale, the island's tallest peak, stands 3370 feet above sea level.

First discovered by Captain Cook's men in 1779, Lanai was long avoided by mariners, who feared its reef-shrouded shores and saw little future in the dry, barren landscape. You can still see testaments to their fear in the rotting hulks that lie off Shipwreck Beach.

Ancient Hawaiians believed Lanai was inhabited only by evil spirits until Kaululaau, son of the great Maui chief Kakaalaneo, killed the spirits. Kaululaau, a Hawaiian-style juvenile delinquent who chopped down fruit trees with the gay abandon of young George Washington, had been exiled for such destructive behavior to Lanai by his father. After the wild youth redeemed himself by making the island safe from malevolent spirits, Lanai was settled by Hawaiians and controlled by powerful Maui chiefs.

Most archaeologists doubt that the native population, which lived from taro cultivation and fishing along the eastern shore, ever exceeded 2500. Even periods of peak population were punctuated by long intervals when the island was all but deserted. Lying in Maui's wind shadow, Lanai's rainfall ranges from 40 inches along its northeast face to a meager 12 inches annually in the barren southwest corner.

Like Molokai, its neighbor to the north, Lanai for centuries was a satellite of Maui. (Even today it is part of Maui County.) Then in 1778 it was overwhelmed by the forces of Kalaniopuu, the king of the Big Island. Later in the century, an even more powerful monarch, Kamehameha the Great, set up a summer residence along the south coast in Kaunolu.

During the 19th century, Lanai was a ranchers' island with large sections of flat range land given over to grazing. Missionaries became active saving souls and securing property in 1835 and by the 1860s one of their number had gained control of Lanai's better acreage. This was Walter Murray Gibson, a Mormon maverick whose life story reads like a sleazy novel. Despite being excommunicated by the Mormon church, Gibson went on to become a formidable figure in Hawaiian politics.

Gibson was not the only man with a dream for Lanai. George Munro, a New Zealand naturalist, came to the island in 1911 as manager of a plantation complex that originally tried to grow sugar on the island and then turned to cattle raising. While his herds grazed the island's tablelands, Munro worked in the rugged highlands. He extended the native forest, planting countless trees to capture moisture and protect eroded hillsides. He restored areas ravaged by feral goats and imported the stately Norfolk pines that still lend a mountain ambience to Lanai City. And, most important, Munro introduced an ecological awareness that hopefully will continue to pervade this enchanting island.

The land that Gibson and Munro oversaw changed hands several times until James Dole in 1922. Dole, descended from missionaries, was possessed of a more earthly vision than his forebears. Pineapples. He converted the island to pineapple cultivation, built Lanai City, and changed the face of Lanai forever.

Filipinos, now about 50 percent of the island's population, were imported to work the fields. Until a few years ago they were bent to their labors all over Lanai, wearing goggles and gloves to protect against the sharp spines that bristle from the low-lying plants. Pineapples are cultivated through plastic sheets to conserve precious water and harvesting is done by hand. Up until the early 1990s, you could see hundreds of acres covered in plastic. Downtown Lanai would roll up the streets at 9 p.m., but the lights would burn bright in the pineapple fields as crews worked through the night loading the hefty fruits onto conveyor belts.

That was yesterday, back when Lanai retained something of an ambiguous reputation. Most tourists, hearing that Lanai was nothing but pineapples and possessed only 20 miles of paved roads and a single ten-room hotel, left the place to the antelopes and wild goats.

Now, however, the sleeping midget is beginning to awaken. You still rent your car in an old gas station with scuffed floors and deer trophies on the wall. And there are still only three paved roads on the island. But nothing else here will ever be the same.

Stores are being renovated, old plantation homes are receiving fresh coats of paint, and new housing developments are going up. Castle & Cooke, the conglomerate that now owns the island, has poured $350 million into the place, building two resorts and transforming little Lanai into luxurious Lanai. The Manele Bay Hotel, a 250-room oceanfront extravaganza, opened in 1991 just one year after the christening of the Lodge at Koele, a rustic but refined 102-room resort situated along Lanai's forested mountain slopes.

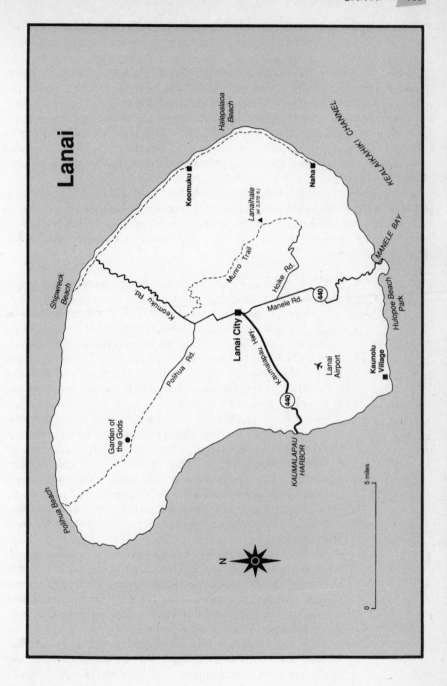

Lanai

Shipwreck Beach

Polihua Beach

Garden of the Gods

Polihua Rd.

Keomuku Rd.

Keomuku ■

Halepalaoa Beach

Munro Trail

Lanaihale (el 3,370 ft.)

Naha ■

KEALAIKAHIKI CHANNEL

MANELE BAY

Holke Rd.

Manele Rd.

440

Lanai City

Kaumalapau Hwy.

Lanai Airport

Kaunolu Village

Hulopoe Beach Park

440

KAUMALAPAU HARBOR

5 miles

0

N

Meanwhile the island's pineapple cultivation is declining precipitously from a peak of about 18,000 acres to a period in the near future when it will total a mere 200 acres, sufficient to supply island needs and give visitors a glimpse at what life was like "back when." Fields are being converted to alfalfa and oats; cattle raising is being reintroduced; and the island's Filipino and Japanese population is quitting the plantation and going to work for the tourist industry.

In the midst of all the construction, and despite the disturbing changes in the lifestyle of the local people, this lovely little isle retains its charm. Even now only a fraction of Lanai's 140 square miles is developed. The rest of the island is covered with a network of jeep and hiking trails guaranteed to keep the heartiest adventurer happy.

Here is an entire island that fits the description "hidden Hawaii." Almost all of Lanai's 2400 citizens live in rustic Lanai City at the island's center and most tourists are concentrated here or along a single beach at the Manele Bay Resort. Just beyond these clusters lie mountains, ranchlands and remote beaches—untouched realms ripe for exploration.

Lanai City

▼▼▼▼▼▼▼▼▼▼ Situated at 1645 feet, **Lanai City** is a trim community of corrugated-roof houses and small garden plots. Tourist brochures present the place as a quaint New England village, but until the Lodge at Koele was built the town was rather drab. Most of the houses were constructed around the 1920s in traditional company-town fashion. They are square boxes topped with tin roofs and tend to look alike. Norfolk pines break the monotony, and now that Lanai is much more self-conscious, many homes are freshly painted in a rainbow assortment of hues.

It is still a company town, but today the company is harvesting tourists instead of planting pineapples. Several housing developments and condominium complexes have been built on the outskirts to house hotel employees and the airport is about to undergo major expansion. With everything centered around the town square, Lanai City embraces almost the entire population of the island. Situated at the center of the island at an elevation midway between the beach and the mountain peaks, it is cool and breezy with a temperate climate.

Nevertheless, the really interesting places on Lanai lie outside town, and most require driving or hiking over jeep trails. It's advisable to get specific directions wherever you go, since the maze of pineapple roads can confuse even the most intrepid pathfinder. Where possible, I've included directions; otherwise, check with the jeep rental shop in Lanai City or at the hotels.

To be extra safe, ask about road conditions, too. The slightest rain can turn a dusty jeep road into a slick surface, and a downpour can transmogrify it into an impassable quagmire. I once dumped a jeep into a three-foot ditch when the trail to Polihua Beach collapsed. It had been raining steadily for three days and the soft shoulder couldn't support the weight of a vehicle. I was 11 miles from Lanai City with the wheels hopelessly embedded and an hour left until dark.

The way back led past pretty menacing country, heavily eroded and difficult to track through. Rain clouds brought the night on in a rush. I gathered up my poncho and canteen, convinced myself that the worst to come would be a cold and wet night outdoors, and began trekking back to civilization. Fortunately, after five miserable hours I made it. But the entire incident could have been avoided if I had first checked road conditions and had allowed at least several hours of daylight for my return.

This shouldn't discourage you, though. With the proper precautions, exploring Lanai can be a unique experience, challenging but safe. To make things easy, I'll start with a journey to the island's northeastern shore, part of which is over a paved road. Then I'll continue clockwise around the island.

LODGING

Prior to the 1990s the only inn on the entire island was the **Hotel Lanai,** a modest mountain retreat. Set 1600 feet above sea level and surrounded by Norfolk pines, it offers clean, medium-sized rooms equipped with private baths. The lodge was built in the '20s, as was most of Lanai City, but was refurbished several years ago when it passed to new management. It features a restaurant and lounge, and is a local gathering place. A lot of folks hang out in the lobby here, making for a warm, friendly atmosphere, and the staff is congenial. Choose between small standard rooms, medium-sized accommodations, and rooms with lanais. There are only ten units in this U-shaped hostelry, so reservations can be troublesome if even a dozen of tourists or locals descend on the island. It's advisable to arrange transportation with the hotel at the time of making reser-

LANAI EXPERIENCES

- Stay at the **Hotel Lanai,** a 1920s-era retreat that until a few years ago was the only hotel on the entire island. (p. 167)
- Search for glass fishing balls and nautilus shells on a strand named for the rusting hulls offshore—**Shipwreck Beach.** (p. 171)
- Follow the **Munro Trail** to the top of Lanai for a crow's nest view of Oahu, Maui, Molokai and Hawaii. (p. 172)
- Look but don't jump from **Kahekili's Leap,** where ancient Hawaiian warriors once plunged from a cliff. (p. 175)
- Hike through the **Garden of the Gods,** whose eroded landscape makes it Hawaii's answer to the Dakota Badlands. (p. 176)

vations. ~ P.O. Box 520, Lanai City, HI 96763; 565-7211, 800-321-4666, fax 565-4713. DELUXE.

The **Lodge at Koele**, a fashionable 102-room hideaway, is a study in style and decorum. The most noteworthy feature is the lobby, a vaulted-ceiling affair faced on either end with a stone fireplace that rises to the roofline. Etched-glass skylights extend the length of the room, illuminating the "great hall." The Victorian guest rooms are done with four-poster beds, lacquer boxes, statuettes and decorative plates. To make sure you remember that even here amid the Norfolk pines you are still in Hawaii, an overhead fan beats the air in languid motions.

Backdropped by mountains and surrounded by miles of pineapple fields, the emphasis at the Lodge is on staying put. There are cloisters lined with wicker chairs, a croquet court, a swimming pool and two jacuzzis that look out on field and forest, and a congenial staff to take care of every request. ~ P.O. Box 774, Lanai City, HI 96763; 565-7300, 800-321-4666, fax 565-3868. ULTRA-DELUXE.

DINING

The **Hotel Lanai** offers wholesome meals at modest prices. The dinner menu features an assortment of steak, seafood and other platters, plus sandwiches and burgers. Decorated with island photographs along the knotty pine walls, this is a cozy place to share a meal. You can strike up a conversation with a local resident, sit back and enjoy the mountain air or bask in the glow of the restaurant's two fireplaces. Watch the hours, though, or you'll get shut out. Continental breakfast is served only from 7:00 to 9:30 a.m., and dinner from 5:30 to 9 p.m. ~ Lanai City; 565-7211. MODERATE TO DELUXE.

If the hotel restaurant is closed, Lanai City has two alternatives. The first is **S. T. Property**, a luncheonette that serves breakfast, lunch and dinner. ~ 711 Lanai Avenue; 565-6537. BUDGET.

HIDDEN ►   Your second alternative, the **Blue Ginger Café**, rests in an old plantation house and serves three solid meals a day. Simple draw-

You can discover for yourself whether **Dreams Come True on Lanai**. That's what Michael and Susan Hunter, two local jewelry makers, claim can happen when you stay in the six-bedroom house they transformed into one of the island's only bed and breakfasts. Set in Lanai City and surrounded by fruit trees and flowering gardens, the house is decorated with hand-carved screens and furniture that the owners transported from Sri Lanka and Bali. There's a large living room for guests as well as a selection of single and double rooms, some with canopied four-poster beds. ~ 547 12th Street, Lanai City; 565-7065, 800-566-6961. MODERATE.

ings of tropical fish adorn the place and the red paint on the cement floor has worn away almost completely. But the white walls shine and the dinners are served piping hot. Breakfasts and plate lunches are pretty standard, but the evening meal is sophisticated enough to include sirloin steak, *saimin*, shrimp Cantonese and lemon chicken. ~ 409 7th Street; 565-6363. MODERATE.

On Lanai, isolation is the engine of ingenuity. Confronted with all that land and so few people, The Lodge at Koele transformed sections of the island into an organic garden, hog farm and cattle ranch. After adding a master chef, they had the ingredients for two gourmet restaurants that would be the pride not only of tiny Lanai but any island. Meals in The Terrace and The Formal Dining Room (jackets required) are as enticing as the hotel's sumptuous surroundings.

The Terrace serves breakfast, lunch and dinner in a more casual atmosphere. Here the day begins with sweet rice waffles and *lilikoi*-coconut chutney, breakfast bread pudding, or bacon and eggs fresh from the farm. By evening the chef progresses to steamed seafood gyoza, and oven-braised lamb shank with herbed polenta, as well as vegetarian specialties. ~ 565-7300. DELUXE.

The Formal Dining Room serves dinner only; feast on roasted rack of lamb or Lanai venison loin with mashed sweet potatoes. Both restaurants overlook the back of the lodge grounds, with views of the fishpond, fountain and orchid house. ~ 565-7300. ULTRA-DELUXE.

GROCERIES For standard food needs, try **Richard's Shopping Center**. This "shopping center" is really only a small grocery store with a dry goods department. Richard's is open Monday through Saturday from 8:30 a.m. to noon and from 1:30 to 6:30 p.m. ~ 8th Street, Lanai City; 565-6047.

If, by some strange circumstance, you can't find what you're seeking here, head down the street to **Pine Isle Market**. Open daily from 8 a.m. to noon and 1:30 to 7 p.m. Closed Sunday. ~ 565-6488.

SHOPPING Granted, it doesn't have much competition (in fact it doesn't have any competition), but **Heart of Lanai Art Gallery** in Lanai City would be remarkable regardless of where it was located. Many of the paintings and sculptures were done by local artists and depict the plantation culture that was once Lanai's lifeblood but is now fast becoming its legacy. Closed Sunday. ~ 363 7th Street; 565-6678.

Otherwise, you will have to seek out the gift shop at The **Lodge at Koele** (565-7300) or the **Hotel Lanai** (565-7211).

NIGHTLIFE Visitors find this a great spot to get the sleep they missed in Lahaina or Honolulu. If rest isn't a problem, Lanai may be a good place to catch up on your reading or letter writing. One thing is certain— once the sun goes down, there'll be little to distract you. You can have a drink while listening to local gossip at the **Hotel Lanai** (565-7211) or while mixing with the gentry at **The Lodge at Koele** (565-7300), where the lounge possesses a kind of gentlemen's library atmosphere with an etched-glass-and-hardwood interior. But on an average evening, even these night owl's nests will be closed by 10 o'clock. In addition to its plush lounge, The Lodge at Koele features hula dancers on weekends at lunchtime or other live entertainment in the lobby (The Grand Hall) at night.

Northeast—Shipwreck Beach and Naha

From Lanai City, Route 430 (Keomuku Road) winds north through hot, arid country. The scrub growth and red soil in this barren area resemble a bleak southwestern landscape, but the sweeping views of Maui and Molokai could be found only in Hawaii.

By the way, those stones piled atop one another along the road are neither an expression of ancient Hawaiian culture nor proof of the latest UFO landing. They were placed there by imaginative hikers. Each one is an *ahu*, representative of a local tradition in which columns of three or so stones are built to help ensure good luck.

Near the end of the macadam road you can turn left onto a dirt road. This track leads past colonies of intermittently inhabited squatters' shacks, many built from the hulks of vessels grounded on nearby **Shipwreck Beach**. The coral reef paralleling the beach has been a nemesis to sailors since whaling days. The rusting remains of a barge and a 1950s-era oil tanker still bear witness to the navigational hazards along this coast. Needless to say, this is one of the best areas in Hawaii for beachcombing. Look in particular for the Japanese glass fishing floats that are carried here on currents all the way from Asia.

HIDDEN ► At the end of the dirt road, a path marked with white paint leads to clusters of ancient **petroglyphs** depicting simple island scenes. Those interested in extensively exploring the coast can hike all the way from Shipwreck eight miles west to Polihua Beach along jeep trails and shoreline.

Back on the main road (continuing straight ahead as if you had never made that left turn that led to Shipwreck Beach) you will discover that the macadam gives way to a dirt road that leads along the northeast shore for 12 teeth-clicking miles. It was along this now-deserted coast that the ancient Hawaiian population lived. Numbering perhaps 2000 in pre-Western times, they fished the coast and cultivated taro.

The ghost town of **Keomuku**, marked by a ramshackle church that is being refurbished, lies six miles down the road. It's another mile and a half to **Kahea Heiau**, a holy place that many claim is the reason Keomuku was deserted. It seems that stones from this temple were used to build the nearby Maunalei Sugar Company plantation despite warnings against disturbing the sacred rocks. So when the plantation failed in 1901 after its sweet water mysteriously turned brackish, the Hawaiians had a heavenly explanation. It was shortly after this incident that most of the rest of Lanai's populace moved up to Lanai City, leaving only spirits along the coast.

Club Lanai, the waterfront complex that caters to day visitors from Maui, is located along the beach nearby. One way to spend just a day on Lanai is to catch a round-trip catamaran ride from Lahaina with this outfit. You'll land at a seven-acre visitor park along a sandy beach on the island's eastern shore. This private facility provides a dining area and bar as well as an array of equipment for beach and water sports. Guests snorkel on a coral reef, learn Hawaiian arts and crafts, and stroll along the strand. They do not, however, get an opportunity to tour around the island. Meals are provided. All you do is show up at Pier 4 in Lahaina Harbor at 6:45 a.m. to board a catamaran that returns you to Lahaina around 3:30 p.m. ~ 871-1144.

Several miles farther, past numerous salt-and-pepper-colored beaches, the road ends at the old Hawaiian village of **Naha**. Today nothing remains of this once prosperous colony.

> When James Dole bought Lanai in 1922, he paid $1.1 million for the entire island.

BEACHES & PARKS

SHIPWRECK BEACH This strand is actually a string of small sandy patches that stretches for eight miles along the north coast, all the way to Polihua Beach. The glass fishing balls, driftwood and occasional nautilus shells on the beach make this a beachcomber's paradise. The remains of misguided ships that gave the beach its name also add to the allure. It's often windy. You can swim here but the water is shallow and you must beware of sharp coral—a protecting reef is 200 yards offshore. Snorkeling is not advised because of sharks. There's good diving for lobsters, but again, be cautious! You'll find good fishing for *ulua*, *papio* and octopus in the area between the squatters' houses and the petroglyphs. There are no established facilities at the beach. ~ Located ten miles north of Lanai City. Head north on Route 430 (Keomuku Road) and turn left at the end of the paved road. See the "Northeast—Shipwreck Beach and Naha" section above for more details.

HALEPALAOA BEACH AND NAHA BEACH A string of salt-and-pepper-colored sand beaches lies along the 12-mile dirt road to Naha. While most are unattractive and crowded with shoals, they do offer great views of Molokai, Maui and Kahoolawe. The Naha road winds in and out along the seafront, with numerous access roads leading to the shore. The prettiest strand is Halepalaoa Beach, a mile-long white-sand corridor partially bordered by sand dunes. Club Lanai, a day-trip center for visitors from Maui, is located here. These are swimming beaches; most are well-protected by shoals, but the waters are shallow. Snorkeling is a possibility here but beware of currents. You can also fish here. Several beaches, including Naha, have small picnic areas ~ Take Route 430 north from Lanai City and continue on after it turns southward and becomes a dirt road. The dirt road extends for about 12 miles, ending at Naha; Halepalaoa Beach is about seven miles out along the dirt road.

Munro Trail

HIDDEN ►

Named for New Zealand naturalist George Munro, this seven-mile jeep trail climbs through rainforest and stands of conifers en route to **Lanaihale**, the highest point on Lanai. From this 3370-foot perch you can see every major Hawaiian island except Kauai.

On the way to Lanaihale, about two miles up the trail, you'll pass **Hookio Gulch**. The ridge beyond is carved with a defense work of protective notches made by warriors who tried futilely to defend Lanai against invaders from Hawaii in 1778.

A footpath leads to an overlook above 2000-foot deep **Hauola Gulch**, Lanai's deepest canyon. Here you may see axis deer clinging to the sharp rockfaces, seeming to defy gravity as they pick their way along the heights.

This knife-edge ridge, little more than 100 feet wide in places, is studded with ironwood and eucalyptus trees, as well as the stately Norfolk pines that New Zealand naturalist George Munro personally planted along the heights. From this aerie the slopes fall away to reveal the twin humps of Maui. The Big Island rests far below you, anchored in open ocean. The sea itself is a flat, shimmering expanse.

From Lanaihale you can either turn around or continue and descend through open fields to Hoike Road, which connects with Route 440. The Munro Trail begins in Koele off Route 430 (Keomuku Road) about a mile north of Lanai City. Be sure to check road conditions and try to go early in the morning before clouds gather along the ridgetop. While it's rough going at times, the trail affords such magnificent views from its windswept heights that it simply must not be ignored by the adventurous sightseer.

Southeast— Manele Bay

HIDDEN ►

Heading south from Lanai City on Route 440 (Manele Road), you'll be traveling through the Palawai Basin, the caldera of the extinct volcano that formed the island. This was also the heart of Lanai's once extensive pineapple plantation.

The explorer can detour off the main highway to the **Luahiwa petroglyphs**. Finding them requires obtaining explicit directions, then driving through a field, and finally climbing a short distance up a steep bluff. But the Luahiwa petroglyphs—portraying human figures, deer, paddles and turtles—are among the finest rock carvings in Hawaii and are definitely worth the search. As you approach each cluster of boulders, you'll see pictographic stories begin to unfold. One in particular depicts a large outrigger canoe, sails unfurled, being loaded Noah-style with livestock. Preparing, perhaps, for the ancient migration north to the Hawaiian Islands? To locate the petroglyphs, head south from Lanai City on Route 440. Turn left at the first dirt road. Follow the lower road as it curves along the bottom of the hillside. After passing below a watertank and pipeline, the road forks and you follow the left fork. The road goes into a horseshoe curve; when you come out of the curve there will be black boulders on the hillside above you to the left. Spread across a few acres, they contain the petroglyphs.

Covered in scrub vegetation along much of its surface, Lanai still supports several rare endemic bird species as well as axis deer, mouflon sheep and pronghorn antelope.

The main road leads through agricultural fields and winds down to the twin bays at **Manele Small Boat Harbor** and **Hulopoe Bay**, which together comprise a marine life conservation area. Just offshore from the cinder cone that separates these two harbors is a sea stack, **Puu Pehe**, known not only for its beauty but its legends as well. Puu Pehe was a lovely Maui girl kidnapped by a Lanai warrior who kept her hidden in a sea cave. One day when he went off in search of water, a huge sea wave swept the girl to her death. Stricken with grief and remorse, the young warrior buried her on top of the rock island and then jumped to his death from its heights.

The small-boat harbor at Manele, rimmed by lava cliffs along the far shore, contains ruins of ancient Hawaiian houses. You'll also see an old wooden chute protruding from the rocks, a loading platform used years ago to lead cattle onto ships. Today this rock-rimmed anchorage is a mooring place for fishing boats and yachts. Hulopoe offers the island's finest beach, a crescent of white sand with gentle waves, crystalline waters and a fine park facility. You'll find the stone ruins of an ancient Hawaiian home and canoe house at the north end of the beach. Just above the beach, on the grounds in front of the plush Manele Bay Hotel, stands the remains of an *ahu* or traditional Hawaiian shrine.

LODGING

While The Lodge at Koele is situated at 1600-feet elevation in Lanai City, eight miles from the ocean, Lanai's other fashionable new resort, the **Manele Bay Hotel** is a traditional beachfront resort. Set on a bluff overlooking the best beach on the island, it is a 250-room extravaganza designed along both Asian and Mediterranean lines and surrounded by artistically planted gardens. Elegance here is in no way subdued: It speaks from the stone floors and white columns, the dark-paneled library and the recessed ceilings. The two-tiered lobby combines art deco windows with traditional Hawaiian murals; the lower level is a terrace with glass doors that open onto ocean views.

Guest rooms look out either on the beach or the grounds, which are sculpted into five different theme gardens—Japanese, Bromeliad, Hawaiian, Chinese and Cosmopolitan. Each room is spacious, done in pastel hues and decorated with Asian armoires and color sketches of Hawaiian flora. The four-poster beds are accented with quilts and upholstered throw pillows. Add a four-leaf clover-shaped pool, six tennis courts, spa and workout room and you will realize that sleepy little Lanai is never going to be the same again. ~ 565-7700, 800-321-4666, fax 565-3868. ULTRA-DELUXE.

DINING   Outside Lanai City the dining choices, a grand total of three, are concentrated at the Manele Bay Hotel. Here, ladies and gentlemen, lunch is served at the **Pool Grille** on a bougainvillea-covered terrace. Set poolside just above the beach, this patio dining facility features island salads, including a seasonal fruit offering. There is also a standard assortment of sandwiches, as well as grilled mahimahi on *nori* bread and other specialties. Lunch only. ~ 565-7700. MODERATE.

This spacious resort offers more formal dining in the **Hulopoe Court Restaurant**, a high-ceiling dining room with glass doors that open onto a veranda overlooking the ocean. Island murals adorn the walls and pineapple motif chandeliers dominate the room. The decor blends Asian and Polynesian styles and the menu features Hawaiian regional cuisine. Breakfast and dinner only. ~ 565-7700. DELUXE.

Sweeping views of Hulopoe Bay star at the **Ihilani Dining Room**. The menu features French-Mediterranean cuisine and specializes in duck, lamb and fresh fish dishes. The service is formal, and the wine list extensive. Dinner only. ~ 565-7700. ULTRA-DELUXE.

NIGHTLIFE   Down along Hulopoe Beach at the Manele Bay Hotel, the **Hale Ahe Ahe Lounge** combines several different settings, each equally inviting. The lounge itself has dark textured walls, a hardwood bar and a clubby ambience. It features piano or contemporary Hawaiian music nightly. Out on the terrace you can settle into a comfortable armchair or lean against the rail and enjoy the ocean view. The adjacent Holokai Room is a game room complete with backgammon board and an air of relaxed elegance. ~ 565-2000.

BEACHES & PARKS   **HULOPOE BEACH PARK** Lanai's finest beach also possesses the island's only fully developed park. Set in a half-moon inlet and fringed with *kiawe* trees, this white-sand beach is an excellent spot for all sorts of recreation. It is also the site of the 250-room Manele Bay Hotel, which rests on a bluff about 50 yards above the waterfront. Part of a marine life conservation area, Hulopoe has a lava terrace with outstanding tidepools along its eastern point. There is also a wading area for children at this end of the park. If you continue a short distance along this eastern shoreline you'll also encounter **Puu Pehe Cove**, a small beach with abundant marine life that is excellent for swimming and snorkeling. Little wonder that Hulopoe is the island's favorite picnic spot. It's also recommended for surfing and fishing. Prime catches are threadfin, *ulua*, and bonefish. This is the most accessible surf-casting beach on the island. There are permanent restrooms and showers. ~ To get there take Route 440 (Manele Road) south from Lanai City for eight miles.

▲ This is it—the only campground on the island! There are six campsites at the far end of the beach. Expect to pay a $5 registration fee plus a charge of $5 per camper per day. Permits are issued by the Lanai Company. ~ P.O. Box 310, Lanai City, Lanai, HI 96763; 565-8200.

MANELE BAY 🏊 ⛵ 🐟 Primarily a small-boat harbor, this cliff-fringed inlet is populated by sailboats from across the Pacific. Carouse with the crews, walk along the jetty or scramble up the rocks for a knockout view of Haleakala on Maui. It's a very good place for swimming since the harbor is well protected, but you need to be wary of boat traffic. Because Manele Bay is part of a marine preserve the snorkeling is notable and the fishing is limited. Only pole fishing is allowed—no nets. There's a park for picnicking, and just around the corner at Hulopoe Beach are facilities for camping, swimming and other sports. ~ Located Route 440 south of Lanai City.

▼▼▼▼▼▼▼▼▼▼▼▼▼▼▼▼▼▼
Southwest—Kaumalapau Harbor and Kaunolu

A southwesterly course along Route 440 (Kaumalapau Highway) will carry you steadily downhill for about six miles to **Kaumalapau Harbor**. This busy little harbor was built by pineapple interests and used primarily to ship the fruit on barges to Honolulu. During the heyday of Lanai's pineapple industry, more than a million pineapples a day were loaded onto waiting ships. On either side of Kaumalapau, you can see the *pali*, which rises straight up as high as 1000 feet, protecting Lanai's southwestern flank. These lofty sea cliffs are an ideal vantage point for watching the sunset.

The most interesting point along this route involves a detour near the airport and a journey down a *very* rugged jeep trail to **Kaunolu Village**. A summer retreat of Kamehameha the Great and now a national historic landmark, this ancient fishing community still contains the ruins of more than 80 houses as well as stone shelters, petroglyphs and graves. Pick your way through it carefully, lest you step on a ghost. Kamehameha's house, once perched on the eastern ridge, looked across to **Halulu Heiau** on the west side of Kaunolu Bay. Commanding a dominant view of the entire region, these rocky remains are bounded on three sides by cliffs that vault 1000 feet from the ocean.

◄ HIDDEN

From nearby **Kahekili's Leap**, warriors proved their courage by plunging more than 60 feet into the water below. If they cleared a

15-foot outcropping and survived the free fall into 12 feet of water, they were deemed noble soldiers worthy of their great king.

Just offshore from this daredevil launching pad lies **Shark Island**, a rock formation that bears an uncanny resemblance to a shark fin. Could it be that warriors skilled enough to survive Kahekili's Leap had then to confront the malevolent spirit of a shark?

Northwest – Polihua Beach

HIDDEN ►

From Lanai City, a graded pineapple road that disintegrates into an ungraded dirt track leads about seven miles to the **Garden of the God**. This heavily eroded area resembles the Dakota Badlands and features multihued boulders that change color dramatically during sunrise and sunset. A fantasy land of stone, the Garden of the Gods is planted with ancient lava flows tortured by the elements into as many suggestive shapes as the imagination can conjure. The colors here vibrate with psychedelic intensity and the rocks loom up around you as though they were the gods themselves—hard, cold, dark beings possessed of untold power and otherworldly beauty.

Past this surreal and sacred spot, Polihua Trail, a rugged jeep road, descends several miles to the ocean. **Polihua Beach**, stretching more than a mile and a half, is the longest and widest white-sand beach on the island. Once a prime nesting beach for green sea turtles, it is an excellent spot to watch whales as they pass close by the shoreline

BEACHES & PARKS

HIDDEN ►

POLIHUA BEACH   A wide white-sand beach situated along Lanai's northwest shore, this isolated strand, with a stunning view of Molokai, rivals Kauai's trackless beaches. Swimming is allowed here but exercise caution—strong winds and currents prevail throughout this region. The water here is sometimes muddy but when it's clear, and when the Fish and Game Division declares it "in season," you can dive for lobsters. According to local fishermen, this is the best spot on the island for fishing. Common catches include *papio*, *ulua*, bonefish, threadfin and red snapper. There are no facilities here. ~ It's about 11 miles from Lanai City through pineapple fields and the Garden of the Gods. The last half of the drive is over a rugged jeep trail. For specific directions and road conditions, check with the jeep rental garages.

Outdoor Adventures

CAMPING

With so much virgin territory, Lanai should be ideal for camping. But here, as on the other islands, landowners restrict outdoors lovers. The villain is the outfit that manages the island. It permits island residents to camp where they like, but herds visitors into one area on the south coast. This campsite, at Hulopoe Beach, has facilities for six sites. Once filled to capacity, no other camping is permitted on the entire island! So make reservations early.

The premier course on the island is one designed by Greg Norman and Ted Robinson, **The Experience at Koele**. ~ 565-7300.

The nine-hole **Cavendish Golf Course**, also in Lanai City, is open to the public as well. ~ No phone.

Or try **Challenge at Manele**, a newly opened 18-hole golf course at the Manele Bay Hotel. ~ 565-7700.

GOLF

Call the County Department of Parks and Recreation for information on the public courts in Lanai City. ~ 565-7878.

Courts are available at **The Lodge at Koele** ~ Lanai City; 565-7300; and the **Manele Bay Hotel** ~ near Hulopoe Beach; 565-7700.

TENNIS

The Lodge at Koele offers horseback riding and equestrian tours. Choose between five rides that take you on various trails around the lodge. The Koele Ride is an hour-long leisurely walking ride that follows a wooded trail and gives riders stunning views of Maui, Molokai and Lanai City. ~ 565-7300.

RIDING STABLES

Given the lack of paved roads, bicycle use is somewhat restricted on Lanai. There are a few nice rides from Lanai City, but all are steep in places and pass over pockmarked sections of road. One goes south eight miles to Manele Bay and the beach at Hulopoe, another diverts west to busy little Kaumalapau Harbor, and the last heads north 14 miles to Shipwreck Beach.

Lanai City Service Inc. is a good place to obtain information concerning Lanai roads. ~ 565-7227.

BICYCLING

Hikers on Lanai are granted much greater freedom than campers. Jeep trails and access roads are open to the public; the only restriction is that hikers cannot camp along trails. Since most of the trails lead either to beaches or points of interest, you'll find them described in the regional sightseeing and "Beaches and Parks" sections above.

In addition to these listings, there are two other trails to consider. The **Ancient Graveyard Trail** (.5 mile) winds to a picturesque graveyard that has been used since ancient times.

The **Koloiki Ridge Trail** (5 miles) leads through forest lands and the Cathedral of Pines (a group of pines resembling a gothic church) to a ridge that runs between Naio Gulch and Maunalei Valley. This moderately difficult hike provides views of Molokai and Maui.

HIKING

Planes to Lanai land at **Lanai Airport** amid an endless maze of tilled fields four miles from downtown Lanai City. This tiny landing strip, slated for major expansion, currently has a small gift shop and a courtesy telephone for car rentals (you'll be picked up in a shuttle). There are no lockers or public transportation. A few rooms house airline offices. Hawaiian

▼▼▼▼▼▼▼▼▼▼▼

Transportation

BY AIR

Airlines offers jet service to the islands; Aloha Island Air flies propeller-driven planes and features competitive rates. ~ 565-6757.

If you're staying at any of the island hotels, they will provide transportation into town, as will any of the island's car rental agencies if you're renting a vehicle from them.

BY BOAT

A ferry service called **Expeditions** operates out of Maui and links Lahaina with Manele Bay on Lanai. There are five boats per day in each direction. The 45-minute crossing provides a unique way to arrive on the island. ~ P.O. Box 10, Lahaina, HI 96767; 661-3756.

CAR & JEEP RENTALS

Lanai City Service Inc., which is affiliated with Dollar Rent A Car, rents automatic compact cars with free mileage. But renting a car on Lanai is like carrying water wings to the desert: there's simply nowhere to go. Rental cars are restricted to pavement, while most of Lanai's roads are jeep trails: four-wheel drive is the only way to fly. ~ 1036 Lanai Avenue; 565-7227.

The first time I visited the island of Lanai, I rented a vintage 1942 jeep. The vehicle had bad brakes, no emergency brake, malfunctioning windshield wipers and no seat belts. It was, however, equipped with an efficient shock absorber—me. Today, Lanai City Services Inc., described above, rents new and reliable jeeps. (Be aware that the rental car collision insurance provided by most credit cards does not cover jeeps.)

BOAT TOURS

There are boat tours of Lanai offered by several Maui-based outfits. Among them are **Trilogy** (661-8110), and **Sentinel Yacht Charters** (661-4743).

HITCHING

Officially, it's illegal, but actually it's common. The folks in these parts are pretty friendly, so rides are easy to get. The trick lies in finding someone who's going as far as you are—like all the way out to Shipwreck Beach or out to the Garden of the Gods.

ELEVEN

Molokai

Between the bustling islands of Oahu and Maui lies an isle which in shape resembles Manhattan, but which in spirit and rhythm is far more than an ocean away from the smog-shrouded shores of the Big Apple. Molokai, Hawaii's fifth-largest island, is thirty-eight miles long and ten miles wide. The slender isle was created by three volcanoes that mark its present geographic regions: one at West End where the arid Mauna Loa tableland rises to 1381 feet, another at East End where a rugged mountain range along the north coast is topped by 4970-foot Mount Kamakou, and the third, a geologic afterthought, which created the low, flat Kalaupapa Peninsula.

Considering that the island measures a modest 260 square miles, its geographic diversity is amazing. Arriving at Hoolehua Airport near the island's center, travelers feel as though they have touched down somewhere in the American Midwest. Red dust, dry heat and curving prairie surround the small landing strip and extend to the west end of Molokai. This natural pastureland gives way in the southcentral region to low-lying, relatively swampy ground and brown-sand beaches with murky water.

The prettiest strands lie along the western shore, where Papohaku Beach forms one of the largest white-sand beaches in the state, and at the east end around Halawa Valley, a region of heavy rainfall and lush tropic vegetation. To the north is the vaunted pali, which rises in a vertical wall 2000 feet from the surf, creating the tallest sea cliffs in the world. Here, too, is an awesome succession of sharp, narrow valleys cloaked in green moss.

Kaunakakai, a sleepy port town on the south shore, is the island's hub. From here a road runs to the eastern and western coasts. Kalaupapa and the northern *pali* are accessible overland only by mule and hiking trails.

Even in a region of islands, Molokai has always been something of a backwater. To the early Hawaiians it appeared desiccated and inhospitable and they named it *molo*, "barren," *kai*, "sea." The rich Halawa Valley was settled in the 7th century and the island developed a haunting reputation for sorcery and mystical occurrences. In ancient times it was also called *pule-oo*, or "powerful prayer," and was revered for the potency of its priests.

When Captain James Cook "discovered" the island in November 1778, he found it bleak and inhospitable. Not until 1786 did a Western navigator, Captain George Dixon, bother to land. When Kamehameha the Great took it in 1795, he was actually en route to the much grander prize of Oahu. His war canoes are said to have loomed along four miles of shoreline when he attacked the island at Pakuhiwa Battleground and slaughtered the island's outnumbered defenders.

The next wave of invaders arrived in 1832 when Protestant missionaries introduced the Polynesians to the marvels of Christianity. Around 1850 a German immigrant named Rudolph Meyer arrived in Molokai, married a Hawaiian chieftess, and began a reign as manager of the Molokai Ranch that lasted for almost a half-century.

Leprosy struck the Hawaiian Islands during the 19th century, and wind-plagued Kalaupapa Peninsula became the living hell to which the disease's victims were exiled. Beginning in 1866, lepers were torn from their families and literally cast to their fates along this stark shore. Here Father Damien de Veuster, a Belgian priest, the Martyr of Molokai, came to live, work and eventually die among the afflicted.

For years Molokai was labeled "The Lonely Isle" or "The Forgotten Isle." By 1910 a population that once totaled 10,000 had decreased to one-tenth the size. Then in 1921, Polynesians began settling homesteads under the Hawaiian Homes Act, which granted a 40-acre homestead to anyone with over 50 percent Hawaiian ancestry. Molokai eventually became "The Friendly Isle," with the largest proportion of native Hawaiians anywhere in the world (except for the island of Niihau, which is closed to outsiders). With them they brought a legacy from old Hawaii, the spirit of aloha, which still lives on this marvelous island. Young Hawaiians, sometimes hostile on the more crowded islands, are often outgoing and generous here. And of all the islands, Molokai offers you the best opportunity to "go native" by staying with a Hawaiian family.

During the 1920s, while Hawaiians were being granted the hardscrabble land that had not already been bought up on the island, Libby (which later sold out to Dole) and Del Monte began producing pineapples across the richer stretches of the island. The company towns of Maunaloa and Kualapuu sprang up and Molokai's rolling prairies became covered with fields of spike-topped fruits. Over the

years competition from Asia became increasingly intense, forcing Dole to shut its operation in 1975 and Del Monte to pull out in 1982.

As elsewhere in Hawaii, the economic powers realized that if they couldn't grow crops they had better cultivate tourists. During the 1970s thousands of acres along the island's western end were allocated for resort and residential development and the sprawling Kaluakoi Resort was built. While this hotel and condominium complex has only been marginally successful, a master plan for future development, bitterly opposed by native Hawaiians and environmentalists, is still in the works. In 1996, vandals destroyed five miles of water pipes on Molokai Ranch, which had earlier closed access to several beaches and evicted a number of former plantation workers from their homes.

Today the island's population numbers about 7000. It still does not possess a single traffic light or elevator and the weak economy has saved it from the ravages of development that plagued the rest of Hawaii during the 1980s. Change is coming, but like everything on Molokai, it is arriving slowly. Time still remains to see Hawaii as it once was and to experience the trackless beaches, vaulting seacliffs, sweeping ranchlands and forested mountains that led ancient Hawaiians to believe in the mystical powers of Molokai.

▼▼▼▼▼▼▼▼▼▼▼▼▼▼▼▼▼▼
Kaunakakai to East End

You don't need a scorecard, or even a map for that matter, to keep track of the sightseeing possibilities on Molokai. Across its brief expanse, the Friendly Isle offers several rewards to the curious, none of which are difficult to find.

First of course is the falsefront town of Kaunakakai, a commercial hub that more resembles a way station on the road to Dodge City. From here a simple two-lane road, Route 450 (Kamehameha V Highway), threads its way along the southern shore in search of the Halawa Valley at the far east end of the island.

It is only too appropriate that **Kaunakakai** gained its greatest fame from someone who never existed. Known for a song written about "The Cock-eyed Mayor of Kaunakakai," the town has in fact had only one mayor—whether he was cock-eyed, no one will say. This somnolent village, with its falsefront buildings and tiny civic center, is administered from Maui. Poor but proud, it possesses a population of fewer than 3000, and has a main drag (Ala Malama Street) that extends a grand total of three blocks but still represents the hub of Molokai.

Nearby is the **wharf**, extending seaward almost a half-mile and offering a mooring place for a few fishing boats, charter outfits, and private sailboats. A good place to gaze out on the island of Lanai, it is also an ideal vantage from which to take in the velvet green slopes that rise toward the ridgeline of Molokai.

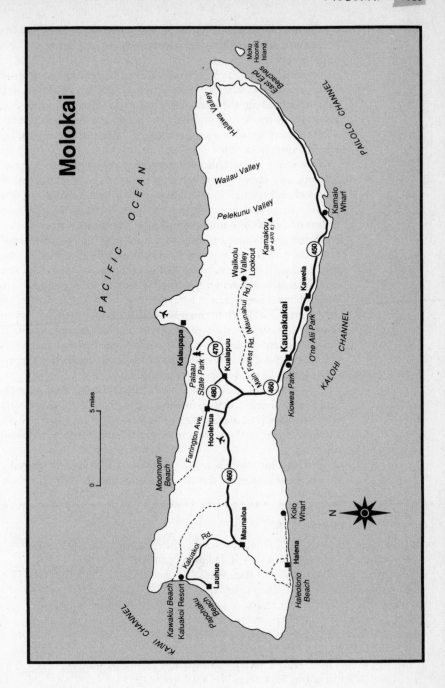

Molokai

Close to the pier landing rest the rocky remains of **Kamehameha V's Summer Home**, where Hawaii's king luxuriated during the late-19th century.

From Kaunakakai to Halawa Valley, a narrow macadam road leads past almost 30 miles of seascapes and historic sites. Route 450 runs straight along the south shore for about 20 miles, presenting views across the Kalohi and Pailolo channels to Lanai and Maui. Then the road snakes upward and curves inland before descending again into Halawa Valley.

Due to the calm, shallow waters along the southeastern shoreline, this area once supported one of the greatest concentrations of fishponds in Hawaii. Numbering as many as five dozen during the pre-Western period, these ancient aquaculture structures were built of lava and coral by commoners to raise fish for Hawaiian royalty. Small fish were trapped within these stone pens, fattened and eventually harvested. You will see the rebuilt remains of several as you drive along the coast, including **Kalokoeli Fishpond**, two miles east of Kaunakakai, **Keawanui Fishpond**, about 12 miles east of town, and **Ualapue Fishpond**, a mile farther east.

About five miles from town lies Kawela, once an ancient city of refuge, now known as the place where two battles were fought at **Pakuhiwa Battleground**. In his drive to become Hawaii's first monarch, Kamehameha the Great launched a canoe flotilla that reportedly extended four miles along this shore.

This is also the site of **Kakahaia National Wildlife Refuge**, a 42-acre habitat that is a nesting area for a dozen species of coastal and sea birds. Centered around Kakahaia Beach Park, the preserve includes a 15-acre freshwater pond that rests immediately inland from the coast.

Just past the ten-mile marker (indicating that you are ten miles east of Kaunakakai), a dirt road leads to **Kamalo Wharf**, an old

MOLOKAI EXPERIENCES

- Ride a mule down the world's highest seacliffs along a harrowing succession of switchbacks to the windblasted **Kalaupapa Peninsula**. (p. 198)
- Cruise to Maui aboard the 118-foot **Maui Princess** while watching the waters for dolphins and humpback whales. (p. 202)
- Try the Molokai honey, bread and pastries at **Kanemitsu's Bakery** then step out onto the main street of a town that has no traffic lights. (p. 187)
- Have an early evening drink, catch a Molokai sunset and "talk story" with local folks at the **Pau Hana Inn**. (p. 189)
- Wander the beach in **Halawa Valley** and explore a luxurious agricultural region inhabited by Hawaiians for 1300 years. (p. 186)

pineapple and cattle shipping point. This natural harbor, once a major commercial center (by Molokai standards!), is now a gathering place for occasional fishermen and boats.

It's a half-mile farther to **St. Joseph Catholic Church**, a tiny chapel built by Father Damien in 1876. A statue of the bespectacled priest, clad in a cape and leaning on a cane, graces the property. A small cemetery completes this placid tableau.

A monument (past the 11-mile marker) designates the **Smith and Bronte Landing**, an inhospitable spot where two aviators crash-landed after completing the first civilian transpacific flight in 1927. The 25-hour flight from California, scheduled to land in Honolulu, ended abruptly when the plane ran out of gas. (An opening in the trees past the 12-mile marker reveals the aforementioned Keawanui Fishpond, one of Molokai's largest.)

Set back from the road in a clearing framed by mountains is **Our Lady of Seven Sorrows Catholic Church** (14 miles east of Kaunakakai). Originally built by Father Damien in 1874 and reconstructed almost a century later, it's a pretty chapel surrounded by coconut trees and flanked by a small cemetery.

One of the largest temples in the islands, **Iliiliopae Heiau**, rests hidden in the underbrush on private land just inland from the highway. Measuring about 100 yards in length and 30 yards in width, it was once a center of sorcery and human sacrifice that today consists of a stone platform and adjoining terraces. This is also the trailhead for the Wailau Valley Trail. According to legend, the *heiau*'s stones were all transported from this distant valley and assembled in a single night. ~ 15 miles east of Kaunakakai; for permission and directions, call Pearl Petro at 558-8113.

◄ *HIDDEN*

The best way to visit this ancient site is on the **Molokai Wagon Ride**, a horse-drawn tour conducted by several delightful local fellows. ~ Located at Mapulehu Mango Grove, 15 miles east of Kaunakakai; 558-8380.

The Molokai Wagon Ride also visits the nearby **Mapulehu Mango Grove**, a stand of 2500 fruit trees that were planted during the 1930s and now represent one of the largest such groves in the world. The wagon ride winds up at a picturesque beach where guests enjoy a Molokai-style lunch on the beach complete with coconut husking and Hawaiian net throwing.

At the **Mapulehu Glass House** you can tour a somewhat overgrown funky old garden. Spanning ten acres and centered around a greenhouse, it features flowering ginger and other exotic plants as well as poorly tended patches. ~ 15 miles east of Kaunakakai, marked by a flagpole and mailbox number 800; 558-8160.

The ruins of the island's first **sugar mill** stand near Route 450's 20-mile marker. All that remains of this early factory, which burned down about a century ago, is a solitary stack.

Just beyond the 20-mile marker is Kumimi Beach, which presents your first view of **Moku Hooniki Island** as well as otherworldly vistas of Maui.

The road now begins a sinuous course along a string of pearl-white beaches, then climbs above a rocky coastline. As you curve upward into Molokai's tropical heights, the roadside flora becomes increasingly colorful and dense. First you encounter the open pastures and rolling ranchland of 14,000-acre **Puu O Hoku Ranch,** then dive into the tropical foliage of Molokai's windblown northeast coast.

HIDDEN ▶

As the road winds high above **Halawa Valley** it offers several vista points from which to view this V-shaped canyon bounded by green walls. Directly below, tropical greenery gives way to white surf and then aquamarine ocean. A river bisects this luxuriant region. At the far end, surrounded by sheer walls, two waterfalls— Hipuapua and Moaula—spill down the mountainside. Obviously East End has withheld its most spectacular scenery until the last.

Archaeologists believe that Molokai's first settlement was established here, possibly as early as the 7th century. The ancient Hawaiians terraced the surrounding slopes, planting taro and living off the largesse of the sea.

In 1946 (and again in 1957) a tidal wave swept through the valley, leveling buildings and leaving salt deposits that destroyed the agricultural industry. Today you can drive down into the valley, where you'll find a park, a lovely curve of sandy beach, fresh-water Halawa Stream, an old church and several other structures. A hiking trail leads to 250-foot Moaula Falls and 500-foot Hipuapua Falls, which lie to the interior of this awesomely beautiful vale. (Please note, however, that at last report this trail had been closed by the landowner and was not open to the public.)

LODGING

HIDDEN ▶

The choicest spot on the island to combine local color with a relaxing atmosphere is the cozy **Pau Hana Inn,** Molokai's oldest hotel. The beachfront is lackluster, but there's a lovely view across the Kalohi Channel to Lanai. You'll find a quiet, lazy ambience here with cottages and buildings spotted about the lawns. Relax and enjoy the lush vegetation, small swimming pool, and the restaurant and bar down near the waterfront.

Standard rooms are budget-to-moderate-priced, small in size, and sport ceiling fans. Deluxe units are larger and newer. Add a fan, lanai, tub and extra double bed and you'll pay something in the deluxe price range. These rooms are a good choice if you're traveling with friends—they can be rented with tiny kitchenettes. ~ 553-5342, 800-423-6656, fax 553-5047. BUDGET TO DELUXE.

There's Polynesian architecture but less island spirit at the Pau Hana's sister property, **Hotel Molokai.** Set on a small unappealing beach two miles east of Kaunakakai, this hotel charges a moderate price for a very tiny room with twin beds. I found spotty mirrors, bumpy rugs, shared lanai and a tacky interior of shingled (yes, shingled) walls. All that's okay in a low-rent hostelry, but why pay more for less? Actually, you're probably paying for what's outside: a shrub-rimmed lawn with coconut trees, and along the shore a pool and thatch pavilions. Amid all this splendor you'll find a cluster of brown-shingle buildings with elegantly curved Polynesian roofs and plate-glass windows reflecting the view. These are the deluxe rooms; they have wood paneling, high-beamed ceilings and a much more appealing atmosphere. ~ 553-5347, 800-423-6656, fax 553-5047. MODERATE TO DELUXE.

If privacy is what you're after, you'll love **Kamalo Plantation Bed & Breakfast.** Set on five acres of orchards and tropical gardens, the inn features a large secluded cottage in the middle of the grounds and two guest rooms in the open, airy house. Screen windows let in the tropical smell of the flowering trees, and each room has a private lanai. Breakfast consists of homemade bread and fresh fruit from the orchard. ~ HCO1 Box 300, Kaunakakai, HI 96748; phone/fax 558-8236. MODERATE.

CONDOS

If you're traveling with several folks or want kitchen facilities, there are also condominiums: **Molokai Shores** (553-5954, 800-535-0085, fax 800-633-5085) and **Wavecrest Resort** (558-8103, 800-535-0085, fax 558-8206). Both offer oceanfront accommodations with full kitchen, lanai and color television. Each is a series of low-slung buildings that forms a U-shaped configuration around a landscaped lawn extending to the beach. Within the grounds are palm trees, a swimming pool, shuffleboard and barbecue areas. Of the two, Wavecrest (rates from $109), 12 miles east of Kaunakakai, is the better bargain; in addition to a few extra features including tennis courts and a dishwasher, the rates are slightly lower than those at Molokai Shores (rates from $125), just one mile east of Kaunakakai.

DINING

A gourmet will starve on Molokai, but someone looking for a square meal at fair prices should depart well-fed. The budget restaurants are clustered along Ala Malama Street in Kaunakakai.

If you're into Filipino fare, try **Oviedo's Lunch Counter.** This mom-and-pop restaurant serves up spicy steaming dishes at low prices. You'll find plank board walls surrounding a few plastic chairs and yellow formica tables. The steam-tray cuisine includes chicken papaya, pig's feet, turkey tail adobo and mango beans. Open for lunch and early dinner. ~ 553-5014. BUDGET.

HIDDEN ▶   **Kanemitsu's Bakery** serves tasty meals at appetizing prices. A local institution, it's a simple café with molded seats, formica tables and an interesting folk art mural presenting a map of Molokai. The lunch special varies but the price is low whether you are dining on pork chops, beef teriyaki, breaded mahimahi or fried chicken. Kanemitsu's is a favorite with the breakfast crowd, which is drawn in by the bakery as well as a menu of omelettes, hot cakes and egg dishes served with Portuguese sausage or that island favorite, Spam. No dinner served. Closed Tuesday. ~ 553-5855. BUDGET.

Outpost Natural Foods has a take-out counter at the back of its tiny health food store. Here you can fuel up with delicious sandwiches, salads and smoothies that are both nutritious and inexpensive. There are also burritos and daily specials. Open for lunch only. Closed Saturday. ~ 70 Makaena Street; 553-3377. BUDGET.

The **Pau Hana Inn** is Molokai's classic Hawaiian retreat. The lingua franca at this local hangout is pidgin English and the password is *laid-back*. While enjoying a meal at the **Banyan Tree Terrace Restaurant** you'll find all the accoutrements to furnish a tropical dream, from overhead fans to Hawaiian altos plucking slack-key guitars. Charm is the Pau Hana's middle name, which is why it's such a popular spot among savvy travelers. Meals are served in a spacious dining room overlooking a century-old banyan tree that faces the ocean. The lunch and dinner menus offer standard fare and come with a salad bar; breakfast is also served. ~ Pau Hana Inn; 553-5342. MODERATE.

GROCERIES   The nearest Molokai approaches to a supermarket is **Misaki's**, a medium-sized grocery store on Kaunakakai's main drag, Ala Malama Street. The prices are higher and the selection smaller here than at the chain markets, so it's wise to bring a few provisions from the larger islands. Open 8:30 a.m. to 8:30 p.m., Sunday 9 a.m. to noon. ~ 553-5505.

Outpost Natural Foods, down the street and around the corner from Misaki's, offers a friendly atmosphere as well as juices, herbs, dried fruit, fresh local produce and other health food items. Closed Saturday. ~ 70 Makaena Street; 553-3377.

Try **Kanemitsu's Bakery** for delicious Molokai honey, bread and pastries. ~ 553-5855.

On the East End, **Wavecrest Resort**, 12 miles out, has a "general store" with a very limited supply of groceries (primarily canned goods) and a hearty stock of liquor.

SHOPPING   You needn't worry about falling into the shop-till-you-drop syndrome on Molokai. Long before you have even begun to think about being tired you will have visited every store on the island. Shopping is still an adventure here, since the few stores operating are all owned by local people and provide a window into life on Molokai.

Ala Malama Street, Kaunakakai's main street, offers a modest row of shops. **Molokai Island Creations** specializes in clothing, jewelry, glassware and gift items made by Molokai artists. ~ 553-5926.

Imports Gift Shop features casual wear, cultured and mabe pearls, and Hawaiian heirloom jewelry. Closed Sunday. ~ 553-5734.

For beachwear you can try **Molokai Surf**. Closed Sunday. ~ 553-5093.

Molokai Fish & Dive, "home of the 'original' Molokai T-shirt designs," features its signature clothing and souvenirs as well as beach items and sporting equipment. ~ Kaunakakai; 553-5926.

The Kahua Center (Wharf Road) has a couple interesting stores. **Dudoit Imports** (no phone) features local arts and crafts, antiques and jewelry, and **Lorenzo's Gallery of Fine Art and Molokai Treasures** (553-3748) has a beautiful collection of paintings by local artists. Closed weekends.

Confirmed partygoers will find Molokai a pretty dead scene. Probably the best place around is the venerable **Pau Hana Inn** in Kaunakakai. It's certainly popular among the local folks. The Pau Hana Inn blazes with local color weeknights and cranks up the band on weekends when they charge a cover. The ocean view stars nightly. ~ 553-5342.

NIGHTLIFE

O'NE ALII PARK This spacious park features a large grass-covered field and coconut grove plus a narrow beach with an excellent view of Lanai. A reef far offshore makes this area very shallow and affords ample protection. It's excellent for children. Snorkeling, though, is only mediocre. As for surfing, all the action is far out on the reef and it's rarely any good. Surf-casting isn't bad here but it's even better farther to the east. The most common catches are *manini*, red and white goatfish, parrotfish, *papio*, *ulua*, milkfish and mullet. The facilities here include a picnic area, restrooms, showers and electricity at the pavilion. ~ Located four miles east of Kaunakakai on Route 450.

BEACHES & PARKS

▲ Mainly tent camping; no hookups. Very popular and therefore sometimes crowded and noisy. County permit required.

KAKAHAIA BEACH PARK This is a long, narrow park wedged tightly between the road and the ocean. Near a national wildlife refuge, Kakahaia is an important nesting area for native and migratory birds. Picnicking, swimming, snorkeling, surfing and fishing are much the same as at O'ne Alii Park. Day use only. ~ Head east on Route 450 from Kaunakakai for six miles.

PUKOO BEACH This crescent-shaped strand is mirrored by another curving beach just to the west. Maui lies directly across the channel and there are also marvelous views of Lanai. With a shallow, rocky bottom, this beach provides only mediocre swimming.

However, it's very popular with fishermen. There are no facilities here. ~ The old Neighborhood Store 'n' Snack Bar (now closed), located on Route 450 near the 15-mile marker, is your landmark. Just past here, traveling east, turn into the second driveway on the right. This access road leads a short distance to the beach.

KUMIMI BEACH, POHAKULOA POINT, AND OTHER EAST END BEACHES Beginning near the 18-mile marker on Route 450, and extending for about four miles, lies this string of small sandy beaches. These are among the island's loveliest, featuring white sands and spectacular views of the islands of Maui and Lanai. The swimming is very good, but beware of heavy currents and high surf. Plentiful coral makes for great snorkeling and good lobster diving. There are numerous surfing breaks throughout this area. Pohakuloa Point (or Rock Point), located eight-tenths of a mile past the 20-mile marker, is one of Molokai's top surfing spots. These are also good beaches for surfing. Barracuda are sometimes caught in the deeper regions. Also bonefish, mountain bass, threadfin, *manini*, red and white goatfish, *ulua*, *papio*, parrotfish, milkfish, and mullet. There is a small market near the 15-mile marker. ~ These pocket beaches are located along Route 450 between the 18- and 22-mile markers.

HALAWA BEACH PARK Set in lush Halawa Valley, one of Molokai's most splendid areas, the park is tucked neatly between mountains and sea on a grassy plot dotted with coconut palms and ironwood trees. Cliffs, waterfalls, two pocket beaches—altogether a heavenly spot, though sometimes rainy and almost always windy. This is a very good place to swim because it is partially protected by the bay. But exercise caution anyway. Snorkeling is good, though the water is sometimes murky. It's one of the very best spots on the island for surfing. Fishing is also notable; the reefs studding this area make it a prime locale for many of the species caught along East End Beaches. The park is a bit weatherbeaten and overgrown and although there are a picnic area and restrooms, the running water must be boiled or treated chemically. ~ Located at the far end of Route 450, about 30 miles east of Kaunakakai.

▲ Not permitted in the park, but people camp on the other side of Halawa Stream on property owned by Puu O Hoku Ranch. You will have to park and carry your gear to where you want to camp.

Kaunakakai to West End

Generally, if you are not pointed east on Molokai, you are headed westerly. The thoroughfare that carries you across the prairie-like plains of west Molokai is Route 460, also called the Maunaloa Highway, another two-lane track. Along the way you can venture off in search of the plantation town of Kualapuu and the vista point overlooking Kalaupapa, but eventually you will arrive at road's end out in the woodframe town of Maunaloa. From this red-dust municipality it's a short jaunt to Papohaku Beach, Molokai's western shore.

Just a mile west of the cock-eyed town of Kaunakakai on Route 460 is the **Kapuaiwa Grove**, planted in the 1860s by Kamehameha V. This magnificent stand of coconut palms, once 1000 in number, consists of particularly tall trees. The grove creates the sensation of being in a tropical dream sequence, with hundreds of palm trees flashing green and yellow fronds and extending to the lip of the ocean. Some appear to stand in columns, but others have bent so far to the wind they have fallen out of formation.

According to legend, Molokai was the child of the god Wakea and his mistress Hina, whose cave still lies along the southeastern edge of the island.

Strung like rosary beads opposite the grove are seven tiny churches. This **Church Row** includes Protestant, Mormon, Jehovah's Witness and several other denominations. Like sentinels protecting the island from the devil, they too are gathered in rows. The most intriguing are the oldest, tiny woodframe structures with modest steeples. These one-room chapels lack worldly frills like stained glass and are furnished with creaky wooden pews that seat a few dozen parishioners. Stop by and inquire about services; visitors are always welcome.

A side trip along Route 470 leads past the tinroof town of **Kualapuu**. Filled with modest plantation houses, it harkens back to an earlier era when Molokai cultivated pineapples rather than tourists. Today its claim to fame is a 1.4 million gallon reservoir that is reportedly the largest rubber-lined water tank in the world.

Farther up Route 470, Kalai is home to the R. W. Meyer Sugar Mill, which is the highlight of the new **Molokai Museum and Cultural Center**. There is an 1878 steam-generated operation that has been restored in sparkling fashion. The mule-driven cane crusher, copper clarifiers and dependable old steam engine are ready and waiting for Molokai to return to its old ways. There are also well-presented displays and heirlooms of the German immigrant family that owned the mill, as well as native Molokai artifacts. Admission. ~ Route 470; 567-6436.

Route 470 ends at the **Kalaupapa Lookout**. Here cliffs as green as Ireland fall away in dizzying fashion to reveal a softly sloping tableland 1600 feet below, the Kalaupapa Peninsula. Fringed by white-sand beaches, this geologic afterthought extends more than two miles out from the foot of the *pali*. A lighthouse and landing strip occupy the point of the peninsula. Nearer the cliffs, a cluster of houses comprises the famous leper colony; while neighboring Kauhako Crater, a nicely rounded circle far below you, represents a vestige of the volcano that created this appendage. Ringed by rock and water, protected by the tallest sea cliffs in the world, Kalaupapa Peninsula is a magnificent sight indeed.

A short hike from the lookout, **Phallic Rock** protrudes obscenely from the ground amid an ironwood stand as thick as pubic hair. This geologic formation, so realistic it almost seems sculpted, was said to represent the Hawaiian fertility god, who was turned to stone when his wife caught him admiring a beautiful young girl. Legend says that a woman offering gifts and spending the night here will return home pregnant.

Molokai's West End was once a rich adze quarry. The rock, vital to a Stone Age society, was fashioned into tools that were in turn used to create weapons, canoes, bowls and other necessities.

Route 480 will take you into the town of Hoolehua, where you'll find **Purdy's Natural Macadamia Nut Farm**. Located right behind the island's only high school, this small grove of 70-year-old macadamia nut trees is open to the public for free tours and tastings. The owner will explain the growing cycles of the trees and demonstrate harvesting and cooking techniques. Visitors can taste the raw product and also sample the nut after it's been naturally roasted, a process that cuts down greatly on the fat and calories found in nuts sold in stores. ~ Lihipali Avenue; 567-6601.

Route 460 continues over dry rolling plains toward Molokai's West End. This arid plateau, windswept and covered by deep red, iron-rich soil, was once planted in pineapple. Today Molokai Ranch, which still owns much of the region, has turned to hay cultivation to feed cattle.

If nothing else, the West End is rich in myth and history. As Hawaiian storytellers recount, the region around Maunaloa, the volcano that formed this side of the island, was once a cultural focus of the Polynesians. It was here that the hula originated; from the slopes of Maunaloa the goddess Laka spread knowledge of the sensuous dance to all the other islands.

Like the pineapple industry itself, Route 460 ends in **Maunaloa**. With the departure of Dole's operations in 1975, this company town assumed the dusty, falsefront visage of the Wild West after the mines petered out and the saloons shut down. In true revival spirit, however, local craftspeople and artists have converted a few buildings into shops and galleries. Besides these more recent additions to the rustic landscape, the old post office remains and there is a classic general store. Framed by Norfolk pines and filled with 1920s-era tinroof plantation houses, Maunaloa itself is a classic.

Perhaps the island's most unexpected and exotic feature is the nearby **Molokai Ranch Wildlife Conservation Park**. Part of Molokai Ranch's sprawling 52,000-acre spread, this 350-acre game preserve is roamed by about 80 African and Asian animals. Barbary sheep, eland, Indian blackbuck, rhea, wild turkeys, zebra, crown crane, giraffe and oryx are among the species that have transformed Molokai's West End into a kind of "Little Africa." Tours feature a "giraffe picnic" where you can feed and pet the curious critters. Horseback riding is also available. The Malihini Rodeo happens every Wednesday and Friday, and any adventurous soul 16 years or older can learn rodeo skills from Hawaiian cowboys. Admission. ~ P.O. Box 259, Maunaloa, HI 96770; 552-2741.

Any tour of West End should of course finish at the west end. **Papohaku Beach,** a sparkling three-mile long swath of white sand, would be a fitting finale to any tour. Reached by taking Kaluakoi Road from Route 460 and driving through the rolling hills of sprawling Kaluakoi Resort, Papohaku is one of the largest beaches in the state. During World War II troops practiced shore landings along this coast. But today you will have the beach and surrounding sand dunes almost entirely to yourself.

MOLOKAI'S OUTBACK For a splendid tour of Molokai's mountainous interior, take a drive or hike on the Main Forest Road (located four miles west of Kaunakakai). This bumpy dirt road requires four-wheel-drive vehicles along its ten-mile-length.

◄ *HIDDEN*

Deer, quail, pheasant, doves and chukkar partridge populate the route. Numerous secondary roads and trails lead to the very edge of the mammoth Molokai Forest Reserve, through which the main road passes. These side roads offer excellent possibilities for adventurous hikers.

After nine miles, the main road passes **Lua Moku Iliahi,** known to the English-speaking world as the **Sandalwood Measuring Pit.** This depression, dug into the earth to match the hull size of an old sailing vessel, was used by 19th-century Hawaiians to gauge the amount of sandalwood needed to fill a ship. It's another mile to **Waikolu Picnic Grove,** a heavily wooded retreat ideal for lunching or camping. Here you'll find picnic facilities and an outhouse. (State permit required to camp.) Across the road, **Waikolu Valley Lookout** perches above Waikolu Valley, which descends precipitously 3000 feet to the sea.

Here you can also explore **Kamakou Preserve,** a 2774-acre sanctuary managed by The Nature Conservancy. Home to more than 200 plants that live only in Hawaii, the preserve is a lush rainforest from which Molokai draws most of its water supply. There are several forest birds, including the *apapane* and *amakihi.* For information on visiting the reserve or to check the condition of the Main Forest Road (which may be closed in wet weather), call 553-5236.

To reach the Main Forest Road, take Route 460 west from Kaunakakai. There is a white bridge a little more than three-and-a-half miles from town, just before the four-mile marker. Take a right on the dirt road right before the bridge and you're on the Main Forest Road.

Far from the madding crowd on the west end of Molokai, you'll find a 6700-acre master-planned complex, the **Kaluakoi Resort.** Divided into the 103-room **Kaluakoi Hotel and Golf Club** (552-2555, 800-777-1700, fax 552-2821), the cottage-like condos of

CONDOS

Kaluakoi Villas (552-2721, 800-525-1470, fax 552-2201), and two other condominium complexes, it is set near a luxurious three-mile-long beach. This is Molokai's premier resting spot, offering both seclusion and comfort.

Here you'll find the essence of plush living: wasp-waisted pool, tennis courts, golf course, a view of Oahu across the channel, and an oceanfront lounge and restaurant. The hotel rooms are located in a two-story building and have all the necessities: lanai, color television, tile bathroom, overhead fan, rattan furniture. For an ultra-deluxe price tag, you can buy a piece of that ocean view in a studio unit with a kitchenette. The villas are more spacious, also include a kitchenette and are priced deluxe.

Ke Nani Kai, a 120-unit condominium located within Kaluakoi Resort, has one- and two-bedroom units starting at $95 per night. From December through March there's a four-night minimum. The complex includes a pool, tennis courts and an outdoor party area with barbecues. ~ 552-2761, 800-888-2791, fax 552-0045.

Nearby **Paniolo Hale**, has 31 units starting at $95 per night. These also include all the amenities and access to a pool, barbecue area and paddle tennis. ~ 552-2731, 800-367-2984, fax 552-2288.

DINING

HIDDEN ►

Everyone has heard of fast food but what about slow food? **Kualapuu Cook House** bills itself as the international headquarters for a "slow food chain." Set in an old plantation house, it serves *saimin*, chili and hamburgers. If you want to get serious about it, there is chicken stir-fry, teriyaki plate and mahimahi—even New York steak. The pies are homemade and the place is bright with local color. Closed Sunday. ~ Route 480, Kualapuu; 567-6185. BUDGET TO MODERATE.

Out in Maunaloa, there's a gathering spot called **Jojo's Café**. Its menu includes a variety of ethnic and all-American dishes. At lunchtime, sandwiches are available; for dinner, you'll find an array of fresh fish and curries. Like many of the mom-and-pop businesses on Molokai, it is located in a tinroof plantation house. You can expect old plantation photos, an antique bar and booths, homespun decor and an easy friendly atmosphere. Closed Sunday. ~ Maunaloa; 552-2803. BUDGET TO MODERATE.

The aforementioned Kaluakoi Hotel, on the island's far west end, has a pennysaver **snack bar** with sandwiches. That's just light artillery to back up the hotel's big gun, the **Ohia Lodge**, Molokai's finest restaurant. This multilevel, handsomely appointed establishment (high-beamed ceiling, rattan furnishings) looks out on the distant lights of Oahu. You can order from an extensive surf-and-turf menu that includes orange-glazed almond chicken, medallions of mahimahi, tenderloin of beef with bordelaise sauce and roast breast of duck. Seeking a place to splurge? Well, this is it. Breakfast and dinner. ~ 552-2555. DELUXE.

Out West End way, **Maunaloa General Store**, in Maunaloa a few **GROCERIES**
miles away from Kaluakoi Resort, has a limited stock of grocery
items. Open 9 a.m. to 7 p.m. except Sunday (10 a.m. to 2 p.m.). ~
552-2868.

Over on Molokai's West End in the red-dust town of Maunaloa **SHOPPING**
you'll stumble upon two great shops that share the same building
and the same telephone, 552-2364. **Big Wind Kite Factory** has an
astonishing assortment of high flyers. There are diamond kites,
dancer kites, windsocks and rainbow tail kites. You can even pick
up flags and banners here. At **The Plantation Gallery** there are
aloha shirts, batik sarongs, tribal art, shell necklaces and other original pieces by over 30 Molokai craftspeople. They also have the
largest collection of books about Hawaii and Hawaiian culture on
the island.

There are also a few shops at **Kaluakoi Hotel** down the road in
the Kaluakoi Resort complex. One of them is the **Laughing Gecko**,
a boutique offering antiques, artwork, and a variety of local hand-
icrafts such as *lauhala* mats and *koa* bracelets. ~ 552-2320.

To step out in style, head west to Kaluakoi Hotel's **Ohia Lounge**. **NIGHTLIFE**
The rattan furnishings, carpets, overhead fans and marvelous view
of Honolulu, not to mention the band on the weekends, make it *the*
place. ~ 552-2555.

KIOWEA PARK Watch for falling coconuts in the beau- **BEACHES &**
tiful Kapuaiwa Grove, which is the centerpiece of this beach park. **PARKS**
Towering palm trees extend almost to the water, leaving little space
for a beach. The swimming here is only okay; the water is well-protected by a distant reef, but the bottom is shallow and rocky, and
the water is muddy. This also makes for mediocre snorkeling.
Common fish catches include mullet, *manini*, parrotfish, milkfish,
and *papio*, plus red, white, and striped goatfish; crabbing is good
in the evening. (This park is generally restricted to homesteaders,
but if you stop for a picnic you may be allowed by the locals to
stay.) A nice place to visit, but I wouldn't want to fall asleep in the
shade of a coconut tree. Facilities include picnic area, restrooms and
pavilion. ~ Located one mile west of Kaunakakai on Route 460.

▲ Camping is usually restricted to homesteaders. If the park is
vacant however, the Hawaiian Homelands Department in Hoolehua will issue permits for $5; hours are Monday through Friday
from 7:45 a.m. to 4:30 p.m. ~ 567-6104.

PALAAU STATE PARK Set in a densely forested area, this 233-acre
park is ideal for a mountain sojourn. Several short trails lead to petroglyphs, a startling phallic rock, and the awesome Kalaupapa
Lookout. The trail down to Kalaupapa Peninsula is also nearby.
There are picnic area, restrooms and pavilion. ~ Take Route 460 six

miles west from Kaunakakai, then follow Route 470 (Kalae Highway) about six more miles to the end of the road.

▲ State permit required. Tent camping only.

HIDDEN ▶ **MOOMOMI BEACH** 🏊 ⛵ 🏃 ⚓ A small, remote beach studded with rocks and frequented only by local people—what more could you ask? While Moomomi is a small pocket beach, many people use the name to refer to a three-mile length of coastline that extends west from the pocket beach and includes two other strands, Kawaaloa Beach and Keonelele Beach. Moomomi offers good swimming, but use caution because the bottom is rocky and the beach is only partially protected. The snorkeling is very good along reefs and rocks. As for surfing, there are fair breaks at the mouth of the inlet. There's good surf-casting from the rocky headland to the west. Keonelele Beach forms the coastal border of the Moomomi Dunes, a unique series of massive sand dunes that extend as far as four miles inland, covering Molokai's northwestern corner. Also known as the Desert Strip, this unique ecosystem is overseen by the Nature Conservancy (553-5236), which can provide information and tours. The preserve protects five endangered plant species and is a habitat for the endangered Hawaiian green sea turtle. You'll find no facilities at the park. ~ To get there take Route 460 west from Kaunakakai to Hoolehua. Go right on Route 481 (Puupeelua Avenue), then left on Farrington Avenue. Farrington starts as a paved road, then turns to dirt. After two-and-two-tenths miles of dirt track, the road forks. Take the right fork and follow it a half-mile to the beach. A four-wheel drive vehicle may be required.

▲ Camping on a grassy plot elevated from the beach is allowed on weekends. Obtain permit and keys at Molokai Ranch.

HIDDEN ▶ **HALENA AND OTHER SOUTH COAST BEACHES** 🏊 ⛵ 🏃 ⚓ Don't tell anyone, but there's a dirt road running several miles along a string of trackless beaches on the south shore. (Note, however, that at last report this road was closed to the public.) The first one, **Halena**, is a very funky ghost camp complete with a dozen weather-beaten shacks and a few primitive facilities. To the west lies **Haleolono Beach**, with its pleasant bay and lagoon. To the east is **Kolo Wharf** (an abandoned pier collapsing into the sea), plus numerous fishponds, coconut groves and small sand beaches. This is an excellent area to explore, camp, hike, fish (bass, threadfin, inenui, red goatfish) and commune with hidden Hawaii. The swimming is also good if you don't mind muddy water. It's wise to boil or chemically treat the water. Note: You need the permission of Molokai Ranch to get to these beaches. ~ To get there take Route 460 to Maunaloa. As you first enter town (before the road curves into the main section), you'll see houses on the left and a dirt road extending perpendicularly to the right.

Now, to get to Halena, take a right at the fork, then a quick left (there are signs posted), then drive a few hundred yards to the end. The shore is nearby; simply walk west along the beach several hundred yards to the shacks.

To get to Haleolono Beach, walk about a mile west along the beach from Halena.

To get to Kolo Wharf and the other beaches, go straight where the road forks. Kolo is two miles east over an equally rugged road. Sand beaches, coconut groves and fishponds extend for another six miles past Kolo. Then the road turns inland, improving considerably, and continues for seven miles more until it meets the main road two miles west of Kaunakakai.

For current information about road access contact Molokai Ranch. ~ 552-2767. At last report, the roads in this region were closed to the public.

KAWAKUI BEACH This idyllic spot is my favorite Molo-   ◄ HIDDEN
kai campground. Here a small inlet, tucked away in Molokai's northwest corner, is edged by a beautiful beach with a sandy bottom. Nearby is a shady grove of *kiawe* trees, fringed by the rocky coastline. On a clear night you can see the lights of Oahu across Kaiwi Channel. This is a very good place to swim because the inlet offers some protection, but exercise caution. Snorkeling is good in summer near the rocks when the surf is low. People fish here for mountain bass, threadfin, inenui and red goatfish. There are no facilities here. Try Kaunakakai. ~ Take Route 460 west from Kaunakakai for about 12 miles. Then take a right onto the dirt road that leads downhill. Follow this bumpy dirt road about seven miles to the beach. The road forks a few hundred yards before the ocean. Take the right fork to Kawakui; the left fork leads to a series of white-sand beaches offering excellent possibilities for exploring and swimming.

▲ That shady grove is a perfect site to pitch a tent.

PAPOHAKU BEACH This splendid beach extends for three miles along Molokai's west coast; it's an excellent place to explore, collect puka shells, or just lie back and enjoy the view of Oahu. Backed by *kiawe* trees and low sand dunes, Papohaku is the largest beach on the island, averaging 100 yards in width. Swimming is excellent, but use caution. There's not much rock or coral here so the snorkeling is only mediocre. You'll find good breaks for surfing when the wind isn't blowing from the shore. Use caution, especially in the winter months. The beach is also popular with bodysurfers. The fishing is good here, usually for mountain bass, threadfin, inenui and red goatfish. There are picnic areas, restrooms and showers; the Kaluakoi Hotel, with snack bar and restaurant, is about a half-mile away. ~ To get to the beach, take Route 460 for about 14 miles from

Kaunakakai. Turn right onto the road to the Kaluakoi Resort. Continue past the hotel (don't turn onto the hotel road) and down the hill. Follow this macadam track, Kaluakoi Road, as it parallels the beach. Side roads from Kaluakoi Road and Pohakuloa Road (an adjoining thoroughfare) lead to Papohaku and other beaches.

▲ Tent only. County permit required.

Kalaupapa

The ultimate Molokai experience is the pilgrimage to the Kalaupapa leper colony along the rugged north shore of the island. Isolated on a 12-square-mile lava tongue that protrudes from the north shore, this sacred and historic site can be reached only by foot, mule or plane.

Here about 68 victims of Hansen's Disease live in solitude. Doctors have controlled the affliction since 1946 with sulfone drugs, and all the patients are free to leave. But many are 60 to 90 years old, and have lived on this windswept peninsula most of their lives.

Their story goes back to 1866 when the Hawaiian government began exiling lepers to this lonely spot on Molokai's rain-plagued north coast. In those days Kalaupapa was a fishing village, and lepers were segregated in the **old settlement** at Kalawao on the windy eastern side of the peninsula. The place was treeless and barren—a wasteland haunted by slow death. Lepers were shipped along the coast and pushed overboard. Abandoned with insufficient provisions and no shelter, they struggled against both the elements and disease.

HIDDEN ►

To this lawless realm came Joseph Damien de Veuster, Father Damien. The Catholic priest, arriving in 1873, brought a spirit and energy that gave the colony new life. He built a church, attended to the afflicted and died of leprosy 16 years later. Perhaps it is the spirit of this "Martyr of Molokai" that even today marks the indescribable quality of Kalaupapa. There is something unique and inspiring about the place, something you'll have to discover yourself.

To visit Kalaupapa, you can fly, hike or ride muleback; there are no roads leading to this remote destination. Once there you must take a guided tour; no independent exploring is permitted. And no children under 16 are allowed. Flights and hiking tours are organized by **Damien Tours** (567-6171) and **Molokai Mule Ride** (567-6088). For flight information, check **Aloha Island Air** (567-6115), **Molokai Shuttle** (567-6847) or **Paragon Air** (244-3356) from Maui.

As far as I'm concerned, the mule ride is the only way to go. The Molokai Mule Ride conducts tours daily, weather permitting. You saddle up near the Kalaupapa Lookout and descend a 1664-foot precipice. Kalaupapa unfolds below you as you switchback through lush vegetation on a three-mile-long trail. The ride? Exhilarating, frightening, but safe. And the views are otherworldly.

On the tour you will learn that Kalaupapa has been designated a national historical park. Among the points of interest within this refuge are numerous windblasted structures, a volcanic crater and

several monuments. You'll also visit Saint Philomena Church, built
by Father Damien in the 1870s, and Kalawao Park, an exotically
beautiful spot on the lush eastern side of the peninsula.

Definitely visit Kalaupapa. Fly in and you'll undergo an unfor-
gettable experience; hike and it will become a pilgrimage.

Outdoor Adventures

CAMPING

With so little development and such an expanse
of untouched land, Molokai would seem a haven
for campers. Unfortunately, large segments of the
island are owned by Molokai Ranch and other private interests;
with the exception of a few beaches on Molokai Ranch property,
these tracts are closed off behind locked gates.

There *are* a few parks for camping. A county permit is required
for Papohaku Beach and O'ne Alii Park. Permits cost $3 per person
a day (50 cents for children) and are obtained at the County Parks
and Recreation office in Kaunakakai. Hours are 8 a.m. to 4 p.m.,
Monday through Friday, so get your permit in advance. ~ 553-3204.

Permits for Kiowea Park, when available, are issued by the Hawaiian Homelands Department in Hoolehua. The fee is $5 per night
at Kiowea for a group of any size. ~ 567-6104.

Camping at Palaau State Park is free but requires a permit from
the Department of Land and Natural Resources (243-5354) on
Maui, or from the park ranger (567-6083).

For information on camping at Molokai Ranch, contact the
Outfitters Center, Molokai Ranch, Monday through Friday 8 a.m.
to 4:30 p.m. ~ P.O. Box 259, Maunaloa, HI 96770; 552-2741.

Molokai Fish & Dive in Kaunakakai sells camping gear. ~ 553-
5926.

For camping gear rentals go to **Fun Hogs Hawaii.** ~ Kaluakoi
Hotel and Golf Club; 552-2555.

SCUBA & SKIN-DIVING

If you're not traveling with gear, the following outfitters can rent
you snorkeling equipment. Several provide snorkeling trips to prime
spots around the island, and you might check with them regarding
other activities such as scuba diving, kayaking and sailing. The best
place for snorkeling on Molokai is at the 20-mile marker on the east
side of the island. Here you're likely to see sturgeon, trumpetfish
and a few green turtles.

Check out **Molokai Fish & Dive** for masks, fins and snorkels. ~
Kaunakakai; 553-5926.

Bill Kapuni's Snorkeland Dive Adventure rents snorkel equipment and is the only dive outfitter on the island. He leads dives to
spots around Molokai where it's not uncommon to see tiger sharks,
hammerhead sharks and countless green turtles. He also teaches
PADI classes. ~ 553-9867.

Molokai Action Adventures offers snorkeling expeditions and
leads kayaking trips. ~ Kaunakakai; 558-8184.

Fun Hogs Hawaii offers kayaking, snorkeling and catamaran excursions. ~ Kaluakoi Hotel and Golf Club; 552-2555.

SAILING   Providing Molokai's only sailing adventure, Molokai Charters operates **Satan's Doll**, a 42-foot sloop that is docked on the wharf in Kaunakakai. Step aboard for sunset cruises, whale-watching tours and snorkeling excursions to Lanai. ~ 553-5852.

FISHING   Depending on the weather, deep-sea fishing charters will take you to various spots that are within ten to twenty miles of Molokai. Here you're likely to catch mahimahi, tuna, marlin and *ono*.

Contact **Alyce C Commercial and Sport Fishing** (558-8377), **Shon-A-Lei II** (553-5242) or **Molokai Action Adventures** (558-8184), all in Kaunakakai.

RIDING STABLES   **Molokai Wagon Ride** sponsors wagon and saddle tours to scenic and historic sites at Mapulehu on eastern Molokai; this outfit also rents horses with guides. ~ 558-8380.

Molokai Ranch offers a two-hour horseback ride to a secluded beach on the island's west end where you stop to kayak, swim and snorkel before heading back. ~ 552-2741.

BICYCLING   Traffic is light and slow-moving, making Molokai an ideal place for two-wheeling adventurers. The roads are generally good, with some potholes out East End near Halawa Valley. The terrain is mostly flat or gently rolling, with a few steep ascents. Winds are strong and sometimes make for tough going. For mountain bike rentals and excursions, contact **Fun Hogs Hawaii**. ~ Kaluakoi Hotel and Golf Club; 552-2555.

HIKING   Molokai features some splendid country and numerous areas that seem prime for hiking, but few trails have been built or maintained and most private land is off-limits to visitors. Some excellent hiking possibilities, but no official trails, are offered along the beaches described above. Palaau State Park also has several short jaunts to points of interest.

The only lengthy treks lead to the island's rugged north coast. Four valleys—Halawa, Wailau, Pelekunu and Waikolu—cut through the sheer cliffs guarding this windswept shore.

The **Pelekunu Trail** begins several hundred yards beyond the Waikolu Valley Lookout (see the section on "Molokai's Outback"). It is unmaintained and extremely difficult. Traversing Nature Conservancy property, the trail leads to a lookout point and then drops into the valley.

The **Wailau Trail** is another very difficult trail; it takes about 12 hours and passes through some muddy rainforest regions. The trailhead is off Route 450 about 15 miles east of Kaunakakai. The trail extends across nearly the entire island from south to north. Dangers include deep mud and wild boar. To hike it, you must obtain permission from Pearl Petro. Send a self-addressed stamped envelope. ~ P.O. Box 25, Kaunakakai, HI 96748; 558-8113.

The **Kalaupapa Trail** is the easiest and best-maintained trail descending the north *pali*. A trail description is given in the "Kalaupapa" section in this chapter. To hike here you must obtain permission and pay $30 for a mandatory tour of the leper colony. Call Damien Tours for permission and information. ~ 567-6171.

The only valley accessible by car is Halawa. The **Halawa Valley Trail** (which at last report was closed to the public), one of Molokai's prettiest hikes, extends for two miles from the mouth of the valley to the base of Moaula Falls. This 250-foot cascade tumbles down a sheer cliff to a cold mountain pool perfect for swimming. Hipuapua Falls, a sister cascade just a third of a mile north, shoots 500 feet down the *pali*.

The trail is marked near the end of Route 450 a short distance from the beach. There is a parking area, and the attendant will give you information concerning the status of public access to the trail.

Transportation

BY AIR

When your plane touches down at **Molokai Airport**, you'll realize what a one-canoe island you're visiting. There's a snack bar and adjoining lounge, which seem to open and close all day, plus a few car rental and airline offices. It's seven miles to the main town of Kaunakakai. There is no public transportation available. However, shuttle service can be arranged through some of the hotels, and taxis are available.

The airport is served by several airlines: Hawaiian Airlines carries passengers in turbo prop planes. Aloha Island Air and Molokai Shuttle fly small prop planes and are the most exciting way to reach Molokai. To fly direct from Honolulu to Kalaupapa, try Aloha Island Air, which can always be relied upon for friendly service.

BY BOAT

If you'd prefer to arrive by boat, **Sea Link of Hawaii** provides round-trip service from Maui aboard the 118-foot *Maui Princess*. The one-and-a-half-hour cruise provides a unique opportunity to travel between the islands by sea. ~ 553-5736.

CAR RENTALS

The existing companies are: **Dollar Rent A Car** (567-6156, 800-800-4000 from the mainland, 800-342-7398 in Hawaii) and **Budget Rent A Car** (567-6877, 800-451-3600).

JEEP RENTALS

Budget Rent A Car rents jeeps, but requires that you drive them only on paved roads! ~ 567-6877, 800-451-3600. (Be aware that the rental car collision insurance provided by most credit cards does not cover jeeps.)

Index

Lodging Index

Dining Index

HIDDEN GUIDES

Adventure travel or a relaxing vacation?—"Hidden" guidebooks are the only travel books in the business to provide detailed information on both. Aimed at environmentally aware travelers, our motto is "Adventure Travel Plus." These books combine details on unique hotels, restaurants and sightseeing with information on camping, sports and hiking for the outdoor enthusiast.

THE NEW KEY GUIDES

Based on the concept of ecotourism, The New Key Guides are dedicated to the preservation of Central America's rare and endangered species, architecture and archaeology. Filled with helpful tips, they give travelers everything they need to know about these exotic destinations.

ULTIMATE FAMILY GUIDES

These innovative guides present the best and most unique features of a family destination. Quality is the keynote. In addition to thoroughly covering each destination, they feature short articles and one-line "teasers" that are both fun and informative.

Order Form

Ulysses Press books are available at bookstores everywhere. If any of the following titles are unavailable at your local book store, ask the bookseller to order them. Or you can order them directly from Ulysses Press.

Hidden Guidebooks

___ Hidden Boston and Cape Cod, $9.95
___ Hidden Carolinas, $15.95
___ Hidden Coast of California, $15.95
___ Hidden Colorado, $12.95
___ Hidden Florida, $14.95
___ Hidden Florida Keys and
Everglades, $9.95
___ Hidden Hawaii, $15.95
___ Hidden Idaho, $13.95

___ Hidden Maui, $12.95
___ Hidden New England, $15.95
___ Hidden Oregon, $12.95
___ Hidden Pacific Northwest, $15.95
___ Hidden Rockies, $16.95
___ Hidden San Francisco and
Northern California, $15.95
___ Hidden Southern California, $15.95
___ Hidden Southwest, $16.95

The New Key Guidebooks

___ The New Key to Belize, $14.95
___ The New Key to Cancún and
the Yucatán, $13.95
___ The New Key to Costa Rica, $15.95

___ The New Key to Ecuador and
the Galápagos, $15.95
___ The New Key to Guatemala, $14.95

Ultimate Family Guidebooks

___ Disneyland and Beyond, $11.95

___ Disney World and Beyond, $12.95

Mark the book(s) you're ordering and enter the total cost here ⇨

California residents add 8% sales tax here ⇨

Shipping, check box for your preferred method and enter cost here ⇨

❑ Book Rate   FREE! FREE! FREE!

❑ Priority Mail $3.00 First book, $1.00/each additional book

❑ UPS 2-Day Air $7.00 First book, $1.00/each additional book

Billing, enter total amount due here and check method of payment ⇨

❑ Check ❑ Money Order

❑ VISA/MasterCard _____

Name_____Phone _____

Address_____

_____

Money-back guarantee on direct orders placed through Ulysses Press.

ABOUT THE AUTHOR

RAY RIEGERT Ray Riegert is the author of eight travel books, including *Hidden San Francisco and Northern California*. His most popular work, *Hidden Hawaii*, won both the coveted Lowell Thomas Travel Journalism Award and the Hawaii Visitors Bureau Award for Best Guidebook. In addition to his role as publisher of Ulysses Press, he has written for the *Chicago Tribune*, *Saturday Evening Post*, *San Francisco Examiner & Chronicle* and *Travel & Leisure*. A member of the Society of American Travel Writers, he lives in the San Francisco Bay Area with his wife, travel publisher Leslie Henriques, and their son Keith and daughter Alice.

ABOUT THE ILLUSTRATOR

SANDRA WONG Sandra Wong received her bachelor of fine arts degree from the San Francisco Art Institute. Her work has been shown in Los Angeles, San Francisco and China. She currently lives in Oakland, California.